Communication
and Negotiation

SAGE ANNUAL REVIEWS OF COMMUNICATION RESEARCH

SERIES EDITORS

Suzanne Pingree, *University of Wisconsin—Madison*
Robert P. Hawkins, *University of Wisconsin—Madison*
John M. Wiemann, *University of California—Santa Barbara*

EDITORIAL ADVISORY BOARD

Books in This Edited Series:

Editors

Linda L. Putnam
Michael E. Roloff

Communication and Negotiation

Sage Annual Reviews of Communication Research

Volume 20

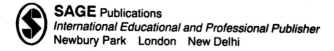

SAGE Publications
International Educational and Professional Publisher
Newbury Park London New Delhi

For information address:

SAGE Publications, Inc.
2455 Teller Road
Newbury Park, California 91320
E-mail: order@sagepub.com

SAGE Publications Ltd. .
6 Bonhill Street
London EC2A 4PU
United Kingdom

SAGE Publications India Pvt. Ltd.
M-32 Market
Greater Kailash I
New Delhi 110 048 India

Printed in the United States of America

Library of Congress Cataloging-in-Publication Data

Main entry under title:

Communication and negotiation / editors, Linda L. Putnam, Michael E.
    Roloff.
        p.   cm. — (Sage annual reviews of communication research; v.
    20)
    Includes bibliographical references and index.
    ISBN 0-8039-4011-4 (cloth). — ISBN 0-8039-4012-2 (pbk.)
    1. Negotiation in business. I. Putnam, Linda. II. Roloff,
Michael E. III. Series.
HD58.6.C66   1992
658.4—dc20   92-6398

97 98 99 00 01 02 8 7 6 5 4 3

Sage Production Editor: Astrid Virding

We dedicate this book to our spouses and daughters for their patience and support throughout the long hours of reading, revising, and editing these chapters.

Thomas M. Putnam and daughter, Ashley,

and

Karen Roloff and daughters, Erika, Katrina, and Carlissa

CONTENTS

ACKNOWLEDGMENTS

This book grew out of numerous conversations and convention panels that centered on the role of speech communication in studying conflict and negotiation. Discussions with colleagues, both inside and outside our field, heightened our awareness that no volume exists to describe and synthesize the conceptual perspectives that communication scholars bring to the study of negotiation. These perspectives employ a different language and different ways of seeing negotiation than do studies in cognate fields of social psychology, political science, anthropology, sociology, organizational behavior, economics, and law. Although communication scholars are not uniform in their approaches to negotiation nor do they have a monopoly on social interaction research, their perspectives, rooted in communication and rhetorical theory, distinguish them from scholars outside the field. The desire to articulate the conceptual roots and unique features of these perspectives compels the development of this book.

We are indebted to our colleagues in the field of communication and in the interdisciplinary area of conflict research for encouraging us to undertake this project. In particular, we extend our thanks to Suzanne Pingree, John M. Wiemann, and Robert P. Hawkins, the editors of the Sage Annual Reviews of Communication Research, for their advice and encouragement throughout this project. The chapter authors provided the necessary enthusiasm and cooperation to make this project possible. Their responses to requests for revisions in the face of imminent deadlines made the production of 11 chapters occur in a smooth and timely manner. Students in our seminars on communication and negotiation during past years provided excellent insights on the role of communication in bargaining and served as sounding boards for many ideas in this book. We would also like to thank Beverly Robinson and Liz Whitworth at Purdue for typing one of the chapters in this volume and to the Departments of Communication at Purdue and at Northwestern for their support throughout this process. Finally, we are also grateful to the professors who encouraged us to pursue negotiation research during our doctoral education, namely, David H. Smith at the University of South Florida, Ernest G. Bormann at the University of Minnesota, and Bradley Greenberg and Gerald R. Miller at Michigan State University.

COMMUNICATION PERSPECTIVES ON NEGOTIATION

Linda L. Putnam and Michael E. Roloff

> Ours is an age of negotiation. The fixed positions and solid values of the past seem to be giving way, and new rules, roles, and relations have to be worked out. The hard lines and easy cognitive recognition systems of the Cold War have first multiplied and then melted, revealing the necessity . . . of talking things over and out. . . . Negotiation becomes not a transition but a way of life.
>
> —I. W. Zartman, 1976, pp. 2, 3

ALTHOUGH ZARTMAN made this statement in the mid 1970s, his words apply in today's era of rapid political and economic changes, transformations in labor relations, and increasing civil and community disputes. Conflict in this country is a "growth industry" that pervades interpersonal relations, organizational processes, international diplomacy, and media content (R. Fisher & Ury, 1981; Kremenyuk, 1988; Roloff, 1987). Although we typically think of bargaining as a formal activity, negotiation is also prevalent in informal marital interactions, superior-subordinate communication, and customer-merchant exchanges (Galinat & Muller, 1988; G. Morris & Coursey, 1989; Scanzoni & Polonko, 1980). As a ubiquitous activity of modern life, negotiation merits the attention of communication scholars.

In fact, negotiation and communication are inherently intertwined. Logically, negotiation cannot occur without some means of communication. Although negotiation theorists recognize this fact, surprisingly little research centers directly on the role of communication in bargaining. Speech communication researchers began investigations of negotiation

1

in the 1960s and 1970s. At that time communication scholars were making key contributions to conflict research through their work on game theoretical models, persuasion, and interpersonal conflict (Beisecker, 1970; Bennett, 1971; Bostrom, 1968; Frost & Wilmot, 1978; Jandt, 1973; Miller & Simons, 1974). This work combined with empirical studies of restricted and unrestricted communication in negotiations (Greenwood, 1974; Johnson, 1974; Smith, 1969; Steinfatt, Seibold, & Frye, 1974) and the role of communication in labor-management mediation (Keltner, 1965; Taylor, 1973) brought communication scholars into the bargaining arena. Rhetorical studies on persuasion and social conflicts have also paved the way for communication scholars to develop a distinct approach to the study of conflict (Bosmajian, 1972; Bowers & Ochs, 1971; Burgess, 1973; Lanigan, 1970; Scott & Smith, 1969; Simons, 1969, 1972; Tompkins & Anderson, 1971). This work, when combined with contemporary studies of actual bargaining talk, has led to a research tradition that employs a communication lens to examine negotiation interaction (Donohue, 1981a, 1981b; Putnam & Jones, 1982b; Theye & Seiler, 1979).

This volume draws on these historical roots to integrate the research topics and perspectives that communication scholars employ in studying negotiation. This research crosses levels of analysis, methods of inquiry, and subspecialties in the field as scholars focus on negotiation as a common phenomenon of interest. Despite potential fragmentation into specialized domains, communication scholars aim to uncover insights about the way media, messages, and symbols function in the negotiation process. This introduction sets forth definitions of *negotiation* and *communication,* describes the nature and significance of a communication perspective, examines the role of communication within negotiation research, describes alternatives for classifying research on communication and negotiation, and presents the plan for this volume. Through integrating diverse subspecialties in the field, we hope that this volume aids in forming a "meta-perspective" for studying communication and bargaining (Pingree, Wiemann, & Hawkins, 1988, p. 13).

DEFINING COMMUNICATION AND NEGOTIATION

Negotiation, although similar to decision making or joint problem solving, is a special type of social interaction—one distinguished by goals, relationships, and normative practices that differ from other types of communication (Donohue, Diez, & Stahle, 1983). Bargaining entails two or more interdependent parties who perceive incompatible goals and engage in social interaction to reach a mutually satisfactory outcome (Sawyer & Guetzkow, 1965; Stein, 1988). Each party in the relationship must cooperate to reach his or her objective and each party can block the other one from attaining his or her goal (Putnam, 1989). This interdependence, combined with potentially antithetical goals and demands, sets up a mixed-motive relationship in which both parties cooperate by competing for divergent ends. Rules and normative practices of bargaining include specifying preferred outcomes prior to the negotiation, exchanging proposals and counterproposals, and engaging in dynamic movement through social interaction (Donohue et al., 1983; Walton & McKersie, 1965; Zartman, 1976).

These characteristics distinguish bargaining interaction from related types of communication such as group decision making and persuasion. In group decision making, participants do not necessarily develop preset preferences nor do they engage in ritualized proposal exchanges (C. Morris, 1970; Zartman, 1977). Negotiation goes beyond persuasion or getting the opponent to do something that he or she would not ordinarily do (Nemeth & Brilmayer, 1987). That is, negotiation employs problem solving activities and persuasion to reach mutually acceptable agreements, but these activities do not depict the nature of social interaction in bargaining. Negotiation differs from related types of communication by centering on perceived incompatibilities and employing strategies and tactics aimed at reaching a mutually acceptable agreement.

As the definition of *negotiation* implies, communication is central to the bargaining process. Lewicki and Litterer (1985, p. 157) treat social interaction as the "heart of the negotiation process" or "the central instrumental process." Bell (1988) contends that negotiation is primarily a complex process of verbal and nonverbal interaction and Zartman (1976) points out, "Negotiation is by nature a communication encounter, not a physical encounter (like war) or a mechanical encounter (like voting). . . . Controlled communication is the essence of negotiation" (p. 14).

Communication in bargaining entails multiple factors, including verbal messages, nonverbal cues, vocal overtones, information exchange, language, communication media, symbols, and meaning. Strategies and tactics of negotiating, for example, threats, demands, and offers, are expressed through verbal messages, gestures, and vocal overtones. Bargainers rely on both the content and the function of messages to provide information about proposals as well as reveal clues about their opponents' preferences and interests.

Language shapes the instrumental, relational, and identity management functions of negotiation (see Keough, Chapter 5, and Roloff & Jordan, Chapter 1, this volume; Wilson & Putnam, 1990). Language encompasses semantics or word choice, phonetics or the vocal production of syllables and words, and syntax or sentence structure (see Gibbons, Bradac, & Busch, Chapter 7, this volume). Language patterns shape the definition and transformation of proposals (instrumental communication, see Keough, Chapter 5, and Putnam & Holmer, Chapter 6, this volume), the concepts of power and influence (relational communication, see Donohue & Ramesh, Chapter 9, and Gibbons et al., Chapter 7, this volume), and each person's identity or face (identity management communication, see Wilson, Chapter 8, this volume). Language in negotiation also embodies past relationships of the bargainers, the history of the process, and the contextual features that permeate negotiation (Bell, 1988).

Communication media refer not only to the channel for conducting bargaining, for example, through telephone, face-to-face, or electronic systems, but also to the way modes of communication mediate the negotiation process. Media, then, are not simply containers for conducting bargaining or for covering it as a news event; rather they are actively involved in shaping negotiation situations and outcomes (see Douglas, Chapter 11, and Poole, Shannon, & DeSanctis, Chapter 2, this volume).

Social interaction in bargaining also entails "the production, transmission, and interpretation of symbols" and meanings (Roloff, 1987, p. 485). Symbols such as narratives, metaphors, myths, and images enact social meanings. Messages, language, and media are also symbolic in that they are drawn from a social context and from texts of discourse that constitute social meanings (see Douglas, Chapter 11, and Putnam & Holmer, Chapter 6, this volume). Bargainers use social texts and reproduce them in their interactions as they create strategies, tactics, and meanings in negotiations.

In effect, communication approaches to the study of bargaining are not unidimensional. Rather researchers center on select components of communication, namely, verbal and nonverbal messages, information exchange, language, media, symbols, and meaning. These components provide a lens to tap into other dimensions of bargaining, such as negotiator goals and characteristics, the climate of the interaction, the search for alternative settlements, the evolution or development of the bargaining process, negotiator relationships, and the role of audiences in the negotiation process. Communication research, then, is not simply the inclusion of different channels or several premanipulated messages into empirical designs. "Rather communication scholarship sets forth a perspective for understanding the negotiation process, for examining bargaining interaction as a system, and for exploring the micro elements and subtleties that frequently alter the course of negotiations" (Chatman, Putnam, & Sondak, 1991, p. 159).

THE ROLE OF COMMUNICATION IN NEGOTIATION

Although social interaction is a central element in bargaining, much of the extant literature and many theoretical perspectives are insensitive to the role that communication plays in negotiation. Bargaining research is dominated by work that seeks to predict outcomes to the neglect of the interaction that precedes, enacts, and sets up alternatives for settlements (Stein, 1988). Scholars also differ in the ways that they classifying bargaining and communication in different schools of research.

Zartman (1988) identifies five "families" of negotiation analysis: structural, strategic, process, behavioral, and integrative. *Structural analysis* focuses on the distribution of power or the relative strength of the parties. Communication in this perspective links power and reward strategies to negotiated outcomes (Donohue, 1978; Steinfatt et al., 1974). *Strategic analysis* employs game theory approaches to examine preset utilities and options. Game theory typically models utilities while reducing the number of options that players can consider at once. Studies that examine tacit communication or merge matrix games with opportunity to communicate adopt this analytical approach (Greenwood, 1974; Harris & Smith, 1974). *Process analysis* focuses on links between concession behavior and negotiated outcomes. Communication studies that center on offers and counteroffers, rates of concessions, and variance between initial and final offers fall into this approach. Tutzauer (Chapter 3, this volume) provides a critique of this perspective and offers alternatives for reconceptualizing this process.

Although research on communication falls into each of these families, most studies of bargaining interaction exemplify the behavioral or the integrative approaches. Behavioral analysis focuses on the goals, personality traits, and predispositions of negotiators. Research on cooperative-competitive orientations, levels of aspiration, and argumentativeness as a personality trait operate within behavioral analysis

(Keough, Chapter 5, this volume; Donohue, 1978; Tutzauer & Roloff, 1988). *Integrative analysis* centers on negotiation as a process that develops either through set stages or through changes in bargaining over time (Gulliver, 1979, 1988). Communication studies that examine phase development in negotiation, reciprocity in bargaining strategies and tactics, issue development, and escalating and de-escalating conflict work within this analytical approach (Bednar & Curington, 1983; Donohue & Diez, 1985; Donohue, Diez, & Hamilton, 1984; Putnam & Jones, 1982a; Putnam, Wilson, & Turner, 1990; Wilson & Putnam, 1990). Holmes (Chapter 4, this volume) reviews and critiques the negotiation literature on phase development and posits new frameworks and methods for conducting phase research.

Another alternative for classifying negotiation research stems from disciplinary arenas. Specifically, Bazerman, Lewicki, and Sheppard (1991) identify seven different disciplinary approaches to the study of negotiation, namely, behavioral decision theory, economics, social psychology, sociology, political science, communication, and anthropology. The study of social interaction in bargaining, however, is not limited to scholars in one field. Communication scholars have joined researchers from a variety of disciplines to study tactics and strategies, verbal and nonverbal messages, arguments, and influence patterns in negotiation.

In the 1960s and 1970s, a number of scholars from psychology, political science, marketing, and industrial relations used coding schemes to examine bargaining talk (see, for example, Angelmar & Stern, 1978; Axelrod, 1977; Dyar, 1977-1978; Hopmann, 1974; Landsberger, 1955; Lewis & Fry, 1977; McGrath & Julian, 1963; Morley & Stephenson, 1977; Osterberg, 1950; Pruitt, 1971; Pruitt & Lewis, 1975; Rackham & Carlisle, 1978a, 1978b; Walcott & Hopmann, 1975; Zechmeister & Druckman, 1973). These studies, even though they highlight the significance of social interaction in negotiation, typically place communication in a secondary role to other interests, for example, levels of aspiration, power relationships, international conflict, and integrative or successful settlements. Moreover, the coding schemes used to analyze interaction often fail to capture the subtle nuances that surface in actual communication.

Even though communication scholars are indebted to this early work, they departed from it in the 1980s by centering on message systems, sequences of communicative behavior, and language use as the essence of negotiation (Donohue, 1981a, 1981b; Putnam & Jones, 1982a). Message systems are not simply categories of verbal and nonverbal behaviors. Rather they reflect a coherent framework drawn from communication and rhetorical theory. For example, communication scholars develop argumentation categories from the way language generates knowledge, redefines issues, and enacts policies. These category systems extend beyond those that treat arguments as reflecting values or as illustrating different types of claims (Axelrod, 1977; see Keough, Chapter 5, this volume; Zechmeister & Druckman, 1973). Communication scholars also study the regularities, sequences, and patterns of messages as essential features of bargaining interaction. Moreover, the study of language illustrates how word choice, vocal overtones, and conversational structures embody the subtle nuances and complexities that characterize turning points in negotiation.

In effect, three key features distinguish a communication approach to negotiation. First, scholars examine bargaining through micro elements of verbal utterances, nonverbal cues, channels, language, and symbols. These micro elements form patterns, regularities, and subtle meanings that frequently alter the course of negotiation. Moreover, these micro processes occur in context; hence, bargainers produce message and meaning systems jointly through interactions that occur in situ. The context of communication, then, spans across previous and subsequent messages, communication patterns over time, bargaining context and relationships, and the larger social context from which language systems are derived.

Second, communication scholars center on the dynamic features of negotiation; hence they address such concerns as how goals, strategies, and tactics change over time; how information processing occurs; how offers are formulated and modified; how issues and disputes are transformed; how power and authority are redefined through communication styles and strategies; and how conflict in negotiation escalates and de-escalates (Bednar & Curington, 1983; Bell, 1988; Gulliver, 1979; Putnam & Jones, 1982a; Stein, 1988). As Chatman et al. (1991) contend, "To understand negotiation as an effective form of dispute resolution, researchers need to place investigations of the dynamic aspects of bargaining in the highest priority. The pieces of this complex and mysterious process puzzle appear to reside with the communication perspective" (p. 160).

A third feature that constitutes a communication approach is an effort to uncover systems of meaning in the bargaining process. Systems of meaning stem from many elements in the bargaining situation, including the negotiators' interpretations, covert verbal and nonverbal cues, the evolving patterns of behavior, past and normative practices, and societal texts (Bell, 1988; Stein, 1988). Because communication scholars focus on language and discourse, they can assess systems of meaning from individual, interpersonal, situational, and cultural perspectives. Individual or cognitive approaches to meaning center on negotiators' attributions, expectations, and intentions, while interpersonal approaches focus on co-orientation or the joint constructing of meaning through shared interpretations. Situational meanings stem from past practices, relationships among disputants, procedural and normative behaviors, prenegotiation history, genesis and evolution of the conflict, and organizational context. Finally, societal and cultural meanings impinge on bargaining through stereotypes of the activity, cultural language, legal and political constraints, constituents and audiences to the negotiation process, power relationships in society, and mass media coverage of bargaining events.

In effect, a communication perspective on negotiation operates from different assumptive ground than does a political, economic, or psychological view of bargaining. This assumptive ground derives from attention to elements that are typically ignored in extant literature, specifically, the microprocesses and patterns of bargaining interaction; the dynamic or evolving nature of negotiation; and the systems of meaning enacted through individual, situational, and cultural factors that shape the process. A communication perspective also leads to classifying extant literature differently than do scholars who track the historical development of bargaining or the analytical frameworks of theorists.

CLASSIFYING COMMUNICATION
AND BARGAINING RESEARCH

Two approaches for classifying communication and bargaining research surface in the literature. The *effects approach* treats communication as a variable in the bargaining process and the *key components approach* highlights the communication ingredients that researchers select to conduct particular studies. In the effects approach, researchers examine the way communication influences bargaining outcomes (Chatman et al., 1991). The models that researchers employ, however, link communication to bargaining outcomes in different ways. The limited effects model conceives of communication as noise or error that contaminates psychological, structural, or cultural predictors of negotiated outcomes. Hence, researchers try to control communication through designs that isolate bargainers from each other, treat communication as a mysterious "black box," and limit bargaining to short "one-shot" experiments. Although the limited effects model aids in studying bargaining inputs, it offers disputants little guidance once the process begins.

In contrast, three other models treat communication as an essential variable in predicting negotiated outcomes. The mediating effects model examines the way psychological, structural, or cultural variables produce communicative behaviors that, in turn, influence negotiated settlements. In this model, researchers study communication as a critical part of the causal sequence that links antecedents to outcomes. The moderating effects model treats communication not as a variable that adds to the causal sequence but as a contingency that moderates links between antecedent variables and outcomes. For example, cooperative orientations may shape high joint gains if certain communicative behaviors, like open and honest information exchange, occur during the negotiation.

Finally, the independent effects model treats communication as directly influencing outcomes. For example, frequent use of a particular type of policy arguments increases the likelihood of reaching integrative or distributive outcomes. The independence approach gains an advantage over the other two models by centering on bargaining as an emergent process. This model, however, unlike the mediating and moderating approaches, ignores the psychological, structural, and cultural factors that address why certain outcomes occur.

Using effects models to classify communication and bargaining literature assumes that the primary role communication plays in bargaining is to aid prediction and control. Other approaches emphasize the role of communication in understanding or making sense of negotiation as a complex social phenomenon or constituting negotiation rather than reflecting it as an objective experience (Jonsson, 1990). The *key components approach* is uniquely communicative in focusing on ingredients of communication as the basis for classifying research. This approach clusters bargaining research into B. Fisher's (1978) four perspectives for studying human communication: mechanistic, psychological, system-interaction, and interpretive-symbolic (Chatman et al., 1991; Putnam & Jones, 1982b; Putnam & Poole, 1987). This classification scheme emanates from the way researchers highlight the different components of communication, for example, sender, receiver, message, channel, and transmission (Krone, Jablin, & Putnam, 1987; Chatman et al., 1991). Jonsson (1990) employs a variation of this approach in his classification scheme of manipulative, cognitive, and cybernetic categories. The mechanistic perspective adopts a conduit metaphor by centering on the sending of information through communication channels, for example, opportunity to communicate or comparison of written, face-to-face, and electronic channels (Greenwood, 1974; Steinfatt et al., 1974) while the psychological approach accents the attributes or motivational aspects of negotiators that influence verbal and nonverbal messages (Johnson, McCarty, & Allen, 1976; Tutzauer & Roloff, 1988). Both approaches typically treat communication as a variable that moderates or mediates negotiated outcomes.

In contrast, the systems-interactional and the interpretive-symbolic approaches focus on communication as a way of understanding how negotiation is constituted. Researchers who adopt a systems-interactional view concentrate on the sequence, the development, or the recurring patterns of verbal and nonverbal messages that enact the process (Donohue et al., 1984; Putnam & Jones, 1982a). The interpretive-symbolic approach focuses on meanings that are created, maintained, or modified through bargaining interaction. This work typically examines language, conversational structures, or symbols as indices of meanings that bargainers jointly construct from their situational or cultural context (Diez, 1986; Neu, 1988, Putnam, Van Hoeven, & Bullis, 1991).

Both approaches reveal the goals and assumptions of researchers. However, both the effects model and the key components approach limit the role of communication in bargaining. The effects model reduces communication to a variable aimed at predicting outcomes. This approach eludes studies that see communication as socially constructing the bargaining process. The key components approach suffers from its inability to classify perspectives that overlap, for example, studies that combine psychological and system-interaction approaches. Moreover, the study of a particular construct in negotiation, for example, negotiator power, typically crosses all four perspectives (see, for instance, Donohue & Ramesh, Chapter 9, this volume). Finally, this typology operates primarily at an interpersonal level that minimizes socio-historical and critical approaches to the study of bargaining. B. Fisher's (1978) typology, then, is useful for classifying dyadic bargaining but is limited in addressing the situational and contextual features of negotiation.

PLAN OF THIS VOLUME

Rather than adopt a pure form of these approaches, this volume clusters research on communication and negotiation into three sections that unite bargaining arena and communication perspectives. Part I of this book focuses on the negotiation process, specifically on the strategies and tactics embedded in social interaction, the effects of communication media on the negotiation process, and the evolution of bargaining from prenegotiation to settlement. This section of the book examines the research that crosses mechanistic, psychological, and system-interactional perspectives on communication and negotiation. In Chapter 1, Roloff and Jordan explore the content of negotiation plans. Plans entail the actions and interactions that bargainers devise for reaching commodity, relational, and face-related goals. Strategies and communicative tactics, however, often change as negotiators revise their plans, anticipate their opponents' plans, and develop collaborative plans through prenegotiation and use of procedural messages during formal bargaining.

Poole, Shannon, and DeSanctis in Chapter 2 illustrate how types and combinations of communication media aid in the movement of negotiation through differentiation to integration. In particular, they examine the way different media impact on conflict intensity, the synchronization of strategies, issue definition, solution search, face saving, climate, and the balance of power between negotiators. This chapter concludes by recommending a multimedia approach to bargaining and by posing queries for determining when and how to use multimedia in negotiation.

In Chapter 3, Tutzauer reframes traditional research on offers and counteroffers in bargaining by reviewing the strengths and weaknesses of models of concession behavior. Operating from the assumptions that offers change over time and that bargainers influence each other, he introduces a communication framework for examining concession behavior either as strings of offers and responses, or as unidimensional points on a continuum, or as small changes that induce catastrophic variations. With a similar focus on the dynamic elements of negotiation, Holmes in Chapter 4 reviews and critiques the models of phase development in bargaining. He defines a *phase* as a coherent period of interaction characterized by a dominant constellation of communication acts. Drawing from distinctions between phases as stages and phases as episodes, Holmes presents alternative frameworks and methods for examining multidimensional phases in negotiation research.

Part II of this book shifts to the research on language and meaning in negotiation. This work draws from the interpretive-symbolic perspective for studying communication and negotiation. In particular, it centers on the role of language and meaning in the use of arguments, the framing and reframing of issues, the expression of threats and promises, and the use of facework in negotiations. In Chapter 5, Keough reviews rhetorical and conversational approaches to the use of arguments in bargaining. She challenges the traditional use of persuasive arguments as strategies used to gain coherence from opponents and sets forth the position that arguments in negotiation produce knowledge and generate ideas. They serve instrumental, relational, and identity management functions and can be judged for their effectiveness and appropriateness in the negotiation process.

Putnam and Holmer in Chapter 6 add to Keough's view by treating arguments as frames for conceptualizing issues in negotiation. *Frames* are biases, interpretive schemes, or meaning systems that are indexed through language use. Putnam and Holmer compare and contrast three approaches to the study of framing in negotiation: cognitive heuristics, frame categories, and issue development. They introduce concepts from Bateson's and Goffman's notions of framing to enrich the three approaches and to add communicative features to the study of reframing in bargaining.

Language is the central theme of Gibbons, Bradac, and Busch's approach to the study of threats and promises in Chapter 7. The language of threats is revealed through semantics, syntax, and phonetics as well as propositions. Issues of intentionality and control are central in making sense of threats in bargaining. They advocate the use of language dimensions such as polarization, intensity, immediacy, diversity, and style to examine threats in negotiation.

Wilson in Chapter 8 reviews the research that employs the social psychological and the discourse traditions for studying facework in negotiation. Communicative tactics and discourse patterns are ways that bargainers defend and protect their own and the other person's face during negotiations. These face management interactions are critical to maintaining the bargainer's identity. Wilson advocates merging the two research traditions and linking face concerns to negotiated outcomes.

In Part III of this book, situational context and the socio-historical conditions dominate the treatment of communication and bargaining. This section treats negotiator-opponent relationships as sequences of interchanges that occur over an extended time; negotiator-constituent relationships as messages between bargainers and their constituencies; and negotiation audiences as the makers, promoters, assemblers, and consumers of news about negotiations and disputes. In Chapter 9, Donohue and Ramesh review the literature on the affective/cognitive and behavior aspects of bargainer-opponent relationships. Specifically, they center on the role of strategies, tactics, and meaning systems of relationships as expressed through expectations, goals, and feelings. They conclude that bargaining is effective when relational messages go unnoticed or when they are openly discussed rather than covertly expressed.

In Chapter 10, Turner expands relationship beyond the dyad to bargainer-constituent communication. Working within a boundary role perspective, he reviews the literature on communication of expectations, feedback on performance, and the management of distance and trust in caucus sessions. He concludes by presenting a model for linking negotiator-constituent interaction to communication at the bargaining table.

Douglas, in Chapter 11, shifts to the broad arena of public constituencies and media audiences. In particular, she addresses the way news of negotiation is produced, the effects of media on negotiated outcomes, and the role of media in the negotiation process. She concludes that news making performs a middle position between media promoters and consumers and that the media need social conflicts to pursue their own needs for institutional power and profits.

Research on communication and negotiation provides a lens for examining the micro processes in bargaining, for concentrating on the dynamic features of the process, and for understanding individual and social meanings. This volume pulls together research on strategies and tactics; language and meaning; and situational and contextual parameters that influence negotiator-opponent relationships, negotiator-constituent interactions, and media audiences.

A communication perspective, as with any disciplinary approach, has its limitations. As Bell (1988) astutely observes, "Each disciplinary perspective is partial and incomplete, it brings into sharp focus some elements of a phenomena, but blurs, distorts, and masks other features entirely" (p. 235). The topics addressed in this volume illustrate the way communication researchers have coalesced around demarcated zones. These zones provide only minimal treatment of the emerging areas of international and cross-cultural negotiation, multiparty disputes, and interorganizational bargaining. In effect, the research reported in this volume relies too heavily on dyadic negotiations defined through an American model. Even though the chapters in this volume draw from research on hostage negotiation and marital disputes, the majority of work in communication centers on laboratory experiments and labor-management settings. Future studies need to include formal and informal business negotiations, plea bargaining, and multiparty disputes.

Finally, communication researchers need to concentrate on integrating micro and macro levels of analysis. Since communication scholars bring a micro lens to the study of negotiation, finding a way to merge micro processes with macro context is the most significant challenge for future studies. This volume, with its goal of crossing interpersonal, organizational, and mass communication research, is a step in this direction.

REFERENCES

Angelmar, R., & Stern, L. W. (1978). Development of a content analytic system for analysis of bargaining communication in marketing. *Journal of Marketing Research, 15,* 93-102.

Axelrod, R. (1977). Argumentation in foreign policy settings. *Journal of Conflict Resolution, 21,* 727-756.

Bazerman, M. H., Lewicki, R. J., & Sheppard, B. H. (Eds.). (1991). *Research on negotiation in organizations: Handbook of negotiation research* (Vol. 3). Greenwich, CT: JAI Press.

Bednar, D. A., & Curington, W. P. (1983). Interaction analysis: A tool for understanding negotiations. *Industrial and Labor Relations Review, 36,* 389-401.

Beisecker, T. (1970). Verbal persuasive strategies in mixed-motive interactions. *Quarterly Journal of Speech, 56,* 149-160.

Bell, D. V. J. (1988). Political linguistics and international negotiation. *Negotiation Journal, 4,* 233-246.

Bennett, W. (1971). Conflict rhetoric and game theory: An extrapolation and example. *Southern Speech Communication Journal, 37,* 34-46.

Bosmajian, H. A. (Ed.). (1972). *Dissent: Symbolic behavior and rhetorical strategies.* Boston: Allyn & Bacon.

Bostrom, R. N. (1968). Game theory in communication research. *Journal of Communication, 18,* 369-388.

Bowers, J. W., & Ochs, D. J. (1971). *The rhetoric of agitation and control.* Reading, MA: Addison-Wesley.

Burgess, P. G. (1973). Crisis rhetoric: Coercion versus force. *Quarterly Journal of Speech, 59,* 61-73.

Chatman, J. A., Putnam, L. L., & Sondak, H. (1991). Integrating communication and negotiation research. In M. H. Bazerman, R. J. Lewicki, & B. H. Sheppard (Eds.), *Research on negotiation in organizations: Handbook of negotiation research* (Vol. 3, pp. 139-164). Greenwich, CT: JAI Press.

Diez, M. E. (1986). Negotiation competence: A conceptualization of the rules of negotiation interaction. In D. G. Ellis & W. A. Donohue (Eds.), *Contemporary issues in language and discourse processes* (pp. 223-237). Hillsdale, NJ: Lawrence Erlbaum.

Donohue, W. A. (1978). An empirical framework for examining negotiation processes and outcomes. *Communication Monographs, 45,* 247-257.

Donohue, W. A. (1981a). Analyzing negotiation tactics: Development of a negotiation interact system. *Human Communication Research, 7,* 273-287.

Donohue, W. A. (1981b). Development of a model of rule use in negotiation interaction. *Communication Monographs, 48,* 106-120.

Donohue, W. A., & Diez, M. E. (1985). Directive use in negotiation interaction. *Communication Monographs, 52,* 305-318.

Donohue, W. A., Diez, M. E., & Hamilton, M. (1984). Coding naturalistic negotiation interaction. *Human Communication Research, 10,* 403-425.

Donohue, W. A., Diez, M. E., & Stahle, R. B. (1983). New directions in negotiation research. In R. Bostrom (Ed.), *Communication yearbook 7* (pp. 249-279). Beverly Hills, CA: Sage.

Dyar, D. A. (1977-1978). An analysis of negotiation interaction and behaviour. *Industrial Relations Journal, 8,* 61-72.

Fisher, B. A. (1978). *Perspectives on human communication.* New York: Macmillan.

Fisher, R., & Ury, W. (1981). *Getting to yes: Negotiating agreement without giving in.* New York: Houghton Mifflin.

Frost, J. H., & Wilmot, W. W. (1978). *Interpersonal conflict* (1st ed.). Dubuque, IA: William C. Brown.

Galinat, W. H., & Muller, G. F. (1988). Verbal responses to different bargaining strategies: A content analysis of real-life, buyer-seller interaction. *Journal of Applied Social Psychology, 18,* 160-178.

Greenwood, J. G. (1974). Opportunity to communicate and social orientation in imaginary-reward bargaining. *Speech Monographs, 41,* 79-81.

Gulliver, P. H. (1979). *Disputes and negotiations: A cross-cultural perspective.* New York: Academic Press.

Gulliver, P. H. (1988). Anthropological contributions to the study of negotiations. *Negotiation Journal, 4,* 247-255.

Harris, T. E., & Smith, R. M. (1974). An experimental verification of Schelling's tacit communication hypothesis. *Speech Monographs, 41,* 82-84.

Hopmann, P. T. (1974). Bargaining in arms control negotiations: The seabeds denuclearization treaty. *International Organization, 3,* 313-343.

Jandt, F. E. (Ed.). (1973). *Conflict resolution through communication.* New York: Harper & Row.

Johnson, D. W. (1974). Communication and the inducement of cooperative behavior in conflicts: A critical review. *Speech Monographs, 41,* 64-78.

Johnson, D. W., McCarty, K., & Allen, T. (1976). Congruent and contradictory verbal and nonverbal communications of cooperativeness and competitiveness in negotiations. *Communication Research, 3,* 275-291.

Jonsson, C. (1990). *Communication in international bargaining.* New York: St. Martin's.

Keltner, J. W. (1965). Communication and the labor-management mediation process: Some aspects and hypotheses. *Journal of Communication, 2,* 64-80.

Kremenyuk, V. A. (1988). The emerging system of international negotiations. *Negotiation Journal, 4,* 211-218.

Krone, K. J., Jablin, F. M., & Putnam, L. L. (1987). Communication theory and organizational communication: Multiple perspectives. In F. M. Jablin, L. L. Putnam, K. H. Roberts, & L. W. Porter (Eds.), *Handbook of organizational communication* (pp. 18-40). Newbury Park, CA: Sage.

Landsberger, H. A. (1955). Interaction process analysis of the mediation of labor-management disputes. *Journal of Abnormal and Social Psychology, 51,* 552-558.

Lanigan, R. L. (1970). Urban crisis: Polarization and communication. *Central States Speech Journal, 21,* 108-116.

Lewicki, R. J., & Litterer, J. A. (1985). *Negotiation.* Homewood, IL: Irwin.

Lewis, S. A., & Fry, W. R. (1977). Effects of visual access and orientation on the discovery of integrative bargaining alternatives. *Organizational Behavior and Human Performance, 20,* 75-92.

McGrath, J. E., & Julian, J. W. (1963). Interaction process and task outcomes in experimentally created negotiation groups. *Journal of Psychological Studies, 14,* 117-138.

Miller, G. R., & Simons, H. W. (Eds.). (1974). *Perspectives on communication in social conflict.* Englewood Cliffs, NJ: Prentice-Hall.

Morley, I., & Stephenson, G. M. (1977). *The social psychology of bargaining.* London: George Allen & Unwin.

Morris, C. G. (1970). Changes in group interaction during problem-solving. *Journal of Social Psychology, 81,* 157-165.

Morris, G. H., & Coursey, M. (1989). Negotiating the meaning of employees' conduct: How managers evaluate employees' accounts. *Southern Communication Journal, 54,* 185-205.

Nemeth, C., & Brilmayer, A. G. (1987). Negotiation versus influence. *European Journal of Social Psychology, 17,* 45-56.

Neu, J. (1988). Conversational structure: An explanation of bargaining behaviors in negotiations. *Management Communication Quarterly, 2,* 23-45.

Osterberg, W. H. (1950). A method for the study of bargaining conferences. *Personnel Psychology, 3,* 169-178.

Pingree, S., Wiemann, J. M., & Hawkins, R. P. (1988). Editors' introduction: Toward conceptual synthesis. In R. P. Hawkins, J. M. Wiemann, & S. Pingree (Eds.), *Advancing communication science: Merging mass and interpersonal processes* (pp. 7-17). Newbury Park, CA: Sage.

Pruitt, D. G. (1971). Indirect communication and the search for agreement in negotiation. *Journal of Applied Social Psychology, 1,* 205-239.

Pruitt, D. G., & Lewis, S. A. (1975). Development of integrative solutions in bilateral negotiation. *Journal of Personality and Social Psychology, 31,* 621-633.

Putnam, L. L. (1989). Bargaining. In E. Barnouw (Ed.), *International encyclopedia of communication* (Vol. 1, pp. 176-178). Philadelphia, PA: Oxford University Press.

Putnam, L. L., & Jones, T. S. (1982a). Reciprocity in negotiations: An analysis of bargaining interaction. *Communication Monographs, 49,* 171- 191.

Putnam, L. L., & Jones, T. S. (1982b). The role of communication in bargaining. *Human Communication Research, 8,* 262-280.

Putnam, L. L., & Poole, M. S. (1987). Conflict and negotiation. In F. M. Jablin, L. L. Putnam, K. H. Roberts, & L. W. Porter (Eds.), *Handbook of organizational communication* (pp. 549-599). Newbury Park, CA: Sage.

Putnam, L. L., Van Hoeven, S. A., & Bullis, C. A. (1991). The role of rituals and fantasy themes in teachers' bargaining. *Western Journal of Speech Communication, 55,* 85-103.

Putnam, L. L., Wilson, S. R., & Turner, D. B. (1990). The evolution of policy arguments in teachers' negotiations. *Argumentation, 4,* 129-152.

Rackham, N., & Carlisle, J. (1978a). The effective negotiator—Part I: The behaviour of successful negotiators. *Journal of European Industrial Training, 2*(6), 6-11.

Rackham, N., & Carlisle, J. (1978b). The effective negotiator—Part II: Planning for negotiations. *Journal of European Industrial Training, 2*(7), 2-5.

Roloff, M. E. (1987). Communication and conflict. In C. R. Berger & S. H. Chaffee (Eds.), *Handbook of communication science* (pp. 484-534). Newbury Park, CA: Sage.

Sawyer, J., & Guetzkow, H. (1965). Bargaining and negotiation in international relations. In H. C. Kelman (Ed.), *International behavior: A social-psychological analysis* (pp. 466-520). New York: Holt, Rinehart & Winston.

Scanzoni, J., & Polonko, K. (1980). A conceptual approach to explicit marital negotiation. *Journal of Marriage and the Family, 42,* 31-44.

Scott, R. L., & Smith, D. K. (1969). The rhetoric of confrontation. *Quarterly Journal of Speech, 55,* 1-8.

Simons, H. W. (1969). Confrontation as a pattern of persuasion in university settings. *Central States Speech Journal, 20,* 163-169.

Simons, H. W. (1972). Persuasion in social conflicts: A critique of prevailing conceptions and a framework for future research. *Speech Monographs, 39,* 227-247.

Smith, D. H. (1969). Communication and negotiation outcome. *Journal of Communication, 19,* 248-256.

Stein, J. G. (1988). International negotiation: A multidisciplinary perspective. *Negotiation Journal, 4,* 221-231.

Steinfatt, T. M., Seibold, D. R., & Frye, J. K. (1974). Communication in game simulated conflicts: Two experiments. *Speech Monographs, 41,* 24-35.

Taylor, S. A. (1973). Communication and teacher-administration negotiations. *Speech Teacher, 22,* 44-47.

Theye, L. D., & Seiler, W. J. (1979). Interaction analysis in collective bargaining: An alternative approach to the prediction of negotiated outcomes. In D. Nimmo (Ed.), *Communication yearbook 3* (pp. 375-392). New Brunswick, NJ: Transaction-International Communication Association.

Tompkins, P., & Anderson, E. V. B. (1971). *Communication crisis at Kent State: A case study.* New York: Gordon & Breach.

Tutzauer, F., & Roloff, M. E. (1988). Communication processes leading to integrative agreements: Three paths to joint benefits. *Communication Research, 15,* 360-380.

Walcott, C., & Hopmann, P. T. (1975). Interaction analysis and bargaining behavior. *Experimental Study of Politics, 4,* 1-19.

Walton, R. E., & McKersie, R. B. (1965). *A behavioral theory of labor negotiations: An analysis of a social interaction system.* New York: McGraw-Hill.

Wilson, S. R., & Putnam, L. L. (1990). Interaction goals in negotiation. In J. A. Anderson (Ed.), *Communication yearbook 13* (pp. 374-406). Newbury Park, CA: Sage.

Zartman, I. W. (1976). Introduction. In I. W. Zartman (Ed.), *The 50% solution* (pp. 3-41). New Haven, CT: Yale University Press.

Zartman, I. W. (1977). Negotiation as a joint decision-making process. *Journal of Conflict Resolution, 21,* 619-638.

Zartman, I. W. (1988). Common elements in the analysis of the negotiation process. *Negotiation Journal, 4,* 31-43.

Zechmeister, K., & Druckman, D. (1973). Determinants of resolving a conflict of interest: A simulation of political decision making. *Journal of Conflict Resolution, 17,* 63-88.

PART I

STRATEGIES, TACTICS, AND NEGOTIATION PROCESSES

Chapter 1

ACHIEVING NEGOTIATION GOALS: THE "FRUITS AND FOIBLES" OF PLANNING AHEAD

Michael E. Roloff and Jerry M. Jordan

LEWICKI AND LITTERER (1985) observed, "Preparation and planning are the most important parts of negotiation" (p. 47). Indeed, professional negotiators from the United States report that planning skills are the most important traits a bargainer can have (Karrass, 1970) and this view is shared by negotiators from many other countries (Graham & Sano, 1989). Although research verifies that the manner in which bargainers plan affects their outcomes (Bass, 1966; Druckman, 1967, 1968; Morley, 1982), extant scholarship is hampered by its fragmented and descriptive nature. To address these deficits, this chapter reviews scholarship on negotiation planning and concludes with recommendations for future research. It begins by examining the nature of negotiation plans and the planning process.

NEGOTIATION PLANS

Few researchers have studied the most obvious and important aspect of preparation, the content of negotiation plans (Rackham & Carlisle, 1978; Roloff & Jordan, 1991). Researchers rarely ask negotiators to describe their plans, choosing instead to correlate facets of the planning process with outcomes (Bass, 1966; Druckman, 1967, 1968; Kahn & Kohls, 1972; Klimoski, 1972). By not assessing plan content, researchers are unable to identify features that hinder goal accomplishment (cf. Bell & Roloff, 1991; Berger & Bell, 1988).

Plans are the actions that individuals devise to overcome obstacles to goal achievement. Although not all behaviors are planned (cf. Roloff & Berger, 1982) nor are all planned actions performed (Hjelmquist & Gidlund, 1984), this chapter assumes a causal relationship between the plans that bargainers devise and the enactment of behaviors contained therein (cf. Chmielewski, 1982).

Plans are linked to three fundamental elements: goals, obstacles, and means. Goals are desired endstates toward which actors strive (Miller, Galanter, & Pribram, 1960). Plans are tied to the goals they are designed to attain. Regardless of whether goals exist from the outset of the negotiation or emerge during interaction, negotiation behavior aims at their accomplishment and continues until disputants reach or abandon their objectives (Benoit, 1990).

An obstacle constitutes a perceived barrier to goal achievement (Allen, 1984). As a goal is analyzed, obstacles become conspicuous. Hammond (1989) proposes a model of plans that highlights the interrelatedness of goals and obstacles through the organization of plans in memory. Plans are indexed in memory by the goals they satisfy *and* by the problems they avoid. Therefore, a person can develop a plan to achieve current goals while avoiding the problems that inhibit goal attainment. The recollected obstacles serve two functions. They allow old plans to be "debugged" to facilitate goal achievement and they highlight means by which an opponent's plan might be thwarted (cf. Carbonell, 1981).

Planners devise means that are adapted specifically to overcoming obstacles to their objectives. Plans consist of action sequences that are expected to produce desired effects. Since language is used to overcome obstacles to goal achievement (Gibbs, 1986; Roloff & Janiszewski, 1989), negotiators devise interaction behaviors intended to accomplish their goals (Benoit, 1990).

Since plans are aimed at goal attainment, this discussion of plan content focuses on negotiation objectives. Fundamentally, negotiation is a process by which parties attempt to reach an accord that specifies how they will act toward one another (cf. Sawyer & Guetzkow, 1965). Specifically, negotiators try to dictate or clarify the terms of an exchange or the distribution of resources (Wall, 1985). In doing so, negotiators pursue three types of goals: commodity, relational, and face-related. Although negotiators may pursue multiple goals that interact in complex ways, this chapter discusses goals in isolation with an emphasis on their respective characteristics, obstacles encountered in their pursuit, and the means employed to overcome resistance. After discussing each type separately, this chapter examines the pursuit of multiple goals.

COMMODITY GOALS

When the supply of a resource falls outside an optimal range, individuals try to acquire needed quantities (Foa & Foa, 1974). Often they turn to others to acquire commodities such as money, goods, services, or information. When advantageous to do so, people negotiate a resource exchange prior to a transaction (Neale, Northcraft, & Bazerman, 1989).

Characteristics. Scholars suggest four important characteristics of commodity goals. First, negotiators profit from conceptualizing their commodity goals as interests rather than positions. Interests are the desires and concerns that motivate negotiators to develop specific positions on an issue (Fisher & Ury, 1981; Lax & Sebenius, 1986). For example, a professor may plan to demand a given salary level in exchange for services. That position may stem from an underlying interest to maintain a certain standard of living. By focusing on the base interest, the professor can formulate a number of different alternatives through which the university can meet his or her goal (e.g., salary, summer support, consulting opportunities) and can avoid becoming locked in an untenable position (i.e., a single salary level).

Second, negotiators should *operationalize* their commodity goals in a specific fashion. To evaluate the extent to which an offer meets their needs, negotiators should cast their goals in quantitative terms and should set both a target and a resistance point (Lewicki & Litterer, 1985). Thus, a negotiator would identify a range of incomes that could afford a given standard of living. Indeed, such specific objectives are frequently developed prior to negotiation (Putnam, Wilson, & Turner, 1990; Rackham & Carlisle, 1978) and bargainers who try to achieve specific, quantitative goals acquire greater profits than do those whose goals are not precise (Huber & Neale, 1987).

Third, negotiators should be flexible as to the total number of commodities under consideration. A negotiator may be ill-served by seeking only one resource. For example, if a university cannot afford to offer a professor a given salary, the negotiations may reach an impasse. However, the university might offer guaranteed sabbatical or computer equipment as compensation for a lower salary. To the extent that these commodities serve the same function as salary or meet a different interest of at least equal value (i.e., support the professor's research), the professor could modify his or her salary demands. Moreover, some of these options may not be as costly to the university as salary and could be traded away (cf. Tietz & Weber, 1978). By expanding the resources under consideration, both parties could entice each other to fulfill commodity goals and to reach an agreement that integrates their needs (Pruitt, 1981).

Fourth, bargainers should formulate goals to which they can remain committed. Bargainers who are *not* firmly committed to their objectives engage in concession-making that reduces the likelihood of maximizing their outcomes (Pruitt, 1981). For example, group representatives who oppose the majority position during the formulation of objectives or do not participate in the setting of group goals are less committed to the group demands and are more willing to adopt the views of the opposing representative rather than to defend their own groups' objective (Breaugh & Klimoski, 1977; Rabbie & Huygen, 1974).

Finally, negotiators should set goals that are difficult but possible to attain. Difficult goals have an energizing effect on bargainers and, as long as the goals are realistic, they promote behaviors that lead to integrative agreements (Huber & Neale, 1987). Accordingly, bargainers committed to specific and moderately difficult goals are likely to discover integrative potential and to formulate tactics that capitalize on it (Roloff & Jordan, 1991).

Obstacles to Achieving Commodity Goals. Negotiators may encounter three types of obstacles to commodity goal achievement. First, they may discover obstacles that reside within the opposing party. Given that negotiators initially perceive their interests as incompatible (Thompson & Hastie, 1990), they may expect their opponent to resist proposals and set lower prenegotiation commodity goals (Tietz, Weber, Vidmajer, & Wentzel, 1978). Opponents can also create obstacles through argumentative discourse enacted during a negotiation (Putnam et al., 1990). When successful, this discourse reduces the pressure on bargainers to make concessions (Donohue, 1981a, 1981b).

An opponent's resistance may stem from lack of motivation or lack of ability to agree to the negotiator's requests for commodities (cf. Francik & Clark, 1985; Gibbs, 1986). Stubbornness may be based on four things: (1) the negotiator's needs are insufficiently urgent to require action, (2) the opposition has no obligation (legal or moral) to lessen the need, (3)

meeting the need is not advantageous to the opposition's interests, and
(4) the negotiator's proposals will not attenuate the need (cf. Putnam et al.,
1990). However, even if sufficiently motivated, resistance may arise
from inability to meet the stated need. The opposing negotiator may be
perceived to have insufficient resources to meet the expressed needs
or may not have the authority to allocate them (cf. Bies, Shapiro, &
Cummings, 1988).

The second source of obstacles resides with the negotiators themselves. Not all negotiators believe that they can influence their counterparts. Bargainers, who prior to negotiation have information that their
case is not easily defensible, set lower commodity goals (Druckman,
Zechmeister, & Solomon, 1972; Tietz et al., 1978) as do negotiators who
perceive they have inadequate alternative commodity sources (Rabbie
& Visser, 1972). In other instances, negotiators have insufficient confidence in their own abilities to accomplish goals. Bargainers who fail to
achieve their commodity goals in past negotiations set lower goals prior
to bargaining than do those who were successful in the past (Tietz et al.,
1978). Consequently, it is not surprising that bargaining groups spend
time in their initial planning sessions reviewing the merits of their own
case (Putnam et al., 1990).

Finally, individuals may perceive obstacles within the negotiation context such as time pressure. Negotiations are costly in terms of resources
expended to keep them going as well as delays in meeting commodity
goals (Pruitt, 1981). Hence, bargainers cannot afford a protracted negotiation. Bargainers under time pressure set lower resistance and target
points both initially and during negotiation (Pruitt & Drews, 1969; Yukl,
1974a, 1974b). Consequently, discussions during caucus sessions often
focus on the advantage of granting a concession in exchange for a timely
agreement (Putnam, Wilson, Waltman, & Turner, 1986).

Overcoming Commodity Obstacles. Scholars have not uncovered the
link between perceived obstacles to achieving commodity goals and the
means by which negotiators plan to overcome them. However, a secondary analysis of data from a study in which students negotiated the
sale of textbooks to a bookstore (Roloff & Jordan, 1991) provides information to infer such a link.

In this context, negotiators create two strategies to motivate a skep-
tical opponent: unilateral and bilateral. The unilateral strategy is aimed
at convincing the opponent to make concessions from his or her commodity objectives. To do so, 52% of the negotiators aim to advance

arguments based upon the quality of the books, their market value, and need for profit. In essence, they try to entice the opponent to pay their price by stressing the legitimacy of their need and highlighting the advantages of their product. In addition, 18% of the students indicate that they try to create a positive relationship with the opponent by acting friendly, fair, and concerned. Presumably, opponents are more inclined to give in if they like the negotiator than if they dislike him or her. This situation implies that relationship building constitutes a means to an end as well as an end in and of itself. Finally, a few negotiators plan to move the opponent by being coercive (12%) or making promises (6%).

Negotiators also devise a bilateral strategy in which they try to motivate the opponent to change by altering their own position. Overall, 31% report that they intend to make a high initial offer on each book followed by concessions. By starting with a bid that is higher than their goal, negotiators can afford to make concessions that activate a norm of reciprocity (Wall, 1985). As a result, the parties move toward a compromise position (Froman & Cohen, 1970).

A similar percentage (34%) plan to logroll. They treat the three books as a package and trade price concessions on books that are of little value in exchange for opponent's concession on books that are worth more (cf. Tietz & Weber, 1978). Thus, they meet their own needs by attaining higher profits on some books and taking a loss on books of lower priority. This tactic is especially prevalent when the bargaining situation makes it easy to prioritize the relative value of the books and the negotiator has moderately difficult commodity goals (cf. Thompson, 1990a, 1990b).

Negotiators are also aware that the ability to accept a proposal can be an obstacle. For example, 9% of the negotiators aim to *resist* their opponent by citing their lack of authority (i.e., their friend or boss has the final say). In effect, the constituent becomes an obstacle (cf. Friedland, 1983; Rubin, Brockner, Eckenrode, Enright, & Johnson-George, 1980). To counter, 14% indicate they would stress the benefits of their proposal to the opponent's constituency.

Although no strategies or tactics aimed at overcoming self-related or situational obstacles emerge in the plans, bargainers appear sensitive to these problems. Self-related obstacles, as previously noted, stem from having insufficient confidence in the strength of one's case or in one's ability to influence the opponent. When asked what information they would like to possess while creating their plans, bargainers ask for strategic information to use in an upcoming negotiation. Negotiators are sensitive to their need for information to make better arguments for their position, such as the original price for the books (26%), the books' current market value (39%), the condition of the books (21%), their own or opposition's alternatives to reaching agreement (11%), and information about the opponent's strategies and traits (48%). Although participants in this study could not acquire this information during bargaining, it is likely such information seeking normally occurs prior to and during the negotiation and might bolster flagging confidence (Thompson, 1991; Tutzauer & Roloff, 1988).

Finally, a few bargainers are uncertain about situational obstacles; 2% report the need to know how much time they have to negotiate an agreement. Anticipating time pressure may make negotiators lax in preparing extensive arguments (cf. Morley, 1982) and too responsive in concession-making.

Although speculative, these data suggest bargainers recognize obstacles to reaching their commodity goals and create specific yet diverse tactics for overcoming them.

RELATIONAL GOALS

When two negotiators agree to a commodity exchange, they enter into a relationship (cf. Blau, 1967). In some cases, their association is transient. If there are many suppliers of a resource or if repeated exchanges are impractical, then no contact beyond a single transaction is necessary or desirable. However, negotiators may find it advantageous to anticipate or even guarantee that future exchanges occur. A stable supply of needed commodities is attractive and exchange relations may become intrinsically rewarding as partners come to like one another (Lax & Sebenius, 1986). Consequently, negotiators may have goals of cultivating and maintaining relational commitment (see Donohue & Ramesh, Chapter 9, this volume; Greenhalgh, 1987).

Characteristics. Relational goals have three important characteristics. First, relational objectives may cause negotiators to focus beyond individual interests to the welfare of the association as a separate entity. This altruism implies that individuals can separate the needs of their relationship from their own parochial concerns. Indeed, some individuals consider whether their interdependent behavior might harm their relationship apart from its impact on themselves or their partner (cf. Hample & Dallinger, 1990).

Second, due to the potential for future interaction inherent in relationships (Hinde, 1979), relational goals may prompt a future orientation. Instead of merely judging what is best for "the here and now," negotiators must be concerned with future needs and problems. For example, organizational members evaluate their dispute resolution techniques in part by their likelihood of reducing future similar conflicts (Lissak & Sheppard, 1983). Friends employ the same criterion (Senchak & Reis, 1988).

Finally, because relationships entail an emotional quality (Hinde, 1979), relational goals may be aimed at the creation or restoration of trust (see Donohue & Ramesh, Chapter 9, this volume). At a minimum, commitment to an ongoing relationship requires trusting the other party to honor exchange commitments and not to be exploitative (Matthews & Shimoff, 1979).

Obstacles to Achieving Relational Goals. At least three barriers may prevent negotiators from achieving stable exchange relationships. First, negative emotions lessen the likelihood of a cooperative association. Individuals tend to compete with disliked others (McClintock & McNeel, 1967; Swingle & Gillis, 1968) and negative affect leads to a reduced desire for future interaction (Slusher, 1978). Therefore, individuals in exchange relationships may enact behaviors designed to reduce mutual animosity (Lissak & Sheppard, 1983; Senchak & Reis, 1988).

Second, negotiators may perceive that they have little in common. Similar attitudes and interests allow relational partners to engage in joint activity that increases attraction (Davis, 1981). Moreover, value differences may forecast conflicts on the practical issues of an exchange which are difficult to resolve (cf. Druckman, Broome, & Korper, 1988).

Third, alternative relationships might block the desire to form or maintain exchange associations. Relationships in which both partners perceive that they have more attractive alternatives are more likely to suffer disruption than are those in which only one partner perceives better alternatives or neither party does (Udry, 1981). This pattern holds regardless of relational satisfaction.

Overcoming Relational Obstacles. To mitigate or control negative affect, individuals may plan to use nonverbal and verbal cues that express likability or friendliness (cf. Rosenfeld, 1966a, 1966b). However, if negative affect results from prior competitive interactions, they may shift to cooperative behavior to increase both liking and the desire for future interaction (Slusher, 1978). Several approaches can overcome a lack of commonality. A negotiator may plan to express similar attitudes to increase the likelihood of cooperative endeavors (Fahs, 1981). Also, negotiators may neutralize the problems that arise from dissimilarity by agreeing to respect their mutual differences or by agreeing to keep their differences separate from their exchanges (Druckman et al., 1988).

Overcoming obstacles that stem from perceived alternatives can be difficult. Alternative relationships empower bargainers (Bacharach & Lawler, 1976, 1981) and allow them to meet their commodity goals by obtaining concessions from their partners (Komorita & Miller, 1986; Landau & Leventhal, 1976; Yukl, 1976). Consequently, bargainers may negotiate a contract that restricts their use of alternatives (cf. Thibaut, 1968). For example, a low-power bargainer may create a plan to link an attractive exchange agreement (i.e., one that exceeds the powerful person's commodity goals) with a binding contract that commits the parties to an *exclusive* exchange association (Thibaut & Gruder, 1969). In contrast, when mutual alternatives disrupt an exchange relationship, negotiators may plan to stress the stability afforded by a restrictive contract (cf. Thibaut & Gruder, 1969).

Thus negotiators may plan to fulfill their need for a stable exchange relationship in addition to meeting their transient needs for commodities. In doing so, they must devise means to overcome obstacles that arise from the nature of a relationship.

FACE-RELATED GOALS

Exchange relationships not only provide needed commodities but also affect self-concept or face. For example, individuals who perceive that their exchanges with a partner are inequitable often feel a lack of respect that, in turn, threatens their own self-esteem (Schafer, Keith, & Lorenz, 1984). Hence, individuals entering negotiation with the purpose to accomplish image goals must devise tactics to accomplish them (cf. Weinstein, 1966).

Characteristics. A negotiator's face-to-face objectives may take three forms (see Wilson, Chapter 8, this volume; Wilson & Putnam, 1990). First, bargainers may seek to *maintain* or *restore* their self-image. Victims of an inequity may think that their partners see them as weak or as foolish, which may prompt the use of demanding behavior to counter that image (Brown, 1977). Conversely, harm-doers (i.e., individuals who receive disproportional benefits in an exchange) may think that their partners view them as victimizers, which may prompt the use of explanations to justify the inequity (Walster, Walster, & Berscheid, 1978).

Second, negotiators may want to *support* the self-image of their opponents. In particular, the over-benefited partner may apologize and be supportive as a way of restoring his or her image as a fair person and to reduce the likelihood of retribution (cf. Rivera & Tedeschi, 1976).

Finally, bargainers may want to *attack* the self-image of their partner. For example, individuals who initiate a confrontation because of a transgression often want the other person to feel responsible or guilty for the negative consequence (Stutman & Newell, 1990).

Obstacles to Achieving Face-Related Goals. Obstacles to a negotiator's aim to appear strong and capable may accrue from the opponent. When bargainers discover that their opponents view their positions as weak and they receive no other gesture of respect, they feel their personal effectiveness is demeaned and they anticipate that their opponents will try to frustrate them (Tjosvold & Huston, 1978). Similarly, negotiators may infer that their opponents reject their competencies if the partners issue nonnegotiable demands and control the bargaining process (Tjosvold, 1977b, 1978b).

Different obstacles make it difficult to support an opponent's image. Representatives often assume that their constituencies want them to establish a position of relative strength over their opponents (Benton & Druckman, 1974; see also Turner, Chapter 10, this volume). Moreover, negotiators assume that their constituents are more concerned with impressions of strength than they are (Pruitt, Carnevale, Forcey, & Van Slyck, 1986). When monitored by the constituency, bargainers evidence higher concern for appearing strong and engage in contentious behavior that attacks the image of the opponent (Carnevale, Pruitt, & Britton, 1979; Pruitt et al., 1978; Pruitt et al., 1986). A similar effect occurs when a constituency instructs its representative to be concerned only with the group's needs or to resist being intimidated by the opponent (Tjosvold, 1977a, 1977b).

When seeking to attack an opponent's face, a negotiator may perceive the opponent's anticipated response is the primary obstacle. In some cases the expression of a complaint is so indirect that the opposition does not see it as an indictment that requires actions (Newell & Stutman, 1989/ 1990). However, negotiators may expect that overt face attacks prompt defensive reactions and counterattacks. An individual who initiates a confrontation may try to prevent the target person from turning the tables and complaining about the initiator's prior transgressions (Stutman & Newell, 1990).

Overcoming Face-Related Obstacles. As noted earlier, negotiators need to enact behaviors that create certain images. To maintain an image of strength, a negotiator might plan to be contentious and uncompromising. A positive correlation exists between the desire to appear *strong* to the opponent and being argumentative during negotiation (Carnevale et al., 1979). Also, negotiators who want to resist being intimidated by their opponents are often unwilling to compromise during negotiation (Tjosvold, 1977b). Alternatively, bargainers who desire to appear *fair* indicate a willingness to compromise and to consider the opponents' needs (Tjosvold, 1977a). Negotiators may appear both strong and fair by matching the frequency and size of their opponents' concessions (McGillicuddy, Pruitt, & Syna, 1984).

A negotiator's constituency may advocate such a demanding position that it becomes difficult to support the image of the opponent. Therefore, bargainers may devise means to induce their constituents to adopt flexible positions and strategies (Turner, 1990; see also Turner, Chapter 10, this volume).

Finally, a negotiator who wants to attack an opponent's face may anticipate that the target may not understand that a complaint is being made, or may decide to counterattack. To overcome these obstacles, negotiators may rehearse their arguments to present them in a clear and complete fashion during bargaining (cf. Stutman & Newell, 1990) or they may engage in an imagined interaction to anticipate and refute the responses of the opponent (cf. Edwards, Honeycutt, & Zagacki, 1988; Stutman & Newell, 1990).

Thus, negotiators are concerned with more than just commodities or an ongoing relationship. When their face is threatened, they enter negotiations with the intent of overcoming obstacles that might prevent restoring it.

PURSUING MULTIPLE GOALS

Persons frequently pursue multiple objectives within their interactions (Tracy & Coupland, 1990). Bargainers can pursue a number of different types of goals or more than one goal of each type during the same negotiation (Wilson & Putnam, 1990). Even when individuals enter negotiation with a single goal, other objectives can emerge (Wilson & Putnam, 1990). For example, negotiators' concern for face may be heightened by their opponents' behaviors or by feedback from their constituencies (Brown, 1977).

Characteristics. The pursuit of multiple goals adds complexity to negotiation. Goals may interact in diverse ways (Benoit, 1990; Wilensky, 1983). Sometimes goals can be congruent and used to increase the chance that other goals will be fulfilled (Wilensky, 1983). A negotiator who maintains a self-image of relative strength through argumentation is better able to achieve commodity goals than a bargainer who fails to maintain this image (Donohue, 1981a, 1981b). Bargainers who support the face of their opponents will be seen as attractive relational partners (Tjosvold, 1978a; Wayne & Ferris, 1990). However, one goal may constrain a negotiator's ability to accomplish another. For example, developing alternative exchange relationships can provide a powerful lever for achieving commodity goals (Bacharach & Lawler, 1981), but individuals who like their opponents are reluctant to use this tactic (Michener & Schwertfeger, 1972). A negotiator who pursues multiple goals must employ several criteria when formulating tactics (Hample & Dallinger, 1990) and may be unable to use tactics that are effective for achieving a single goal.

Obstacles to Achieving Multiple Goals. Goal conflicts constitute significant obstacles to achieving multiple goals. To maintain face, a negotiator may feel compelled to exploit the opponent (Marlowe, Gergen, & Doob, 1966), which violates rules for friendly relations (Argyle & Henderson, 1984). Bargainers who cling to extreme positions create perceptions of strength but sacrifice an image of fairness (McGillicuddy et al., 1984) and good will for future exchanges (Esser, 1989; Seholm, Walker, & Esser, 1985). In such cases, the means used to overcome an obstacle to one goal create obstacles for attaining another goal.

Overcoming Goal Conflict. Individuals may employ three methods to deal with goal incompatibility (O'Keefe & Delia, 1982). First, they may seek one goal and sacrifice others. Given bargainers often enter negotiation to acquire resources, commodity goals may have priority over relational and face goals. If so, a negotiator may enact behaviors geared to achieving commodity goals with minimal regard to their effect on other goals. When activated, however, other goals can override commodity objectives. Negotiators who are romantically involved sacrifice their individual commodity goals for the sake of relational harmony (Fry, Firestone, & Williams, 1983) and even nonromantic negotiators choose to make concessions on their commodity goals if they promote good will with the opponent (Putnam et al., 1986). Furthermore, bargainers whose opponents make them look weak may retaliate and fail to achieve their own commodity objectives (Brown, 1968).

A second method is to separate goals and try to achieve them at different times. For example, Morley and Stephenson (1977) suggest that different goals are operative at various stages of negotiation. While commodity goals are pursued throughout, bargainers initially aim to build images of legitimacy while attacking their opponents. In later stages, negotiators develop working relationships and assess the implications of agreements for their future association. This pattern allows negotiators to achieve commodity goals by accomplishing different and potentially incompatible goals in separate negotiation phases.

A third method involves behaviors that simultaneously achieve multiple objectives. Although effortful, this approach may be advantageous. Bargainers are most likely to find integrative agreements when they are highly committed to achieving commodity objectives *and* expect to work together in the future than when they do not expect future interactions (Ben-Yoav & Pruitt, 1984a, 1984b). Thus, when both instrumental and relational goals are activated, individuals need not sacrifice one for the other, but instead they can find means of achieving both. For example, planning to ask questions about the opponent's interests and reactions may facilitate the discovery of integrative agreements through learning about the opponent's priorities (Thompson, 1991; Tutzauer & Roloff, 1988) and further the development of a positive relationship by signaling concern for the partner's needs (Donohue, Diez, & Stahle, 1983).

Thus plan content is potentially quite complex. A negotiation plan may include multiple goals, some of which are tangible and directly related to agenda items on commodities. Relational and face-related goals are more concerned with intangibles and may be more difficult to negotiate in a direct fashion than are commodity goals (cf. Blau, 1967), but they can be just as important (Lewicki & Litterer, 1985). Regardless of the number or types of goals, bargainers anticipate obstacles achieving them and devise means of overcoming them. Past research suggests that the planning process has an important impact on bargaining outcomes.

NEGOTIATION PLANNING

Planning is a process in which actors use procedural knowledge about *how* to plan to devise action sequences and anticipate the effects of these actions (Berger, in press; Scholnick & Friedman, 1987; Wilensky, 1983). Planning may occur well in advance of an interaction or may occur on-line in the midst of an encounter (Hayes-Roth & Hayes-Roth, 1979).

Despite the potential importance of plans, negotiators do not always expend great effort in planning (Lewicki & Litterer, 1985) nor are they especially rational when they plan (Neale & Bazerman, 1991). Negotiators are likely to expend planning effort when their goals are personally important. For instance, persons spend more time rehearsing for a confrontation when their relationship with the target is important and the issue is deemed vital (Stutman & Newell, 1990). Also, planning effort is greater when negotiators anticipate difficulty achieving their goals. Hence, negotiators who view their partners as willing and able to provide them with needed commodities may give less thought to an upcoming negotiation than will bargainers for whom a successful outcome is less certain.

Negotiators may also encounter situational factors that constrain their ability to plan. For example, negotiators may have limited time for planning (cf. Morley, 1982) and hence, decide to "play it by ear" once negotiations begin (Lewicki & Litterer, 1985). Unfortunately, bargainers who try to plan during a negotiation encounter severe time constraints. During interactions, individuals are under pressure to respond quickly to their opponents' communication; hence, other cues in the negotiation compete for their attention. As a result, interactants report that fewer than half of their thoughts during a conversation involve planning (Waldron, Cegala, Sharkey, & Teboul, 1990).

Negotiation research suggests that when planning occurs, it can take three forms: adaptive, interactive, and collaborative.

ADAPTIVE PLANNING

Even though negotiators create an initial plan to try to overcome perceived obstacles, the chance of failure always exists. As a result, negotiators need to consider plan revisions to enact if the initial plan should fail. This process of considering alternative paths to a goal is known as *adaptive planning*. When engaging in adaptive planning, negotiators do not need to abandon their initial plan totally, rather they may fix the deficient component (Alterman, 1988). Negotiators may plan to lower their aspirations. As the negotiation continues without agreement, aspirations for commodity goals decrease (Yukl, 1974b) and bargaining groups rationalize making concessions (Putnam et al., 1990). To the extent that bargainers set resistance points for their commodities, planned reductions may still allow negotiators to attain needed resources (Yukl, 1974a).

Negotiators may plan to alter their means of achieving their initial objectives. Coercion is employed as "a measure of last resort" (Tedeschi & Bonoma, 1977), used when other techniques have proved unsuccessful. In the event of failure to achieve their initial commodity goals, negotiators plan shifts from noncoercive techniques to coercive behaviors such as threats (Roloff & Jordan, 1991). Even though applying greater pressure may elicit concessions, coercion may also have undesirable effects on relational and face-related goals.

Pruitt (1981) posits a less coercive method of adaptive planning. Negotiators are advised to start with reasonably demanding commodity goals and to create as many different means of accomplishing them as possible. Should a negotiator be unable to achieve the initial goal, he or she should reduce the objective and create alternative proposals.

This approach has several advantages. First, it allows the negotiator to maintain relatively high goals when encountering resistance. Because the negotiator has backup proposals, he or she feels less pressure to make concessions. Second, by preparing alternatives in advance, the negotiator can respond to obstacles during the bargaining. Negotiations need not be suspended to formulate new proposals. Third, by preparing many different proposals, the negotiator may discover one of high quality. Persons who are instructed to develop as many different solutions to a conflict as possible increase their chances of finding an effective one (D'Zurilla & Nezu, 1980; Nezu & D'Zurilla, 1981).

Although adaptive planning is beneficial, not all negotiators are motivated to do it. Bargainers often overestimate their ability to attain commodity goals (Neale & Bazerman, 1985, 1991). Hence, they may see little reason to engage in adaptive planning and are less prepared if failure occurs.

INTERACTIVE PLANNING

Negotiators vary in the degree to which they anticipate and accommodate the plans of their opponents. Bruce and Newman (1978) posit a distinction between a single actor plan and interacting plans. In the former, individuals consider their own goals and devise actions they can use to overcome obstacles. In the latter, actors consider and incorporate into their own plans the plans of the opponents. Research indicates that approximately half of a sample of negotiators explicitly include some aspect of their opponents' plans in their own planning (Roloff & Jordan, 1991). Moreover, experience with a particular bargaining role (i.e., buyer or seller) facilitates interactive planning (Roloff & Jordan, 1991). Similarly, Putnam et al. (1990) report that in the early stages of negotiation, bargaining groups try to estimate their opponents' priorities and probable reactions to their own proposals.

Interactive planning provides both offensive and defensive advantages. A negotiator may engage in constructive counterplanning by crafting a tactic to overcome obstacles the opponent might raise (Carbonell, 1981). Skilled bargainers plan tactics that appeal to the opposition (Rackham & Carlisle, 1978). Furthermore, bargainers who have information about their own and their opponents' potential profits set goals that are less costly and more acceptable to their opponents than do negotiators who lack this information (Kahn & Kohls, 1972).

Interactive planning allows negotiators to engage in obstructive counterplanning aimed at creating obstacles to the opponents' positions (Carbonell, 1981). Hence, negotiators must not only overcome obstacles to their own proposals but raise objections to their opponents' positions. Individuals who rehearse what they and their partner would say prior to a confrontation are able to generate effective counterarguments (Stutman & Newell, 1990). Also, individuals who create counterarguments prior to receiving persuasive messages are able to resist these influence attempts (Petty & Cacioppo, 1977).

Some researchers suggest that interactive planning also has disadvantages. A bargainer's perceptions of the opponent's plan may not be accurate; these biased judgments can adversely affect bargaining success.

For example, initial perceptions may indicate greater goal incompatibility than is actually present (Thompson & Hastie, 1990) and oversimplify the potential moves of the opponent (Carroll, Bazerman, & Maury, 1988). Moreover, some bargainers evidence inaccurate assessments of their partners' goals even after negotiation begins (Pruitt & Drews, 1969; Thompson & Hastie, 1990). Given that some individuals intentionally seek to mislead their partners (Thompson & Hastie, 1990) and to withhold genuine but socially inappropriate reasons for resistance (cf. Folkes, 1982), it is not surprising that individuals make inaccurate inferences.

The effect of inaccurate information on planning also hinges on a negotiator's own goals (Hamner & Harnett, 1975). Negotiators whose commodity goals are relatively low gain advantage from information since they may discover that their opponents can provide them with more resources than they originally thought. However, information about the opponents' profits may cause negotiators to lower initial commodity goals prior to their first bids and to sacrifice the chance to obtain higher goals. Hence, interactive planning might afford greater benefits to bargainers with initially lower goals than to negotiators with high aspirations (Church & Esser, 1980).

COLLABORATIVE PLANNING

Most research examines planning away from the opposition when negotiators are either in solitude (Rackham & Carlisle, 1978) or in private caucus sessions (Bartos, 1974; Putnam et al., 1990). However, negotiators also engage in collaborative planning in which they develop plans of action in consultation with their opponents. At least two forms of collaborative planning exist.

First, opposing bargainers may meet in prenegotiation sessions to explore the possibility of formal negotiations on issues on which they disagree. Zartman and Berman (1982) argue that one party may have to convince its opposition that a given problem should be managed through negotiation. Some issues may be nonnegotiable. If the parties find a basis for negotiation, then sessions may be held to set up procedures, agenda items, and dates for upcoming talks on main issues (Sawyer & Guetzkow, 1965). This form of collaborative planning is critical since preliminary decisions may specify procedures that determine outcomes in later negotiations (cf. Thompson, Mannix, & Bazerman, 1988).

Because negotiation requires the parties to coordinate their actions, a second type of collaborative planning takes place during formal negotiations as bargainers enact procedural statements or structure their actions through metatalk (Ragan & Hopper, 1981). While negotiating, bargainers frequently propose particular sequences of speakers, the issues to discuss, and the general operating procedures such as voting (McGrath & Julian, 1963). Negotiators who engage in early collaborative planning may facilitate reaching creative and constructive settlements (McGrath & Julian, 1963). Morley and Stephenson (1977) also observe such actions but primarily in later bargaining sessions. They conclude that procedural statements reflect a problem-solving orientation in which negotiators systematically analyze issues. A factor analysis of negotiation behaviors verifies that procedural statements cluster with other problem-solving behaviors (Putnam & Jones, 1982).

Given that individuals may enter negotiation with conflicting plans (Bass, 1966), collaborative planning allows bargainers to merge their plans. For example, Rackham and Carlisle (1978) observe that inexperienced negotiators plan the exact sequence for discussing agenda items while experienced bargainers plan to discuss issues in no particular order. Given that sequential consideration of issues is less effective for reaching goals than simultaneously packaging them (Yukl, Malone, Hayslip, & Pamin, 1976), experienced negotiators who confront inexperienced opponents must find ways to merge their plans with those of their counterparts. Experienced bargainers need to convey the benefits of considering the issues simultaneously. Thus, planning is both a psychological activity reflected in the content of thought and a communication process evident in discourse.

FUTURE DIRECTIONS

Planning research is conducted in a fragmented and descriptive manner. For example, rather than approaching plan content as a coherent structure, research focuses on one element in isolation from other factors. Research exists on the effect of goal setting, but it does not examine the obstacles to attaining goals nor the means of overcoming them. Consequently, researchers must infer from other indicators (e.g., enacted behaviors and outcomes) that other planning elements are present. Moreover, plans for achieving commodity goals receive far more attention than other types of goals. To understand the planning process, research must include measures that directly examine the structure among plan elements and across a variety of goals. Otherwise, researchers cannot evaluate the logic behind actions nor can they assess whether they are predetermined or emergent.

Also, research needs to build theoretical frameworks from which to study negotiation plans and planning. Most studies cited in this review are not conducted with a planning focus. Typically, planning is part of a larger study but is not even highlighted in the title or abstract of the article. When planning is the focus of the study, research is typically exploratory. Scholars need to develop frameworks that predict the kinds of plan content that negotiators develop and to determine what constitutes effective plans.

Furthermore, researchers must avoid the temptation to study plans and planning only prior to negotiation. This approach fosters the misconception that plans are enacted in a fixed or lockstep fashion. Studies that focus on negotiation over time demonstrate that goals change and negotiators plan different arguments as the process unfolds (Putnam et al., 1990; Yukl, 1974b). Such designs show the effects of plans on behavior as well as the influence of behavior on plan modification.

Finally, scholars need to examine when and how plans are carried out. A well-conceived plan that is not enacted, ineptly performed, or thwarted by the opposition is of little practical value. As of this writing, the process by which plans are translated into action has received little attention.

As noted from the outset of this chapter, plans and planning are acknowledged to play critical roles in negotiation. However, understanding of that role is still at an early stage of development. Hopefully, there will be an accelerated maturation.

REFERENCES

Allen, J. (1984). Towards a general theory of action and time. *Artificial Intelligence, 23,* 123-154.

Alterman, R. (1988). Adaptive planning. *Cognitive Science, 12,* 393-421.

Argyle, M., & Henderson, M. (1984). The rules of friendship. *Journal of Social and Personal Relationships, 1,* 211-237.

Bacharach, S. B., & Lawler, E. J. (1976). The perception of power. *Social Forces, 55,* 123-134.

Bacharach, S. B., & Lawler, E. J. (1981). Power and tactics in bargaining. *Industrial and Labor Relations Review, 34,* 219-233.

Bartos, O. J. (1974). *Process and outcome of negotiations*. New York: Columbia University Press.

Bass, B. M. (1966). Effects on the subsequent performance of negotiators of studying issues or planning strategies alone or in groups. *Psychological Monographs: General and Applied, 80,* 1-31.

Bell, R. A., & Roloff, M. E. (1991). Making a love connection: Loneliness and communication competence in the dating marketplace. *Communication Quarterly, 39,* 58-74.

Benoit, P. J. (1990). The structure of interaction goals. In J. A. Anderson (Ed.), *Communication yearbook 13* (pp. 407-416). Newbury Park, CA: Sage.

Benton, A. A., & Druckman, D. (1974). Constituent's bargaining orientation and intergroup negotiations. *Journal of Applied Social Psychology, 4,* 141-150.

Ben-Yoav, O., & Pruitt, D. G. (1984a). Accountability to constituents: A two-edged sword. *Organizational Behavior and Human Performance, 34,* 283-295.

Ben-Yoav, O., & Pruitt, D. G. (1984b). Resistance to yielding and the expectation of cooperative future interaction in negotiation. *Journal of Experimental Social Psychology, 20,* 323-335.

Berger, C. R. (in press). A plan based approach to strategic communication. In D. Hewes (Ed.), *Cognitive bases of interpersonal communication*. Hillsdale, NJ: Lawrence Erlbaum.

Berger, C. R., & Bell, R. A. (1988). Plans and the initiation of social relationships. *Human Communication Research, 15,* 217-235.

Bies, R., Shapiro, D. L., & Cummings, L. L. (1988). Causal accounts and managing conflict: Is it enough to say it's not my fault? *Communication Research, 15,* 381-399.

Blau, P. M. (1967). *Exchange and power in social life*. New York: John Wiley.

Breaugh, J. A., & Klimoski, R. J. (1977). The choice of a group spokesman in bargaining: Member or outsider? *Organizational Behavior and Human Performance, 19,* 325-336.

Brown, B. R. (1968). The effects of need to maintain face on interpersonal bargaining. *Journal of Experimental Social Psychology, 4,* 107-122.

Brown, B. R. (1977). Face-saving and face-restoration in negotiation. In D. Druckman (Ed.), *Negotiations: Social psychological perspectives* (pp. 275-300). Beverly Hills, CA: Sage.

Bruce, B., & Newman, D. (1978). Interacting plans. *Cognitive Science, 2,* 195-233.

Carbonell, J. G. (1981). Counterplanning: A strategy-based model of adversary planning in real-world situations. *Artificial Intelligence, 16,* 295-329.

Carnevale, P. J. D., Pruitt, D. G., & Britton, S. D. (1979). Looking tough: The negotiator under constituent surveillance. *Personality and Social Psychology Bulletin, 5,* 118-121.

Carroll, J. S., Bazerman, M. H., & Maury, R. (1988). Negotiator cognitions: A descriptive approach to negotiators' understanding of their opponents. *Organizational Behavior and Human Decision Processes, 41,* 352-370.

Chmielewski, T. L. (1982). A test of a model for predicting strategy choice. *Central States Speech Journal, 33,* 505-518.

Church, R. J., Jr., & Esser, J. K. (1980). Effects of information on level of aspiration in bargaining. *Representative Research in Social Psychology, 11,* 38-43.

Davis, D. (1981). Implications for interaction versus effectance as mediators of the similarity-attraction relationship. *Journal of Experimental Social Psychology, 17,* 96-116.

Donohue, W. A. (1981a). Analyzing negotiation tactics: Development of a negotiation interaction system. *Human Communication Research, 7,* 273-287.

Donohue, W. A. (1981b). Development of a model of rule use in negotiation interaction. *Communication Monographs, 48,* 106-120.

Donohue, W. A., Diez, M. E., & Stahle, R. B. (1983). New directions in negotiation research. In R. Bostrom (Ed.), *Communication yearbook 7* (pp. 249-270). Beverly Hills, CA: Sage.

Druckman, D. (1967). Dogmatism, prenegotiation experience, and simulated group representation as determinants of dyadic behavior in a bargaining situation. *Journal of Personality and Social Psychology, 6,* 279-290.

Druckman, D. (1968). Prenegotiation experience and dyadic conflict resolution in a bargaining simulation. *Journal of Experimental Social Psychology, 6,* 367-383.

Druckman, D., Broome, B. J., & Korper, S. H. (1988). Value differences and conflict resolution. *Journal of Conflict Resolution, 32,* 489-510.

Druckman, D., Zechmeister, K., & Solomon, D. (1972). Determinants of bargaining behavior in a bilateral monopoly situation: Opponent's concession rate and relative defensibility. *Behavioral Science, 17,* 514-531.

D'Zurilla, T. J., & Nezu, A. (1980). A study of the generation-of-alternatives process in social problem solving. *Cognitive Therapy and Research, 4,* 67-72.

Edwards, R., Honeycutt, J. M., & Zagacki, K. S. (1988). Imagined interaction as an element of social cognition. *Western Journal of Speech Communication, 52,* 23-45.

Esser, J. K. (1989). Agreement pressure and opponent strategies in oligopoly bargaining. *Personality and Social Psychology Bulletin, 15,* 596-603.

Fahs, M. L. (1981). The effects of self-disclosing communication and attitude similarity on the reduction of interpersonal conflict. *Western Journal of Speech Communication, 45,* 38-50.

Fisher, R., & Ury, W. (1981). *Getting to yes: Negotiating agreement without giving in.* Boston: Houghton Mifflin.

Foa, U. G., & Foa, E. B. (1974). *Social structures of the mind.* Springfield, IL: Charles C Thomas.

Folkes, V. S. (1982). Communicating the reasons for social rejection. *Journal of Experimental Social Psychology, 18,* 235-252.

Francik, E. P., & Clark, H. H. (1985). How to make requests that overcome obstacles to compliance. *Journal of Memory and Language, 24,* 560-568.

Friedland, N. (1983). Weakness as strength: The use and misuse of a "my hands are tied" ploy in bargaining. *Journal of Applied Social Psychology, 13,* 422-426.

Froman, L. A., Jr., & Cohen, M. D. (1970). Compromise and logroll: Comparing the efficiency of two bargaining processes. *Behavioral Science, 15,* 180-183.

Fry, W. R., Firestone, I. J., & Williams, D. L. (1983). Negotiation process and outcome of stranger dyads and dating couples: Do lovers lose? *Basic and Applied Social Psychology, 4,* 1-16.

Gibbs, R. W., Jr. (1986). What makes some indirect speech act conventional? *Journal of Memory and Language, 25,* 181-196.

Graham, J. L., & Sano, Y. (1989). *Smart bargaining* (rev. ed.). New York: Harper & Row.

Greenhalgh, L. (1987). Relationships in negotiations. *Negotiation Journal, 3,* 235-243.

Hammond, K. J. (1989). *Case-based planning: Viewing planning as a memory task.* New York: Academic Press.

Hamner, W. C., & Harnett, D. L. (1975). The effects of information and aspiration level on bargaining behavior. *Journal of Experimental Social Psychology, 11,* 329-342.

Hample, D., & Dallinger, J. M. (1990). Arguers as editors. *Argumentation, 4,* 153-170.

Hayes-Roth, B., & Hayes-Roth, F. (1979). A cognitive model of planning. *Cognitive Science, 3,* 275-310.

Hinde, R. A. (1979). *Toward understanding relationships.* New York: Academic Press.

Hjelmquist, E., & Gidlund, A. (1984). Planned ideas vs. expressed ideas in conversation. *Journal of Pragmatics, 8,* 329-343.

Huber, V. L., & Neale, M. A. (1987). Effects of self- and competitor goals on performance in an interdependent bargaining task. *Journal of Applied Psychology, 72,* 197-203.

Kahn, A. S., & Kohls, J. W. (1972). Determinants of toughness in dyadic bargaining. *Sociometry, 35,* 305-315.

Karrass, C. L. (1970). *The negotiating game.* New York: Thomas Y. Crowell.

Klimoski, R. J. (1972). The effects of intragroup forces on intergroup conflict resolution. *Organizational Behavior and Human Performance, 8,* 363-383.

Komorita, S. S., & Miller, C. E. (1986). Bargaining strength as a function of coalition alternatives. *Journal of Personality and Social Psychology, 51,* 325-332.

Landau, S. B., & Leventhal, G. S. (1976). A simulation study of administrators' behavior toward employees who receive job offers. *Journal of Applied Social Psychology, 51,* 291-306.

Lax, D. A., & Sebenius, J. K. (1986). Interests: The measure of negotiation. *Negotiation Journal, 2,* 73-92.

Lewicki, R. J., & Litterer, J. A. (1985). *Negotiation.* Homewood, IL: Irwin.

Lissak, R. I., & Sheppard, B. H. (1983). Beyond fairness: The criterion problem in research on dispute intervention. *Journal of Applied Social Psychology, 13,* 45-65.

Marlowe, D., Gergen, K. J., & Doob, A. N. (1966). Opponent's personality, expectation of social interaction, and interpersonal bargaining. *Journal of Personality and Social Psychology, 3,* 206-213.

Matthews, B. A., & Shimoff, E. (1979). Expansion of exchange: Monitoring trust levels in ongoing exchange relations. *Journal of Conflict Resolution, 23,* 538-560.

McClintock, C. G., & McNeel, S. P. (1967). Prior dyadic experience and monetary reward as determinants of cooperative and competitive game behavior. *Journal of Personality and Social Psychology, 5,* 282-294.

McGillicuddy, N. B., Pruitt, D. G., & Syna, H. (1984). Perceptions of firmness and strength in negotiation. *Personality and Social Psychology Bulletin, 10,* 402-409.

McGrath, J. E., & Julian, J. W. (1963). Interaction process and task outcome in experimentally-created negotiation groups. *Journal of Psychological Studies, 14,* 117-138.

Michener, H. A., & Schwertfeger, M. (1972). Liking as a determinant of power tactic preference. *Sociometry, 35,* 190-202.

Miller, G. A., Galanter, E., & Pribram, K. H. (1960). *Plans and the structure of behavior.* New York: Holt, Rinehart & Winston.

Morley, I. (1982). Preparation for negotiation: Conflict, commitment and choice. In H. Brandstatter, J. H. Davis, & G. Stocker-Kreichgauer (Eds.), *Group decision making* (pp. 387-419). New York: Academic Press.

Morley, I., & Stephenson, G. (1977). *The social psychology of bargaining.* London: George Allen & Unwin.

Neale, M. A., & Bazerman, M. H. (1985). The effects of framing and negotiator overconfidence on bargaining behaviors and outcomes. *Academy of Management Journal, 28,* 34-49.

Neale, M. A., & Bazerman, M. H. (1991). *Cognition and rationality in negotiation.* New York: Free Press.

Neale, M. A., Northcraft, G. B., & Bazerman, M. H. (1989). Cognitive aspects of negotiation: New perspectives on dyadic decision making. In M. A. Rahim (Ed.), *Managing conflict: An interdisciplinary approach* (pp. 149-160). New York: Praeger.

Newell, S. E., & Stutman, R. K. (1989/1990). Negotiating confrontation: The problematic nature of initiation and response. *Research on Language and Social Interaction, 23*, 139-162.

Nezu, A., & D'Zurilla, T. J. (1981). Effects of problem definition and formulation on the generation of alternatives in the social problem-solving process. *Cognitive Therapy and Research, 5*, 265-271.

O'Keefe, B. J., & Delia, J. G. (1982). Impression formation and message production. In M. E. Roloff & C. R. Berger (Eds.), *Social cognition and communication* (pp. 33-72). Beverly Hills, CA: Sage.

Petty, R. E., & Cacioppo, J. T. (1977). Forewarning, cognitive responding and resistance to persuasion. *Journal of Personality and Social Psychology, 35*, 645-655.

Pruitt, D. G. (1981). *Negotiation behavior*. New York: Academic Press.

Pruitt, D. G., Carnevale, P. J. D., Forcey, B., & Van Slyck, M. (1986). Gender effects in negotiation: Constituent surveillance and contentious behavior. *Journal of Experimental Social Psychology, 22*, 264-275.

Pruitt, D. G., & Drews, J. L. (1969). The effect of time pressure, time elapsed, and the opponent's concession rate on behavior in negotiation. *Journal of Experimental Social Psychology, 5*, 43-60.

Pruitt, D. G., Kimmel, M. J., Britton, S., Carnevale, P. J. D., Magenau, J. M., Peragallo, J., & Engram, P. (1978). The effect of accountability and surveillance on integrative bargaining. In H. Sauermann (Ed.), *Bargaining behavior: Contributions to experimental economics* (Vol. 7, pp. 310-342). Tubingen, Germany: Mohr.

Putnam, L. L., & Jones, T. S. (1982). Reciprocity in negotiations: An analysis of bargaining interaction. *Communication Monographs, 49*, 171-191.

Putnam, L. L., Wilson, S. R., & Turner, D. B. (1990). The evolution of policy arguments in teacher's negotiations. *Argumentation, 4*, 129-152.

Putnam, L. L., Wilson, S. R., Waltman, M. S., & Turner, D. (1986). The evolution of case arguments in teachers' bargaining. *Journal of the American Forensic Association, 23*, 63-81.

Rabbie, J. M., & Huygen, K. (1974). Internal disagreements and their effects on attitudes toward in- and outgroup. *International Journal of Group Tensions, 4*, 222-245.

Rabbie, J. M., & Visser, L. (1972). Bargaining strength and group polarization in intergroup negotiations. *European Journal of Social Psychology, 2*, 401-415.

Rackham, N., & Carlisle, J. (1978). The effective negotiator-part 2: Planning for negotiations. *Journal of European Industrial Training, 2*, 2-5.

Ragan, S., & Hopper, R. (1981). Alignment talk in the job interview. *Journal of Applied Communication Research, 9*, 85-103.

Rivera, A. N., & Tedeschi, J. T. (1976). Public versus private reactions to positive equity. *Journal of Personality and Social Psychology, 34*, 895-900.

Roloff, M. E., & Berger, C. R. (1982). Social cognition and communication: An introduction. In M. E. Roloff & C. R. Berger (Eds.), *Social cognition and communication* (pp. 9-32). Beverly Hills, CA: Sage.

Roloff, M. E., & Janiszewski, C. A. (1989). Overcoming obstacles to interpersonal compliance. *Human Communication Research, 18*, 33-61.

Roloff, M. E., & Jordan, J. M. (1991). The influence of effort, experience, and persistence on the elements of bargaining plans. *Communication Research, 18*, 306-332.

Rosenfeld, H. M. (1966a). Approval-seeking and approval-inducing functions of verbal and nonverbal responses in the dyad. *Journal of Personality and Social Psychology, 4*, 597-605.

Rosenfeld, H. M. (1966b). Instrumental affiliative functions of facial and gestural expressions. *Journal of Personality and Social Psychology, 4*, 65-72.

Rubin, J. Z., Brockner, J., Eckenrode, J., Enright, M. A., & Johnson-George, C. (1980). Weakness as strength: Test of a "my hands are tied" ploy in bargaining. *Personality and Social Psychology Bulletin, 6*, 216-221.

Sawyer, J., & Guetzkow, H. (1965). Bargaining and negotiation in international relations. In H. C. Kelman (Ed.), *International behavior: A social-psychological analysis* (pp. 466-520). New York: Holt, Rinehart & Winston.

Schafer, R. B., Keith, P. M., & Lorenz, F. O. (1984). Equity/inequity and the self-concept. An interactionist analysis. *Social Psychology Quarterly, 47*, 42-49.

Scholnick, E. K., & Friedman, S. L. (1987). The planning construct in the psychological literature. In S. L. Friedman, E. K. Scholnick, & R. R. Cocking (Eds.), *Blueprints for thinking* (pp. 3-38). Cambridge, UK: Cambridge University Press.

Seholm, K. J., Walker, J. L., & Esser, J. K. (1985). A choice of alternative strategies in oligopoly bargaining. *Journal of Applied Social Psychology, 15*, 345-353.

Senchak, M., & Reis, H. T. (1988). The fair process effect and procedural criteria in the resolution of disputes between intimate same-sex friends. *Social Justice Research, 2*, 263-287.

Slusher, E. A. (1978). Counterpart strategy, prior relations, and constituent pressure in a bargaining simulation. *Behavioral Science, 23*, 470-477.

Stutman, R. K., & Newell, S. E. (1990). Rehearsing for confrontation. *Argumentation, 4*, 185-198.

Swingle, P. G., & Gillis, J. S. (1968). Effects of the emotional relationship between protagonists in the prisoner's dilemma. *Journal of Personality and Social Psychology, 8*, 160-165.

Tedeschi, J. T., & Bonoma, T. V. (1977). Measures of last resort: Coercion and aggression in bargaining. In D. Druckman (Ed.), *Negotiations: Social-psychological perspectives* (pp. 213-241). Beverly Hills, CA: Sage.

Thibaut, J. (1968). The development of contractual norms in bargaining: Replication and variation. *Journal of Conflict Resolution, 12*, 102-112.

Thibaut, J., & Gruder, C. L. (1969). Formation of contractual agreements between parties of unequal power. *Journal of Personality and Social Psychology, 11*, 59-65.

Thompson, L. L. (1990a). An examination of naive and experienced negotiators. *Journal of Personality and Social Psychology, 59*, 82-90.

Thompson, L. L. (1990b). The influence of experience on negotiation performance. *Journal of Experimental Social Psychology, 26*, 528-544.

Thompson, L. L. (1991). Information exchange in negotiation. *Journal of Experimental Social Psychology, 27*, 161-179.

Thompson, L. L., & Hastie, R. (1990). Social perception in negotiation. *Organizational Behavior and Human Decision Processes, 47*, 98-123.

Thompson, L. L., Mannix, E. A., & Bazerman, M. H. (1988). Group negotiation: Effects of decision rule, agenda, and aspiration. *Journal of Personality and Social Psychology, 54*, 86-95.

Tietz, R., & Weber, H. J. (1978). Decision behavior in multivariable negotiations. In H. Sauermann (Ed.), *Bargaining behavior: Contributions to experimental economics* (Vol. 7, pp. 60-87). Tubingen, Germany: Mohr.

Tietz, R., Weber, H. J., Vidmajer, U., & Wentzel, C. (1978). On aspiration-forming behavior in repetitive negotiations. In H. Sauermann (Ed.), *Bargaining behavior: Contributions to experimental economics* (Vol. 7, pp. 88-102). Tubingen, Germany: Mohr.

Tjosvold, D. (1977a). Commitment to justice in conflict between unequal status persons. *Journal of Applied Social Psychology, 7,* 149-162.

Tjosvold, D. (1977b). Low power person's strategies in bargaining: Negotiability of demand, maintaining face, and race. *International Journal of Group Tension, 7,* 29-41.

Tjosvold, D. (1978a). Affirmation of the high-power person and his position: Ingratiation in conflict. *Journal of Applied Social Psychology, 8,* 230-243.

Tjosvold, D. (1978b). Control strategies and own group evaluation in intergroup conflict. *Journal of Psychology, 100,* 305-314.

Tjosvold, D., & Huston, T. L. (1978). Social face and resistance to compromise in bargaining. *Journal of Social Psychology, 104,* 57-68.

Tracy, K., & Coupland, N. (1990). Multiple goals in discourse: An overview of issues. *Journal of Language and Social Psychology, 9,* 1-13.

Turner, D. B. (1990). Intraorganizational bargaining: The effect of goal congruence and trust on negotiator strategy use. *Communication Studies, 41,* 54-75.

Tutzauer, F., & Roloff, M. E. (1988). Communication processes leading to integrative agreements: Three paths to joint benefits. *Communication Research, 15,* 360-380.

Udry, J. R. (1981). Marital alternatives and marital disruption. *Journal of Marriage and the Family, 43,* 889-897.

Waldron, V. R., Cegala, D. J., Sharkey, W. F., & Teboul, B. (1990). Cognitive and tactical dimensions of conversational goal management. *Journal of Language and Social Psychology, 9,* 101-118.

Wall, J. A., Jr. (1985). *Negotiation: Theory and practice.* Glenview, IL: Scott, Foresman.

Walster, E., Walster, G. W., & Berscheid, E. (1978). *Equity: Theory and research.* Boston: Allyn & Bacon.

Wayne, S. J., & Ferris, G. R. (1990). Influence tactics, affect, and exchange quality in supervisor-subordinate interactions: A laboratory experiment and field study. *Journal of Applied Psychology, 75,* 487-499.

Weinstein, E. A. (1966). Toward a theory of interpersonal tactics. In C. W. Backman & P. F. Secord (Eds.), *Problems in social psychology* (pp. 393-398). New York: McGraw-Hill.

Wilensky, R. (1983). *Planning and understanding: A computational approach to human reasoning.* Reading, MA: Addison-Wesley.

Wilson, S. R., & Putnam, L. L. (1990). Interaction goals in negotiation. In J. Anderson (Ed.), *Communication yearbook 13* (pp. 374-406). Newbury Park, CA: Sage.

Yukl, G. A. (1974a). Effects of situational variables and opponent concessions on a bargainer's perception, aspirations, and concessions. *Journal of Personality and Social Psychology, 29,* 227-236.

Yukl, G. A. (1974b). Effects of the opponent's initial offer, concession magnitude, and concession frequency on bargaining behavior. *Journal of Personality and Social Psychology, 30,* 323-335.

Yukl, G. A. (1976). Effects of information, payoff magnitude, and favorability of alternative settlement on bargaining outcomes. *Journal of Social Psychology, 98,* 269-282.

Yukl, G. A., Malone, M. P., Hayslip, B., & Pamin, T. A. (1976). The effects of time pressure and issue settlement order on integrative bargaining. *Sociometry, 39,* 277-281.

Zartman, I. W., & Berman, M. R. (1982). *The practical negotiator.* New Haven, CT: Yale University Press.

Chapter 2

COMMUNICATION MEDIA
AND NEGOTIATION PROCESSES

Marshall Scott Poole, Dale L. Shannon, and Gerardine DeSanctis

McCLUHAN'S DOCTRINE is that the medium is the message. Even if we do not agree, it is hard to overlook the importance of communication media in negotiations. Negotiations are inherently multi-media, offering a rich mix of written texts, face-to-face confrontations, hallway conversations, telephone consultations, and use of newspapers and television to send indirect messages. It is no surprise that researchers have devoted considerable attention to the impact of various media on negotiation. The possibility of substituting telephone or audio-only channels for face-to-face negotiations has been explored in the classic studies of Morley and Stephenson (1977) and Short, Williams, and Christie (1976). Weeks and Chapanis (1976) add written communication via teletype to the equation. These studies explore the belief that different media have different strengths and weaknesses and could be used selectively, depending on the contingencies of the negotiation.

The possibility of computer-mediated negotiation has also been investigated. Computer models aid in the definition and resolution of negotiation problems in a number of instances, such as the Law of the Sea Treaty (Nyhart & Dauer, 1986; Sebenius, 1981). Research on software to aid negotiation and conflict management has been conducted by Jarke, Jelassi, and Shakun (1987), Jones and Jelassi (1988), and Nyhart and Samarasan (1989). Some studies envision complex systems similar to Group Decision Support Systems (GDSS) (DeSanctis & Gallupe, 1987), which combine communication features, computer technology, and decision process technologies to support face-to-face meetings or computer conferences (Bui, 1987; Nyhart & Samarasan, 1989; Poole, Zappa, DeSanctis, Shannon, & Dickson, 1990). Given these options, what media should negotiators use?

The most common criterion for media choice is "information richness," the amount of information that can be conveyed through the medium (Rice et al., 1984; Trevino, Lengel, & Daft, 1987). The richness of a medium is a function of its ability to handle multiple information cues simultaneously, to facilitate rapid feedback, or to enable the communicator to establish personal presence. On this definition, face-to-face interaction is a very rich medium whereas an impersonal written memo is low in richness. The most common theoretical claim is that for complex, personally involving tasks such as negotiation, richer media will be most effective (Trevino et al., 1987). This claim is consistent with lay views as well: people generally prefer conducting their negotiations face-to-face (Johansen, Vallee, & Vian, 1979). However, the situation is more complex than this generalization implies. The various communication media have many different impacts. As a result, many unanswered questions regarding media effects focus on which media are best under which circumstances.

Other aspects of media can also be discerned. Media may be viewed as a continuous part of the process of communication. Such a view combines the channel of communication with the type of communication support that media provide (e.g., procedures and codes). Media also serve as linking pins for communication networks that vary in the proximity of the parties involved. Such a view of media, for example, distinguishes between local area networks (LAN), which are close, and wide area networks (WAN), which are distant. Use of a medium also carries a symbolic message in itself. For example, using electronic mail may symbolize progressiveness while using handwritten notes may symbolize personal concern and warmth.

This chapter presents the results of studies on media effects in negotiation and considers the current state of this knowledge. After distinguishing among various types of media, we summarize the research on media impacts. Following this section, we briefly consider the implications of this research for the conduct of negotiations and then we specify a research agenda in this growing area.

TYPES OF MEDIA IN NEGOTIATION

Technological advances have greatly increased the range of media for negotiations. To increase the accuracy of reporting results and to

TABLE 2.1   Media Categorization

Media	Short Hand	Media Type	Variants
Face-to-Face	ftf	Channel	Verbal: Nonverbal
Text	text	Channel	Typing; Teletype; Handwriting; VDT
Audio	audio	Channel	Telephone: Audio-conferencing
Video	video	Channel	Video plus Audio: Video-conferencing
Level 1 Computer Support	level 1	Structure	Computer; Text
Level 2 Computer Support	level 2	Structure	Computer; Text; Modeling
Level 3 Computer Support	level 3	Structure	Computer; Text; Modeling; Artificial Intelligence
Decision Room	level 1 or 2 plus ftf	Setting	Level 1; Face-to-Face; Synchronous Meeting
Computer Conference	level 1 or 2 plus text	Setting	Level 1; Dispersed Group; Synchronous or Asynchronous

reduce tiresome hyphenated phrases, we employ abbreviations for various media mentioned in negotiation research, as shown in Table 2.1.

Most negotiations employ face-to-face (ftf) interactions. Research also examines audio-only media (telephone, teleconferencing), video linkages (television, videoconferencing, teleconferencing), and textual media (handwritten notes, teletype, computer conferencing). As Table 2.1 shows, some media include combinations of media types—video, for example, includes audio as well as video in most implementations.

Recent research focuses on computer support of negotiation through modeling programs (Nyhart & Dauer, 1986) or group decision support systems (GDSSs) (DeSanctis & Gallupe, 1987). Computer models either provide a picture of the situation being negotiated, as in the models of sea-floor mining used in the Law of the Sea negotiations (Sebenius, 1981), or help parties analyze solutions and offers (Samarasan, 1988). GDSSs combine communication, computer, and decision technologies to support the decision making and related activities of work groups.

Communication technologies available within a GDSS include electronic messaging, teleconferencing, and store and forward facilities. Computer technologies also employ multiuser operating systems, fourth generation languages, and graphics facilities. Decision support technologies include agenda setting, modeling methods, structured group methods (such as the Nominal Group and Delphi techniques), and rules for directing group discussion (such as parliamentary procedure). A useful distinction among types of computer support, presented by DeSanctis and Gallupe (1987), sets forth three levels. *Level 1* GDSSs provide technical features aimed at removing common communication barriers, such as anonymous input of ideas and preferences, electronic message exchange between members, voting solicitation and compilation, and common viewing screens for idea display. *Level 2* GDSSs add decision modeling and group decision techniques to level 1 methods, thus providing enhanced structure and support. *Level 3* GDSSs are characterized by machine-regulated group communication patterns, such as expert advice in selecting and arranging the rules to be applied during the negotiation or in rule-based guidance through procedural steps. As indicated in Table 2.1, computer-supported media also incorporate procedural structures that guide communication processes. They provide more explicit structure than does video switching technology, for example. Media complexes in various settings, such as computer conferences, also are examined in research. These complexes include not only channels but also physical descriptions of the communication context.

The types of media in Table 2.1 are basic units that differ within types. These within-type differences are smaller than the between type differences. Chapanis, Ochsman, Parrish, and Weeks's study (1972) shows no difference between the impacts of two different types of text media (teletype and remote handwriting). Different types of level 1 GDSSs also reveal consistent affects (Easton, Vogel, & Nunamaker, 1989; Watson, DeSanctis, & Poole, 1988). In this review, complex media configurations are represented as combinations of elementary media. For instance, a computer con- ference is represented as text plus level 1 or 2 support, depending on the computer conferencing system. A videoconference supported by teletype is represented as video plus text. Further, we propose that the influence of complex media combinations can be predicted, at least to some extent, by combining the effects of the units. For example, the influence of computer conferencing is, in part, predictable from a synthesis of studies of text media and of research on levels of computer support. The types thus provide an abstract set of building blocks for potential negotiation support systems.

MEDIA AND THE NEGOTIATION PROCESS

This review of media impacts on negotiation is rooted in a generic model of bargaining that is distilled from processual models of conflict management (Gulliver, 1979; Morley & Stephenson, 1977; Pondy, 1967; Thomas, 1976; Walton, 1969). This model delineates the key aspects of the negotiation process which electronic media may affect positively or negatively. It also suggests functions for media design. No attempt is made to argue that this generic model is the definitive view of negotiation. The model serves as a conceptual framework for presenting research findings.

TWO PROCESSES:
DIFFERENTIATION AND INTEGRATION

Walton (1969) presents a two-phase model of effective conflict management, which is the least common denominator for the plethora of negotiation and conflict models. In the first phase, known as *differentiation*, latent conflicts and issues emerge and are defined, the reasons for differences are stated, and parties recognize the severity of their differences. This phase is characterized by sharp exchanges and open conflict. If managed properly, however, the issues are clarified and the parties are motivated to pursue negotiation. The outcome of a properly conducted differentiation process is a clear understanding of differences between the parties, motivation to negotiate, and a sense of the other party as a legitimate agent whose position must be dealt with, even if the first party does not agree with it.

The second phase, *integration*, logically follows differentiation. It is a period in which "parties appreciate their similarities, acknowledge their common goals, own up to positive aspects of their ambivalences, express warmth and respect, and/or engage in other positive actions to manage their conflict" (Walton, 1969, p. 105). During the integration process, parties finalize the definition of issues, build a productive working climate, explore solutions, and attempt to generate a mutually acceptable solution and means of implementation. If either process is truncated or ineffectively managed, a less satisfactory result may ensue. Often parties go through several cycles of differentiation and integration to achieve an effective resolution. Thus, it is not simply a two-step process, but a progressive movement toward final integration. Indeed, it is possible to dispense with the notion of phases altogether and to regard differentiation and integration as processes which occur with varying degrees of emphasis throughout the negotiation (see Holmes, Chapter 4, this volume, for a review of phase research).

As Folger and Poole (1984) note, in attempting to move through the two processes, parties are walking a tightrope between two problematic interaction patterns. On the one hand, fear of intense conflict may lead parties to avoid or suppress issues and to maintain a false consensus in which some issues are never raised and some needs go unmet. On the other hand, parties may surface differences but be unable to resolve oppositions. Sometimes parties are caught in escalating spirals of ever-intensifying conflict. Alternatively, the conflict may be resolved by a superior force in which the side with the most power wins.

MOVEMENT BETWEEN
DIFFERENTIATION AND INTEGRATION

The movement between the two processes is affected by at least two factors. First, *conflict intensity* varies as parties move from differentiation into integration and vice versa (cf. Gulliver, 1979). An optimal range of intensity may exist such that if the conflict is too intense, the parties will have difficulty moving into integration; but if intensity is too low, differentiation is difficult. Second, as Walton (1969) notes, successful movement from differentiation to integration depends on the *synchronization* of the parties' tendencies to differentiate or to integrate. If the parties are "out of synch," one bargainer's resistance may undermine the other negotiator's willingness to integrate.

Computer-mediated communication can result in more expression of conflict than does ftf interaction. Researchers note that participants in text-only media, such as computer conferences, are more likely to express differences and make negative statements than ftf communicators (Siegel, Dubrovsky, Kiesler, & McGuire, 1986; Turoff & Hiltz, 1982). This tendency may result from a disinhibition or an inability to see the other party and to pick up such cues as status or emotion that might cause bargainers to hold back (Siegel et al., 1986). However, Poole, Holmes, and DeSanctis (1991) report that a level 1 GDSS used in an ftf meeting surfaces more conflict than does a regular ftf meeting. The GDSS facility for simultaneous and anonymous entry of ideas enables parties to see oppositions on a public screen. Williams (1977) summarizes several studies that show more competitiveness with audio negotiations than with ftf interactions. Basically, then, non-ftf media and ftf media with level 1 or 2 capabilities to highlight oppositions are more effective at surfacing differences and preventing avoidance than is ftf bargaining.

How do the various media influence conflict intensity? Both Siegel et al. (1986) and Poole et al. (1991) provide evidence that conflicts enacted through text and level 1 media are more intense and harder to move into integration than those in ftf situations. Sambamurthy and Poole (1991) report that ftf groups with level 2 support utilize integrative conflict management strategies better than do level 1 ftf groups. They suggest that the modeling capabilities of the level 2 system aid the parties in arriving at satisfactory solutions. This finding parallels Nyhart and Samarasan's (1989) and Nyhart and Dauer's (1986) arguments that the process of building a model collaboratively is an inducement to further cooperation among parties. The tendency of higher conflict intensity with text media may be mitigated by communicating via an asynchronous computer conference, in which parties have a chance to consider the implications of their statements prior to entering them (Hiltz & Turoff, 1978). In addition, some evidence suggests that video mediation may highlight separation between the parties. Williams (1975) observes that videoconferences create a "we" versus "they" dynamic in conferencing groups. Barefoot and Strickland (1982) note that video negotiations are less integrative than are ftf efforts. Similarly, Williams (1977) summarizes a study showing that audio negotiations are more likely to break down than are ftf negotiations. Morley and Stephenson (1977) report that video negotiations deadlock more often than do text, audio, or ftf ones. However, any conclusions about audio media must consider the fact that bargainers make a choice to use the telephone in actual negotiations (Rice, 1984, pp. 61-62). This choice may reflect an unexplored advantage of this medium.

Synchronization of movement through bargaining phases is much easier if parties have a set procedure or agenda that coordinates their moves (Poole, 1991; Walton, 1969). All three levels of computer support embody procedures that regulate the parties' activities. Poole (1991) notes that computer mediation of conflict has the advantage of overcoming people's resistance to the use of procedures because the computer system seems impartial and credible. In contrast, if procedures are too canned or restrictive, resistance may occur and computerization may backfire (Silver, 1988). The benefits of procedures are evident in studies by Morley and Stephenson (1977) that show that the side with the stronger case wins more settlements when procedures constrain discussion than when parties have no constraints. Media that slow down the communication process and are less efficient may inhibit synchronization. Text and computer-based media are often slower than ftf, video, and audio (Johansen et al., 1979; Jones & Jelassi, 1988; Siegel et al., 1986; Weeks & Chapanis, 1976). Computer-based media require users to learn the system. Parties who are unfamiliar with computers may be intimidated (Sproull, Zubrow, & Kiesler, 1987), but this reaction presents only minimal problems (Hiltz & Turoff, 1989; Watson et al., 1988). Also important for synchronization is the effort needed to use certain media. Users report that audio media, in particular, are very demanding and tiring (Johansen et al., 1979). All of these difficulties may move negotiations out of synch.

Ultimately, there is a mixture of benefits and costs for all media except video, which seems ineffective in supporting integration. However, research indicates that people naturally prefer richer media, specifically, ftf and video (Johansen et al., 1979). This finding is interesting in light of the deficiencies of video media in managing conflict.

MEDIA IMPACTS ON TASKS

The remaining research summarizes media effects on five tasks that negotiators typically undertake: issue definition, search for solutions, self-presentation, building appropriate climates, and managing power balances.

Issue Definition. Issue definition centers on setting the agenda for negotiations during differentiation and early integration phases. Several properties of issue definition influence progress in negotiations. First, as Putnam and Holmer note in Chapter 6, this volume, the *framing* of issues strongly influences progress in the negotiation. Generally, integration is easier when issues are framed in an impersonal rather than a personal manner (Fisher & Ury, 1981) and as common problems rather than as unique concerns (Folger & Poole, 1984). Second, the degree of *issue linkage* determines whether the negotiation is conducive to logrolling and other tradeoff strategies during integration. Third, the participants' *bargaining range* places constraints on the degree to which integration is possible. Fourth, parties' *aspiration levels* or the levels of outcome they hope for are important determinants of effective negotiation. Generally, the higher the aspiration level, the more favorable the results for bargainers (Pruitt, 1983). Effective issue definition requires parties to share information, to recognize differences, and to use these differences as a foundation for integrative work.

Evidence suggests that video and ftf media are more appropriate than audio for issue definition in complex tasks like negotiation (Johansen et al., 1979), perhaps because the additional visual channel promotes useful feedback. Although text does not provide immediate feedback, it is adequate for complex tasks because it provides a public artifact for common orientation and because composition requires reflective thinking. All levels of computer systems provide support for the generation and evaluation of ideas, problem formulation, and modeling the negotiation situation (Dennis, George, Jessup, Nunamaker, & Vogel, 1988; Poole et al., 1990). Nyhart and Samarasan (1989) argue that these models are useful for issue analysis because they provide a common database and reference point.

Media shape the framing of issues by encouraging or discouraging shared viewpoints. Some media emphasize separating parties to promote framing issues in ways that do not take the other bargainer into account. Evidence previously cited suggests that video, text alone, and to a lesser extent audio, may create this effect. In contrast, ftf, ftf plus computer support, and level 2 support enable parties to define issues together and to develop common ground (Nyhart & Samarasan, 1989; Sebenius, 1981). Level 2 modeling promotes definition of common issues and bargaining ranges and helps the parties clarify their aspirations (Nyhart & Dauer, 1986).

Solution Search. Search for solutions must be broad and thorough to promote effective resolution of the conflict (Fisher & Ury, 1981). One problem that influences solution search is movement toward *premature convergence* on a solution (Folger & Poole, 1984; Hall & Watson, 1970). Time pressures and fear that the conflict will escalate out of control exacerbate this problem. A second process that presents a problem is *commitment dynamics,* whereby parties feel they have "too much invested to quit" and continue to hold inflexible positions while raising conflict intensity (Pruitt & Rubin, 1986). Rigid adherence to demands furthered by fear of backing down from commitments are major barriers to integration. Several studies show differences in the impacts of media on negotiated outcomes. Sheffield (1989) reports that audio negotiations lead to better solutions than do level 1, text-based negotiations, although there he finds no difference between audio and level 1 ftf conditions. Morley and Stephenson (1977) observe that the side with the stronger case is more successful in audio than ftf negotiations.

Some features of computer support also enhance negotiated outcomes. For example, groups with level 1 GDSS support generate more and better ideas than do non-GDSS groups (Easton et al., 1989; Gallupe, DeSanctis, & Dickson, 1988; Steeb & Johnston, 1981). Perhaps anonymous entry of ideas in a level 1 GDSS results in more solutions than does nonanonymous entry (Jessup, Tansik, & Laase, 1988). Using a level 1 GDSS also results in greater commitment to solutions than does non-supported groups (Gallupe et al., 1988; Steeb & Johnston, 1981; but see Watson et al., 1988, for contradictory results). Further, Smith and Vanecek (1988) note that asynchronous computer conferencing has detrimental effects on solution analysis because it makes coordination harder. Level 2 modeling may provide such coordination and increase synthetic thinking that results in key breakthroughs (Nyhart & Dauer, 1986; Nyhart & Samarasan, 1989; Winter, 1985).

Pressure for premature convergence may be reduced through using media that slow down the pace of negotiations. Hiltz and Turoff (1978) observe that text-based computer conferencing allows time for reflection on ideas, which might prevent the formation of bandwagons. Certainly, text-based negotiations are slower than those conducted with other media (Johansen et al., 1979; Kerr & Hiltz, 1982). However, Fanning and Raphael (1986) note that "typed text is not adequate for rich discussions" (p. 305), such as those required in negotiations. In level 1 ftf meetings, critical discussion is greatly enhanced through the anonymous input of ideas (Jessup et al., 1988). This anonymity and slow input may preclude premature convergence, especially in multiparty negotiations.

To the extent that media either promote the hardening of positions or encourage parties to compromise and move, they influence whether a solution emerges. Putting things in writing and crystalizing a public commitment may make positions rigid. Johansen et al. (1979) review studies that show how text-based negotiations take more time and are more susceptible to problems of rigidity than are those conducted through other media. But ftf negotiations are not immune to these problems. Studies show that opinion changes with video and audio messages are greater than they are with ftf; hence, direct personal contact may enhance rigidity (Johansen et al., 1979). Poole et al. (1991), however, report no evidence of rigidity using a level 1 GDSS in ftf meetings. Ideas and votes are displayed publicly, but without identifying who expressed them. Nyhart's reviews of modeling (Nyhart & Dauer, 1986; Nyhart & Samarasan, 1989) indicate how to prevent rigid commitment by providing an external objective model with which the parties can work.

Self-Presentation. Negotiation also entails self-presentation. Parties act toward others on the basis of their perceptions of the other person's power, determination, legitimacy, trustworthiness, and fairness (see Donohue & Ramesh, Chapter 9, this volume; Rubin & Brown, 1975). Hence, parties are faced with the task of presenting themselves in the best possible light, a task usually accomplished through interaction. A second influence on self-presentation is the *attribution process* (Thomas & Pondy, 1977). Negotiators typically attribute more competitive motives to others than to themselves, which promotes escalation and makes integration difficult. Third, *face-saving* processes, as Wilson describes in Chapter 8, this volume, often make differentiation difficult and block efforts to reach integration (Folger & Poole, 1984).

Media change the nature of self-presentation. Namely, text, audio, and, in some cases, computer support prevent parties from using nonverbal means of presenting self. Morley and Stephenson (1977) conjecture that formal media, such as text and computer support, discourage personal expression. However, Kerr and Hiltz (1982) claim that text-based computer conferencing enables self-presentation through the use of graphics and emotional subtleties in writing (Finholt & Sproull, 1990; Hiltz & Turoff, 1978). Other research suggests that there are no differences in self-disclosure between audio and ftf conditions (Janofsky, 1970), even though people may disclose more in computer-mediated communication than they do in ftf meetings.

Kiesler, Siegel, and McGuire (1984) and Siegel et al. (1986) suggest that text-based computer conferencing depersonalizes or deindividualizes communication, which results in two possible effects on self-presentation. First, because the personhood of the other is de-emphasized, parties are less likely to use personality as an explanation for the conflict than they are in ftf meetings. Hence, they will be less likely than in ftf negotiations to attribute competitive motives to the other party. This impact may promote an integrative orientation if parties invest less of themselves in the conflict and reduce the salience of self-presentation and face-saving (Hiltz & Turoff, 1978). Depersonalization, however, may result in exchanging minimal information because the parties do not think the information is important to communicate. In intense conflicts or competitive climates, failure to exchange information may result in attributing extreme motives to the other party, especially in the absence of corrective feedback. These effects apply primarily to text-based media. Williams (1977) reports no differences in the accuracy of impressions between audio, video, and ftf communication.

Climate. A fourth task is to build an appropriate climate for negotiation. While in the integration phase a cooperative climate is more useful, a competitive climate is sometimes helpful during the differentiation phase (Deutsch, 1969; Folger & Poole, 1984). Of the two climates, the cooperative one is harder to create and maintain in the face of differences. One process that builds a cooperative climate is *discovery of similarities in attitudes, values, and goals* by the two parties (Folger & Poole, 1984). Another process that contributes to cooperative climates is *supportive communication.*

Media-related factors also influence the general climate for negotiation. First, media affect the expression of emotion. Siegel et al. (1986) note that there are more incidents of flaming (uninhibited behavior and name calling) in text-mediated computer conferences than in ftf discussions. Other studies, however, find no evidence of flaming in either ftf or text-only conferences (Fanning & Raphael, 1986; Hiltz & Turoff, 1989; Jarvenpaa, Rao, & Huber, 1988; Poole et al., 1991). This inconsistency may stem from a lack of norm formation in groups. Negative expressions may also result from frustration among new users who, with experience, reduce the tendency to flame (Kerr & Hiltz, 1982; Poole et al.,1991).

Second, media may affect the development of a sense of commonality among parties. Jarvenpaa et al. (1988) report that a shared textual display provides a common focus and benefits agreement in ftf groups. This result also occurs in studies of level 2 modeling (Winter, 1985). In a summary of several studies, Kerr and Hiltz (1982) conclude that asynchronous text-based computer conferencing increases affective ties and personal interaction between individuals that allows some parties to bypass the typical social protocols (Finholt & Sproull, 1990). However, on the down side, the need to type while using computer support in ftf situations may reduce listening (Jarvenpaa et al., 1988) and diminish the parties' abilities to discover similarities. However, this limitation may be offset by the tendency to increase self-disclosure with computer support. Video media improve listening since the parties that are communicating over video spend more time on either sending or listening as opposed to doing both at once (Weeks & Chapanis, 1976). Generally, Morley and Stephenson (1977) argue that formal media (text, video, computer support) lead to more attentive listening than do other media.

Media impacts depend on the existing climate. Generally, media with indirect rather than direct contact result in better negotiated outcomes in competitive than in cooperative climates. Text, audio, and media with reduced eye-contact lead to better negotiated outcomes than ftf in competitive or individualistic climates, but not in cooperative ones (Carnevale & Isen, 1986; Lewis & Fry, 1977; Sheffield, 1989). With ftf plus level 2 support for negotiations, parties with low levels of conflict report high degrees of suspicion of the other bargainer while those with high levels of conflict report positive impressions (Jones & Jelassi, 1988). They also note that computer support helps in situations with a competitive climate and hurts in circumstances with a cooperative climate.

Balance of Power. The final task in a negotiation is to manage the balance of power between the two parties. It is not necessary that the two negotiators be equal in power; however, it is necessary that power be kept balanced. Otherwise, the incentive for the powerful party to negotiate is minimal. The low-power party is also likely to resist negotiation if he or she is subjected to the control of the other. Folger and Poole (1984) summarize dilemmas that power imbalances create for both the strong and the weak parties. One factor that influences the balance of power is the amount of *participation by the two parties.* Influence in a discussion is strongly correlated with speaking time. Any mechanism that can balance participation will promote a balance of power. A second factor that affects balance of power is the degree to which the negotiation places *checks on the resources that parties can use.* Ideally, participants should have access to the same or equivalent sets of resources. In this case, reason and discussion are more likely than material resources to determine the outcome of the negotiation (Folger & Poole, 1984).

To exert influence, parties must participate in the discussion. Imbalances in participation often lead to power asymmetries. A noteworthy feature of ftf communication is the tendency for one or a few discussants to dominate the floor, which enhances their ability to control the discussion (Shaw, 1981). Other media may alter participation opportunities and hence shift power. Barefoot and Strickland (1982) observe that video, compared to ftf, weakens the forces of emergent leadership. Three studies of text-based computer conferences, however, report no differences between group members in relative participation or influence (Kerr & Hiltz, 1982; Kiesler et al., 1984; Siegel et al., 1986). This same finding appears in five studies of ftf plus level 1 and 2 GDSSs (Gallupe et al., 1988; Nunamaker, Applegate, & Konsynski, 1988; Turoff & Hiltz, 1982; Vogel & Nunamaker, 1988; Zigurs, Poole, & DeSanctis, 1988). In these studies, the balance of influence results from the procedural constraints that the media place on participation (e.g., video media employ rules for controling the floor) and from technical features that enable simultaneous idea entry and expression. Specifically, a GDSS may support electronic brainstorming in which all members enter ideas simultaneously. These features may not prevent imbalances, as Poole et al. (1991) show. A skillful or powerful member may use the technology to maintain his or her dominance, as Mantei (1988) and Ho, Raman, and Watson (1989) indicate.

Media other than ftf also offer different resources to use for influence attempts. Nyhart and Dauer (1986) refer to "the battle of the printout," in which computers and computer models are used to convince or to confuse the opposition. Kerr and Hiltz (1982) suggest that text-based computer conferencing discriminates in favor of the literate and educated. As previously mentioned, bargainers who are comfortable with computers may have an advantage, at least in the early stages of a negotiation. Johansen et al. (1979) note that in videoconferences, parties with television skills, such as knowledge about the use of camera angles, may be more effective than bargainers who lack these skills. Future research needs to consider which media add and subtract from the influence equation.

SUMMARY OF LITERATURE REVIEW

This review, while in no way exhaustive, suggests trends in the literature on media impacts. These impacts are summarized in Table 2.2. As this table shows, no single medium surpasses the others on all counts. Every medium has strengths and weaknesses for supporting negotiation. This chapter concludes that a multimedia approach to negotiation support is best. Table 2.2 also offers some general conclusions. Points 1 through 4 indicate that ftf is less effective at surfacing conflicts, but more likely

TABLE 2.2   Summary of Propositions of Media Impacts on Negotiation

Impact	Findings	Is Impact Beneficial or Harmful?
1. Surfaces existing conflicts	text, audio, levels 1, 2 > ftf	Beneficial, if conflict managed effectively
2. Conflict intensity	text, level 1 > ftf	Beneficial within bounds; harmful if too intense
3. Creates "we-they" oppositions	text, audio, video > ftf	Harmful
4. More negative emotional expression	text, level 1 > ftf (mixed results)	Beneficial if managed properly; harmful if it polarizes conflict
5. Reduction of status differences	text, audio > ftf (mixed results)	Beneficial
6. Anonymous expression of ideas and opinions	level 1, level 2 permit this	Beneficial
7. Provides time for reflection	text (especially asynchronous) permits this	Beneficial
8. Slows down negotiation	text, level 1, 2 > ftf, video, audio	Beneficial if it leads to reflection; harmful if it frustrates
9. Reduces time spent on listening	text > ftf; video promotes listening	Harmful
10. Physically demanding and tiring	this holds for audio	Harmful
11. Clarifies procedures	level 1, level 2 > ftf	Beneficial
12. Facilitates work on complex tasks	video, level 1, 2 ftf > audio (mixed results)	Beneficial
13. Provides a common focus	level 1, 2, text video, audio	Beneficial
14. Enables work on a common document	level 1, 2 text permit this	Beneficial
15. Encourages rigid positions	text can do this	Harmful
16. Increases number of ideas considered	level 1, 2 > ftf	Beneficial
17. Provides models for generating solutions	level 2 > level 1, ftf	Beneficial
18. Detailed analysis of solutions	asynchronous text may discourage it	Beneficial
19. Commitment to solutions	level 1 > ftf (mixed results)	Beneficial

TABLE 2.2 Continued

Impact	Findings	Is Impact Beneficial or Harmful?
20. Opinion change	audio > ftf; video > ftf (mixed results)	Beneficial
21. Stronger case wins out	audio > ftf	Beneficial
22. Personal expression	ftf > text, audio, level 1	Beneficial if expression is about needs; harmful if it personalizes conflict
23. Accuracy of impressions	equal for all media	Beneficial
24. Counteracts negative climate	text, audio, level 1, 2 > ftf	Beneficial
25. Positive emotional expression	level 1, 2 > ftf	Beneficial
26. Balance participation	video > ftf; Level 1, 2, text (mixed results)	Beneficial
27. Perceived to be best by lay persons	ftf > all other media	Beneficial
28. Amount of gain in negotiation	audio > level 1 (mixed results; usually no difference)	Beneficial

than other media to avoid extreme escalation. Points 5, 6, and 26 point out that nonvisual media, that is, those media that maintain anonymity, will enhance the parties' inputs but will not necessarily balance power. Points 11 and 12 note that computer support clarifies procedures and helps with complex tasks whereas audio is weak in this function. Points 13, 14, 20, 21, and 24 indicate that depersonalization is greater with audio, text, and computer support than with ftf or video. Audio, text, and computer support make it easier to focus on the issues and to counteract negative climates. Points 7, 13, 14, 16, 17, 18, and 19 suggest that solution quality improves with computer support, with the exception of asynchronous conferencing. It is important to note, however, that people prefer to negotiate with face-to-face than with any other media.

This review also shows that this research is outcome-oriented and does not, at this point, deal with the nature of interaction in mediated negotiations. Several studies in this literature suggest that researchers are beginning to turn their attention to communication process and to the role of media in negotiation interaction.

IMPLICATIONS

New and emerging communication technologies could create the following scenario for future negotiations: Parties meet in a multimedia room and work on a computerized negotiation support system (NSS), in which they privately enter and analyze their own goals and positions prior to bargaining. The NSS prompts parties to compare their own positions to the other party's stance, thus encouraging both parties to set high but realistic aspiration levels. Having done their homework, the parties begin discussion after typing in their public, as opposed to privately held, positions and displaying them in two columns on the NSS public screen. Viewing the screen together, they decide their positions are quite divergent; hence, they must build a decision model of the situation. This model precipitates a serious argument and the parties decide to call in a consultant who is in a small office near the room. The consultant recommends that the parties assemble in small breakout rooms and communicate in text-only mode with a conferencing system. She thinks that this medium might cool the parties down and lead to more reflection. Based on the conference, a possible breakthrough emerges, and the parties go back to the table. The consultant helps them test this solution with their model. Once an acceptable resolution emerges, the NSS guides parties as they formalize their agreement in a contract.

Poole et al. (1990) and Nyhart and Samarasan (1989) describe NSSs that offers negotiators the opportunity to take advantage of the strengths of various media and to avoid their weaknesses. To design and use such a system wisely, however, a number of critical research questions must be addressed. These include: (1) Are these impacts general and robust? Weeks and Chapanis (1976) report that media effects are consistent across tasks, but more studies need to verify this finding. (2) What is the cumulative effect of media ensembles on negotiation? Poole et al. (1991) propose a generic approach for predicting and studying the impact of technological ensembles. (3) Do different combinations of the various types (audio, video, GDSS) result in different impacts? (4) How generalizable are these results to third-party situations? What is the role of the human third party in mediated negotiations? How strongly should the third party control the agenda and the operation of a medium? How closely coupled should third-party behavior be to computer systems and other media? (5) How do social interaction processes influence media impacts? Poole and DeSanctis (1990) and Poole et al. (1991) contend that the ways social technologies are used determine their effects. They outline procedures for studying how groups and individuals appropriate technologies and how these decisions alter media impacts. (6) What is the optimal design for an NSS? Our experience with NSSs is so limited that we know little about designing them. More research is needed before we can capitalize on the available options.

REFERENCES

Barefoot, J., & Strickland, L. (1982). Conflict and dominance in television-mediated interactions. *Human Relations, 35,* 559-566.

Bui, T. X. (1987). Co-op: *A group decision support system for cooperative multiple criteria group decision-making.* Berlin: Springer-Verlag.

Carnevale, P. J. D., & Isen, A. M. (1986). The influence of positive affect and visual access on the discovery of integrative solutions in bilateral negotiating. *Organizational Behavior and Human Decision Processes, 37,* 1-13.

Chapanis, A., Ochsman, R. B., Parrish, R. N., & Weeks, G. D. (1972). Studies in interactive communication: I. The effects of four communication media on the behavior of teams during cooperative problem-solving. *Human Factors, 14,* 487-509.

Dennis, A. R., George, J. E., Jessup, L. M., Nunamaker, J. F., & Vogel, D. R. (1988). Information technology to support electronic meetings. *MIS Quarterly, 12,* 591-624.

DeSanctis, G., & Gallupe, B. (1987). A foundation for the study of group decision support systems. *Management Science, 33,* 589-609.

Deutsch, M. (1969). Conflicts: Productive and destructive. *Journal of Social Issues, 25,* 7-41.

Easton, A. C., Vogel, D., & Nunamaker, J. F., Jr. (1989). Stakeholder identification and assumption surfacing in small groups. In R. Blanning & D. King (Eds.), *Proceedings of the Twenty-Second Annual Hawaii International Conference on System Science* (Vol. III, pp. 344-352). New York: IEEE Computer Society Press.

Fanning, T., & Raphael, B. (1986). Computer teleconferencing: Experience at Hewlett-Packard. *Proceedings of the Conference on Computer-Supported Cooperative Work* (pp. 291-306). New York: ACM Press.

Finholt, T., & Sproull, L. (1990). Electronic groups at work. *Organization Science, 1,* 41-64.

Fisher, R., & Ury, W. (1981). *Getting to yes: Negotiating agreement without giving in.* Boston: Houghton Mifflin.

Folger, J. P., & Poole, M. S. (1984). *Working through conflict.* Glenview, IL: Scott, Foresman.

Gallupe, R. B., DeSanctis, G., & Dickson, G. (1988). The impact of computer-based support on the process and outcomes of group decision making. *MIS Quarterly, 12,* 277-298.

Gulliver, P. H. (1979). *Disputes and negotiations: A cross-cultural perspective.* New York: Academic Press.

Hall, J., & Watson, M. (1970). The effects of a normative intervention on group performance and member reactions. *Human Relations, 23,* 299-317.

Hiltz, S. R., & Turoff, M. (1978). *The network nation: Human communication via computer.* Reading, MA: Addison-Wesley.

Hiltz, S. R., & Turoff, M. (1989). Experiments in group decision making, 3: Disinhibition, deindividuation, and group process in pen-name and real name computer conferences. *Decision Support Systems, 5*, 217-232.

Ho, T. S., Raman, K. S., & Watson, R. T. (1989). Group decision support systems: The cultural factor. *Proceedings of the International Conference on Information Systems* (pp. 257-269). New York: ACM Press.

Janofsky, A. I. (1970). Affective self-disclosure in telephone versus face-to-face interviews. *Journal of Humanistic Psychology, 10*, 93-103.

Jarke, M., Jelassi, M. T., & Shakun, M. F. (1987). Mediator: Towards a negotiation support system. *European Journal of Operational Research, 31*, 314-334.

Jarvenpaa, S. L., Rao, V. S., & Huber, G. P. (1988). Computer support for meetings of groups working on unstructured problems: A field experiment. *MIS Quarterly, 12*, 625-644.

Jessup, L. M., Tansik, D. A., & Laase, T. D. (1988). *Group problem solving in an automated environment: The effects of anonymity and proximity on group process and outcomes with a group decision support system.* Unpublished manuscript, Department of MIS, University of Arizona, Tucson.

Johansen, R., Vallee, J., & Vian, K. (1979). *Electronic meetings.* Reading, MA: Addison-Wesley.

Jones, B. H., & Jelassi, T. (1988). *The effect of computer intervention and task structure on bargaining outcomes.* Unpublished manuscript, Decision Sciences Department, University of Hawaii, Honolulu.

Kerr, E. B., & Hiltz, S. R. (1982). *Computer mediated communication systems.* New York: Academic Press.

Kiesler, S., Siegel, J., & McGuire, T. W. (1984). Social psychological aspects of computer-mediated communication. *American Psychologist, 39*, 1123-1134.

Lewis, S. A., & Fry, W. R. (1977). Effects of visual access and orientation on the discovery of integrative bargaining alternatives. *Organizational Behavior and Human Performance, 20*, 75-92.

Mantei, M. (1988). Capturing the capture lab concepts. *Proceedings of the Conference on Computer Supported Cooperative Work* (pp. 257-269). New York: ACM Press.

Morley, I. E., & Stephenson, G. (1977). *The social psychology of bargaining.* London: George Allen & Unwin.

Nunamaker, J. F., Applegate, L. M., & Konsynski, B. R. (1987). Facilitating group creativity: Experience with a group decision support system. In R. Sprague (Ed.), *Proceedings of the Twentieth Annual Hawaii International Conference on System Sciences* (Vol. 1, pp. 422-430). New York: ACM Press.

Nyhart, J. D., & Dauer, E. A. (1986). A preliminary analysis of the uses of scientific models in dispute prevention, management, and resolution. *Missouri Journal of Dispute Resolution,* Vol. 1986, 29-58.

Nyhart, J. D., & Samarasan, D. K. (1989). The elements of negotiation management: Using computers to help resolve conflict. *Negotiation Journal, 5*, 43-62.

Pondy, L. (1967). Organizational conflict: Concepts and models. *Administrative Science Quarterly, 12*, 296-320.

Poole, M. S. (1991). Procedures for managing meetings: Social and technological innovation. In R. A. Swanson & B. O. Knapp (Eds.), *Innovative meeting management* (pp. 53-109). Austin, TX: 3M Meeting Management Institute.

Poole, M. S., & DeSanctis, G. (1990). Understanding the use of group decision support systems: The theory of adaptive structuration. In J. Fulk & C. Steinfield (Eds.),

Organizations and communication technology (pp. 175-195). Newbury Park, CA: Sage.

Poole, M. S., Holmes, M., & DeSanctis, G. (1991). Conflict management in a computer-supported meeting environment. *Management Science, 37*, 926-953.

Poole, M. S., Zappa, J., DeSanctis, G., Shannon, D., & Dickson, G. (1990, August). *A theory and design for a negotiation support system.* Paper presented at the annual meeting of the Academy of Management, San Francisco.

Pruitt, D. G. (1983). Integrative agreements: Nature and antecedents. In M. H. Bazerman & R. J. Lewicki (Eds.), *Negotiating in organizations* (pp. 35-50). Beverly Hills, CA: Sage.

Pruitt, D. G., & Rubin, J. Z. (1986). *Social conflict: Escalation, stalemate, and settlement.* New York: Random House.

Rice, R., and Associates. (1984). *The new media.* Beverly Hills, CA: Sage.

Rubin, J. Z., & Brown, B. (1975). *The social psychology of bargaining and negotiation.* New York: Academic Press.

Samarasan, D. K. (1988). Collaborative modeling and negotiation. In R. B. Allen (Ed.), *Proceedings of the Conference on Office Information Systems* (pp. 9-21). New York: ACM Press.

Sambamurthy, V., & Poole, M. S. (1991). *The effects of the level of sophistication of computerized support on the conflict process and outcomes in groups.* Unpublished manuscript, Department of Management, Florida State University, Tallahassee.

Sebenius, J. K. (1981). The computer as mediator: Law of the sea and beyond. *Journal of Policy Analysis and Management, 1*, 77-95.

Shaw, M. (1981). *Group dynamics: The psychology of small group behavior* (3rd ed.). New York: McGraw-Hill.

Sheffield, J. (1989). The effects of bargaining orientation and communication medium on negotiations in the bilateral monopoly task: A comparison of decision room and computer conferencing communication media. *Chi '89 Proceedings* (pp. 43-48). New York: ACM Press.

Short, J., Williams, E., & Christie, B. (1976). *The social psychology of telecommunication.* New York: John Wiley.

Siegel, J., Dubrovsky, V., Kiesler, S., & McGuire, T. W. (1986). Group processes in computer-mediated communication. *Organizational Behavior and Human Decision Processes, 37*, 157-187.

Silver, M. S. (1988). User perceptions of decision support system restrictiveness: An experiment. *Journal of Management Information Systems, 5*, 51-65.

Smith, J. Y., & Vanacek, M. T. (1988). Computer conferencing and task-oriented decisions: Implications for group decision support. *Information and Management, 14*, 123-132.

Sproull, L., Zubrow, D., & Kiesler, S. (1987). Cultural socialization to computer in college. *Computers in Human Behavior, 2*, 257-275.

Steeb, R., & Johnson, S. C. (1981). A computer-based interactive system for group decision-making. *IEEE Transactions on Systems, Man, and Cybernetics, 11*, 544-552.

Thomas, K. (1976). Conflict and conflict management. In M. Dunnette (Ed.), *Handbook of industrial and organizational psychology* (pp. 889-935). Chicago: Rand McNally.

Thomas, K., & Pondy, L. (1977). Toward an "intent" model of conflict management among principal parties. *Human Relations, 30*, 1089-1102.

Trevino, L. K., Lengel, R. H., & Daft, R. L. (1987). Media symbolism, media richness, and media choice in organizations. *Communication Research, 14*, 553-574.

Turoff, M., & Hiltz, S. R. (1982). Computer support for group versus individual decisions. *IEEE Transactions on Communications, 30,* 82-90.

Vogel, D., & Nunamaker, J. (1988). *Group decision support system impact: Multi-methodological exploration.* Unpublished manuscript, University of Arizona, Tucson.

Walton, R. E. (1969). *Interpersonal peacemaking.* Reading, MA: Addison-Wesley.

Watson, R. T., DeSanctis, G., & Poole, M. S. (1988). Using a GDSS to facilitate consensus: Some intended and unintended consequences. *MIS Quarterly, 12,* 462-477.

Weeks, G. D., & Chapanis, A. (1976). Cooperative versus conflictive problem-solving in three telecommunication modes. *Perceptual and Motor Skills, 42,* 879-917.

Williams, E. (1975). Coalition formation over telecommunications media. *European Journal of Social Psychology, 5,* 503-507.

Williams, E. (1977). Experimental comparisons of face-to-face and mediated communication: A review. *Psychological Bulletin, 84,* 963-976.

Winter, F. W. (1985). An application of computerized decision tree models in management-union bargaining. *Interfaces, 15,* 74-80.

Zigurs, I., Poole, M. S., & DeSanctis, G. (1988). Computer support of group decision making: A communication-based investigation. *MIS Quarterly, 12,* 625-644.

Chapter 3

THE COMMUNICATION OF
OFFERS IN DYADIC BARGAINING

Frank Tutzauer

PERHAPS THE MOST important communications in a bargaining session are those that convey the disputants' offers and counteroffers. Although other types of communication, for example, threats and promises, arguments and counterarguments, or other message strategies, undoubtedly influence the course of the negotiation, it is likely that offers exert the most profound effect on the process. The nature, timing, and pattern of offers, and the concessions they elicit, constitute the very essence of bargaining and negotiation. Indeed, it can be argued that if there are no offers, there is no bargaining. One might even define *bargaining* as the exchange of offers. Consequently, the bid/counterbid process must assume a central place in any theory of bargaining and negotiation.

This chapter reviews theoretical approaches and empirical findings on the communication of offers and counteroffers in dyadic bargaining. The aim is not to present a comprehensive review, but rather, to highlight those studies, theories, and models that emphasize concessional *processes*. This chapter begins by introducing some preliminary notions and basic terms. Then, after a brief review of early concession research, which emphasizes static views of bargaining, the chapter explores the advantages of a communication approach to the study of offers through examining the dynamic and interactive nature of offers and concessions. The chapter concludes with a discussion of the kinds of questions that must be answered to gain a complete understanding of the bid/counterbid process.

PRELIMINARY NOTIONS AND BASIC CONCEPTS

THE NATURE OF OFFERS

This chapter assumes that offers take place in the context of *two-party* bargaining. Although most of the ideas in this chapter generalize to multiparty negotiations, it is easier to track the dynamics of offers in two-party situations. Thus, this chapter defines *bargaining* as a situation in which two parties to a dispute attempt to arrange the terms of agreement between them. Viewed in this manner, bargaining consists of a series of tentative proposals put forth by the parties. These tentative proposals are called *offers*. If the bargainers mutually agree to one of these proposals, then that proposal serves as a *settlement*. If no such proposal is mutually agreeable, then some default option, called an *impasse* or the *disagreement point*, serves as the settlement, and the bargainers reach a *deadlock*.

Although it is easy to understand an offer in the abstract, how does a researcher recognize an offer when he or she sees one? This question is particularly pertinent given that offers may be either *explicit* (overtly stated) or *implicit* (hinted at or otherwise tacitly made). Because explicit offers are much easier to recognize and deal with, many researchers do not consider implicit offers official bids. Such an attitude is understandable, and, for many bargaining scenarios, it is even reasonable.

However, this approach begs the question: What are the linguistic features of offers? The most obvious linguistic feature of an offer is that it is usually, but not always, numerical. For example, the number of missiles in an arsenal, the price of a car, the level of oil production, and the number of years in a plea-bargained sentence are all bargaining issues in which the basic offers consist of numerical properties.

Second, offers demand a response, usually a counteroffer, but sometimes an acceptance or a rejection. Although offers do not always *elicit* a response, a response is nonetheless implicitly required, in the same way that a question, though it may go unanswered, requests an answer. Offers are like *adjacency pairs,* or "utterance units that imply one another," (Ellis, Hamilton, & Aho, 1983, p. 270; also see Keough, Chapter 5, this volume) and lead to the action-reaction nature of bargaining.

A third linguistic feature of offers is that they are fluid. Whenever an offer is put forth, it is always, in some sense, tentative. Thus, they are constantly subject to change and are usually modified over time. Such a modification may be in the form of an outright concession, or it may be in the form of *incorporation,* which "entails adding to one's proposal . . . some element of a proposal made previously by the other party" (Pruitt, 1981, p. 169). In addition to incorporation, the fluidity of offers serves two other bargaining functions: *information exchange* and *heuristic trial and error* (Pruitt, 1981). Information exchange occurs because an offer reveals information about one's motives "in terms of what is demanded in contrast to what might have been asked" (Pruitt, 1981, p. 173). When a proposal is changed, it tells the opponent that those aspects of the proposal that are modified are not as important as those aspects that are retained. Heuristic trial and error, in contrast, is a strategy in which a bargainer frequently changes offers, conceding incrementally and selecting lowest priority issues first. Several studies reveal that heuristic trial and error results in agreements of high joint benefit (see Pruitt, 1981, chap. 5, for a review).

Finally, in a multi-issue scenario, offers might reflect proposals about a single issue, or they might reflect multiple issues. In other words, the offers might arise from *sequential* consideration of the issues, or they might arise from *simultaneous* consideration of the issues. On the one hand, sequential treatment of the issues simplifies bargaining by dividing a complex problem into smaller components. On the other hand, simultaneous consideration of the issues allows for an offer strategy known as *logrolling,* in which trade-offs among the issues can be made. Such trade-offs can lead to settlements that are beneficial to both parties.

Offers, then, are the basic components of bargaining. They tend to be numerical, they require a response, they are constantly changing, and they reflect simultaneous and sequential consideration of issues. These assumptions influence how offers function in various models of the bargaining process.

THE UTILITY OF OFFERS

Because bargaining is a form of joint decision making, certain decision-theoretic assumptions govern each negotiator's actions. First, bargainers have definite preferences about the possible settlements they want and they know what these preferences are. Situations in which a bargainer says, "Gosh, I don't know if I prefer X or Y and I don't know if I'm indifferent between them," are outside the scope of this discussion.

A second assumption is that bargainers behave rationally, that is, bargainers act according to their preferences. The word *rationality* is a loaded one. People often think rationality means that bargainers behave in a cold, calculating fashion with an amoral approach to others. In this chapter, *rationality* simply means that if a bargainer prefers X to Y and is given a choice between them then X will be chosen.

A final assumption is that a bargainer's preferences can be expressed by means of a numerical scale. One advantage that offers have over other message tactics is that offers are often intrinsically numerical. Yet even when offers are not numbers, for example, if a football team offers to give up a future draft choice in exchange for another team's running back, this option can be placed on a numerical scale. One classic result of decision theory is that, given certain reasonable assumptions about the nature of a bargainer's preferences, it is possible to define a *utility function* by assigning a number to each proposal (Luce & Raiffa, 1957). This number is called the proposal's *utility* and it serves as a quantitative indicator of the worth of the proposal. Utility is measured on an interval-level scale. It has the property that if a bargainer prefers proposal A to proposal B, then the utility of A will be larger than is the utility of B.

Utilities are not always fixed, nor are they always known. Although a utility often remains constant, particularly in simple bargaining tasks, it might change as a function of time, the evolution of issues, or the altering of preferences due to time pressures (Livne, 1987). Furthermore, bargainers usually have only partial knowledge about their opponents' utility functions (Harsanyi & Selten, 1972). Although bargainers are not completely uninformed about their opponents, they only rarely have complete information. Usually, bargainers start out with certain reasonable guesses about their opponents' utilities; they modify these estimates on the basis of offers, arguments, and other behaviors. As Bacharach and Lawler (1981) note, "Concessions communicate intentions, aspirations, and the like to the opponent and can, in turn, alter the opponent's intentions, aspirations, or action" (p. 80).

One consequence of treating offers numerically is that it is easy to depict bargaining geometrically. Two geometric representations prove especially useful. First, when the bargainers' interests are diametrically opposed, the various settlements to which the bargainers might agree can be arrayed along a continuum, with one of the bargainers preferring outcomes at one end and with the other bargainer preferring outcomes at the opposite end. In this situation, an offer corresponds to a point on the continuum, and constitutes a demand for a proportion of the goods. The *contract zone* is that region of the continuum between the two bargainers' extreme-most desires.

If, however, the bargainers' interests are not diametrically opposed, but instead, partially overlap, then a different representation is required. In particular, each possible settlement is represented by a point in the Cartesian coordinate plane, with the x-coordinate corresponding to the utility of the settlement to the first bargainer, and the y-coordinate corresponding to the utility to the second bargainer. Thus, the collection of all possible settlements is a set of points in the plane called the *feasible outcome set*. It is like a two-dimensional contract zone since all bargaining takes place within this set. The points in the feasible outcome set are not the settlements themselves, but, rather, the utilities associated with the settlements. For example, in a plea bargaining situation, the prosecutor might offer a complex package consisting of dropping certain counts, reducing others, shortening prison sentences, and requiring certain kinds of victim compensation in exchange for a desired plea. This package has a certain utility to the defendant, say u_1, and another, perhaps different, utility to the prosecutor, say u_2. Then, the offer is represented in the feasible outcome set as the point (u_1, u_2).

Regardless of which geometric representation is used, certain basic features emerge. The *initial offer* is a bargainer's first offer, and a bargainer's *concession magnitude* is the difference between the first offer and the last offer. A bargainer's *concession rate* is the speed with which he or she is conceding. To treat concession rates adequately requires a dynamic model.

DYNAMIC MODELS OF CONCESSION BEHAVIOR

A relatively large body of research examines the connection between concessions and outcome. Early social-psychological research bases its theoretical grounding in level-of-aspiration theory (Siegel & Fouraker, 1960) or in Osgood's (1962) proposal of Graduated Reciprocation In Tension Reduction (GRIT). Level-of-aspiration theory claims that a tough bargaining stance, marked by a high opening bid followed by limited concessions, leads the opponent to lower his or her aspirations and demand less, resulting in a favorable settlement for the tougher bargainer. GRIT assumes that a moderately tough opening, followed by a series of noncontingent concessions, reduces tensions and fosters cooperation. Both GRIT and level-of-aspiration theory have spawned a large body of research on initial offers and concession magnitude. Putnam and Jones (1982), Rubin and Brown (1975), and Tutzauer (1991) provide extensive reviews of this work; hence, their reviews will not be repeated in this chapter. However, one general observation of this early social-psychological research is that it conceives of bargaining as a static phenomenon. Some theorizing about process exists (e.g., when are concessions reciprocated?), but by and large, the research is inherently static, governed by such questions as: What strategy produces what outcome? Furthermore, the variables are gross indicators of behavior, for example, initial offers and concession magnitudes. More sophisticated explanations are possible.

To illustrate, suppose three bargainers have the same initial offer, the same concession magnitude, and make the same number of offers. However, their concession behavior differs for each negotiator. The first bargainer's offers come in a series of equally spaced steps. The second bargainer begins by making very small concessions, and then, toward the end of the negotiation, makes a flurry of very large concessions. The third bargainer concedes everything on the second offer, and then holds firm for the remaining offers. Thus, even though the three bargainers start at the same place, make the same number of offers, and concede the same total amount, the *process* by which they do so differs markedly.

Similarly, the responses of the bargainers to their partners may be different. In one of the dyads, the bargainers may mimic each other, move for move. In another dyad, one bargainer may not respond to what the other negotiator is doing. Finally, in the third dyad, the bargainers may be responsive to each other, but the degree of responsiveness might depend on what offer is made. Bargainers do not negotiate in a vacuum. Concession making is *interactive*; each bargainer's offers influence those of his or her opponent and vice versa.

Although measures such as concession magnitude, initial offer, and number of concessions undoubtedly capture important aspects of concession making, most of the exchange process is missed. The study of offers and concessions could profit from employing a communication framework.

A COMMUNICATION FRAMEWORK

One benefit of examining offers through a communication lens is incorporating the processual and interactive nature of bargaining. A communication framework embodies three explicit assumptions. The models discussed in subsequent sections meet these assumptions to greater or lesser degrees; these assumptions provide a basis for evaluating the various modes.

(1) The communication of offers is a process. This chapter treats the words *process* and *dynamic* as synonyms, thus the phrase *dynamic process* is, in fact, redundant. Obviously, offers change over time. More importantly, however, changes in offers result from what went before; later offers are tied to earlier offers by some linkage. The assumption of process is so critical that all of the models discussed in this chapter attempt to capture it, but the models differ in the linkage that ties one offer to another. For example, in some models a bargainer's offer is predicted from his or her previous offer, whereas in other models the offer of the opponent determines a bargainer's next proposal. Also, some models combine these two systems.

(2) The offer process is interactive. *Interactive* means that bargainers influence each other. Again, all the models in this chapter meet this assumption to some extent. Models that fail to meet the assumption of interactiveness, although they may make important contributions, nonetheless suffer from a serious deficiency. If offers are *not* interactive, then bargaining is essentially a game of chicken, with offers serving only to inform the opponent of a position. Yet, as anyone who has haggled over the price of a car would agree, a bargainer makes an offer not to inform but to persuade. The essence of bargaining, it seems, is the way bargainers shape each other's behaviors via their offers.

(3) Internal and external forces drive the interactive process of making offers. To argue that offers are interactive and processual, however, is merely descriptive not explanatory. Indeed, what makes a bargainer concede at all? Obviously, certain forces impinge on a bargainer, which results in a change of offer. These forces might arise from factors internal to the negotiation, for example, time pressures, the negotiator's arguments, or reciprocity norms, or they might arise from external factors, for example, constituent pressure, economic hardship, or alternatives to a negotiated agreement. What is important is that the forces motivate a bargainer to change his or her offer. They serve as a heuristic with which to postulate and investigate various models of offers and concessions.

TYPES OF MODELS

Differential Equation Models. In a classic experiment, Kelley, Beckman, and Fischer (1967) investigate the pattern of offers that result when bargainers divide a reward and are unaware of each other's minimum necessary share (MNS), a share of the reward that makes the division profitable. In a variety of situations and MNS levels, Kelley et al. observe that the bargainers' offers are remarkably similar when plotted as a function of time. More specifically, all the bargainers exhibit patterns of *exponential decay*: a relatively high starting offer with initially rapid concessions, followed by slower concessions as the bargainer approaches a terminal resistance value. In general, the higher the MNS is, the higher the resistance points and initial offers will be, although the slower the rate at which the bargainers approach their resistance points.

One advantage of a dynamic model is using a *concession rate,* or the speed with which a bargainer concedes, rather than a crude measure of exchange such as concession magnitude. If a bargainer's offers are plotted as a function of time, then, at any time t, the bargainer's concession rate is represented by the slope of the curve at time t—the steeper the slope, the faster the bargainer concedes. Mathematically, in an exponential decay model, a bargainer's concession rate is proportional to his or her current offer. When the offer is high, for example at the beginning of the bargaining, the negotiator concedes very rapidly. As time progresses and the bargainer's offer falls, the concession rate also drops, and the concession curve flattens out.

Kelley et al. (1967) explain their data by appealing to a *resistance force*, that is, a force that deters concession making and must be overcome before a bargainer lowers his or her offer. The most important assumption of this model is the nature of the resistance force vis-à-vis the MNS. First, Kelley et al. assume that resistance increases as the MNS is approached. Thus, the concession rate drops, which results in a flattening of the concession curve as a bargainer nears his or her MNS value. Second, for a given offer, resistance increases as the MNS increases. For example, if two bargainers make identical initial offers but one of them has a high MNS and the other has a low one, then, at the outset of the negotiations, the bargainer with the low MNS would concede faster than would the one with the high MNS.

Although certainly dynamic, this model suffers from two problems. First, the bargaining scenario is extremely simplistic. The researchers tell the bargainers to divide nine points between them; certainly not a very complicated task. Second, and perhaps more importantly, no clear linkage exists between the behaviors of one bargainer and those of his or her partner. The offer-concession curves of Kelley et al. (1967) depict how a bargainer concedes, but they fail to reference the opponent's behavior. Once the initial offer, the resistance point, and the concession rates are chosen, a bargainer's concession behavior is set, *regardless of what the opponent does*. Although this model is dynamic, it is not interactive.

One interactive model is suggested by Bartos (1966, 1974) who bases his work on Richardson's (1960) action-reaction system (see also Druckman, 1977 and Hopmann & Smith, 1977). Bartos's basic argument is that a bargainer's demand depends not only on his or her previous offer (as in the Kelley et al. model) but also on the demand of the opponent (an interactive model). Although Richardson focuses on the arms race rather than negotiation, Bartos adapts Richardson's equations to bargaining settings, thus capturing the notion that a bargainer's offer depends on his or her previous offer and the prior offer of the opponent. Using this model, Bartos (1966, 1974) conducts several experiments and obtains reasonable support for the Richardson (1960) system.

Even though Bartos's model builds interdependence into the equations, offers still exist on a unidimensional continuum. The basic quantities do not recognize what the opponent might gain or lose. To avoid this problem, vector fields can be used to model the communication of offers. Vectors are advantageous because they include bargaining forces explicitly in the model. Specifically, a *self-oriented* force impels a bargainer to seek more for him- or herself, and an *other-oriented* force impels the bargainer to seek more for the opponent. When these two forces combine, the resultant force determines how a bargainer's offers will change over time.

A *force* is a quantity that has magnitude and direction. Consequently, vectors or, equivalently, Cartesian coordinates of points in the feasible outcome set, represent these forces. In particular, a *vector field* associates each point of the feasible outcome set with a two-dimensional column vector. If a point of the feasible outcome set represents an offer, then the vector linked to it indicates the direction and speed with which the offer is changing due to self- and other-oriented forces. Each bargainer has a vector field, and the solutions of these vector fields give the concessional behavior of each bargainer as a function of time.

A recent study (Tutzauer, 1987) supports the use of vector fields in the form $X = Ax + B$. In this equation, X is a two-dimensional column vector that indicates the direction and speed with which a bargainer will concede when he or she makes x as an offer at time t. A is a 2×2 matrix with negative entries on the diagonal and zeroes off the diagonal; B is a two-dimensional column vector with positive entries that determine the MNS. The entries of *A* are concession rates, one in the self-direction, one in the other-direction. Unlike the equivalent Richardson (1960) or Kelley et al. (1967) formulations, however, *x* is not a unidimensional quantity. Instead, it is a vector (specifically, a point of the feasible outcome set), and its components indicate how much a bargainer is claiming for self and how much is being offered to the opponent. The model is premised on the behavior that Kelley et al. note, namely that concessions slow down as the bargainer approaches the MNS. In the vector model, this assumption is two-pronged, since it applies to what a bargainer claims for self and what he or she is willing to give to the opponent.

Vector fields rectify a problem of the Kelley et al. (1967) and Bartos (1966, 1974) formulations, namely, they provide a more satisfying notion than do previous models of what an offer is. The vector field model shares, however, one disadvantage with the Kelley et al. but not the Bartos model: It is not interactive. Although both bargainers are modeled simultaneously with vector field equations and two-dimensional offers, nothing ties the two vector fields together. The bargainers are modeled simultaneously, but independently.

Iterative Dynamics. Chaos theory is a popular topic in both the natural and the social sciences (for introductions see Gleick, 1987; Hofstadter, 1986; May, 1976). Basically, chaos theory focuses on the study of deterministic systems that produce random behavior. Even though it is debatable whether or not bargaining behavior is chaotic, chaos theory nonetheless provides theoretical tools that can represent an interactive view of offers and concessions.

Chaos theorists develop models by using iterated functions. The approach is deceptively simple. The theorist posits an equation that describes system output as a function of system input, and then he or she studies what will happen when he or she "iterates" the function. That is, the theorist studies what happens when outputs are repeatedly fed back into the system as inputs. The result is a description of the long-term, dynamic aspects of the system.

A similar approach can be used to study bargaining. Whenever a bargainer makes an offer, that offer becomes a stimulus that requires a response by the other bargainer, which in turn requires the first bargainer to counter with yet another offer. This process continues until the bargainers either agree or reach an impasse. The key theoretical problem is to determine the relationship between offer and response.

Taking the unit interval as the bargaining continuum, that is, all numbers between 0 and 1 inclusively, the research can chart one bargainer's outcomes at the smaller end of the interval and the other person's settlements at the higher end. This process resembles two bargainers trying to divide a commodity; an offer consists of the proportion of the commodity that goes to one of the bargainers. For example, an offer of .2 is a claim for a 20/80 split, whereas one of .8 demands an 80/20 split. With this model, an *offer-response function* $y = f(x)$ depicts how a response depends on the immediately prior offer. If an initial offer of .2 is met with a counteroffer of .8, then we have .8 = $f(.2)$. We then put .8 into the function f to produce the next response. The process continues in this manner, producing a string of offers and responses which can be compared to a bargainer's actual behavior. If the function produces accurate predictions across a number of bargainers, then evidence would exist that the model is a reasonable predictor of the course of bargaining.

But what offer-response function should a researcher choose? A recent laboratory experiment (Tutzauer, 1986) supports a relationship premised on three assumptions. First, the bargainers typically alternate in making offers. Second, all concessions make progress toward an agreement. In other words, once an offer is made there is no backtracking. Finally, a bargainer's response to a tough offer is tougher than his or her response to a soft offer. One model that meets these assumptions is the elliptical model. A plot of response versus offer yields the upper quarter of an ellipse centered at the origin with the major axis parallel to the x-axis, although different negotiations will produce ellipses of different curvatures.

An ellipse is an appropriate choice for the offer-response function because it is algebraically simple and, by varying its curvature, it can incorporate a wide range of communicative possibilities. Specifically, simpler models, such as linear equations, often require a response to be proportional to the preceding offer; the ellipse model does not. More important, a researcher can give physical interpretations to the two parameters that govern its curvature. In particular, the parameters index two aspects of relative toughness, capitulation, and resistance. If Bargainer 1 prefers the smaller end of the continuum and Bargainer 2 prefers the larger end, then the capitulation parameter indicates how much toughness exists in the system, in the direction of Bargainer 2 due to Bargainer 1's capitulation. Similarly, the resistance parameter measures how much toughness exists in the system due to Bargainer 2's recalcitrance.

A number of implications stem from the model, namely, what the settlement will be if the bargainers agree and what the final offer will be if they deadlock. Furthermore, the model indicates that the bargainers will deadlock only when capitulation equals resistance, and if they agree, the settlement does not depend on the initial offer. Tutzauer (1986) verifies these predictions with nonlinear regressions that demonstrate the model fits the data well. The problems with the model are theoretical rather than empirical. First, the model applies only to unidimensional bargaining situations. The offers are points on a continuum rather than points of a feasible outcome set. Second, there is no clear reason to prefer the elliptical formulation to the simpler $y = ax + b$. Iterating the linear function yields identical predictions regarding the existence and stability of agreements and deadlocks, even though the two models differ in predicting what the agreement will be. As of yet, however, no data exist either to support or to dispute the linear function.

Catastrophe Theory. Catastrophe theory presents an approach to modeling offers and concessions that differs from the models previously discussed, although it shares with these models the benefit of being dynamic. It can also be interactive, depending on how the researcher conceives of the problem and defines the variables. Catastrophe theory is the creation of French mathematician René Thom (1972/1975). A readable description is presented by Isnard and Zeeman (1976). Basically, catastrophe theory is the study of how small, continuous changes in independent variables can cause catastrophic or discontinuous changes in behavior. Thom's classification theorem states that for four or fewer independent variables and for two or fewer dependent variables, a system can undergo discontinuous change in only seven possible ways.

Discontinuity in bargaining is a change in the *pattern* of offers or the way offers are changing, not changes in the offers per se. For example, suppose two bargainers follow the Kelley et al. (1967) exponential decay model and make steady progress toward agreement. If the bargainers become argumentative and begin insulting each other, then the exponential decay model may suddenly shift to outright recalcitrance. Another example comes from the integrative bargaining literature (Pruitt, 1981). In an integrative scenario, the bargainers may plod along nonproductively when, because of a sudden insight, one of them discovers that logrolling leads to high joint benefits. The bargainers then change their approaches to bargaining by employing different patterns of offers.

Catastrophe theory deals with this kind of sudden abrupt change that happens in various systems. In the case of two independent variables, x_1 and x_2, and one dependent variable y, the only type of discontinuity that occurs is the *cusp catastrophe*. Oliva, Peters, and Murthy (1981) use the cusp catastrophe to model union-management bargaining. They assign the behavior of the bargaining system as y, which they conceptualize as being either strike prone or lockout prone. Strike prone behaviors correspond to large values of y, and lockout prone behaviors correspond to low values of y. Oliva et al. make union and management bargaining intensities the independent variables. They operationalize these intensities as scores on questionnaire items that assess success in winning demands, extent of concession making, unwillingness to compromise, emotional involvement, and concerns about equity. Consequently, the variables, although including offers and concessions, are broader than numerical offers.

The factors that precipitate sudden changes are union and management tolerances. If the intensities are high and the union or management tolerances are crossed, then the system can be thrown into a strike or lockout. To test the model, Oliva et al. (1981) have 35 negotiation teams participate in a collective bargaining game and then track their intensities and behaviors over time. In general, the bargaining zones resemble cusps and the model does an adequate, though not superlative, job of predicting lockout and strike behavior.

One problem with the cusp model, at least with the way that Oliva et al. conceptualize it, is that they include only two behaviors, strike prone and lockout prone. The model does not allow for the emergence of compromise. One alternative, inspired by Isnard and Zeeman (1976), is to use the butterfly catastrophe. The butterfly catastrophe differs from the cusp catastrophe primarily in using four rather than two independent variables. This additional flexibility allows for a systems model in which compromise can emerge.

FUTURE DIRECTIONS

The communication of offers is central to the bargaining process; hence an understanding of negotiation requires an understanding of concessional patterns. The study of offers and concessions has a long history. The various models and theories of concession making are among the most sophisticated in the bargaining literature. Nevertheless, gaps in our understanding exist, thus a variety of extensions and modifications of current research would improve our theoretical insights on the role of offers in negotiation.

What theoretical extensions would be most useful? This chapter suggests that research should follow three major directions. First, and most immediately, researchers need to develop models that are interactive and simultaneously permit bargaining interests that partially overlap. Currently, models exist that are interactive, for example Richardson (1960) processes and elliptical models, but in these models, the bargainers have interests that are diametrically opposed and they make offers that are unidimensional. Next, models exist in which the bargainers' interests partially overlap, for example, vector field models, but they lack a clear linkage between the bargainers' behaviors.

Clearly, there is a need to develop models that possess both properties. Two possibilities surface from this review: linked differential equations defined on feasible outcome sets and the iterative dynamics of feasible outcome sets. The first possibility involves defining Richardson-type vector fields so that offers consist of both a self- and an other-component and so that the definitions of the vector fields depend on both bargainers' previous offers. Although certainly feasible in principle, such equations would be very complex. Consequently, researchers might approach the problem, not with Richardson-type vector fields, but with iterative dynamics of feasible outcome sets. Here, as with elliptical models, an input offer produces an output response, which then becomes a new input. But rather than treating offers and responses as points on a continuum, their functions are defined to handle points of the feasible outcome set.

A second direction for future research is further investigation of catastrophe models of bargaining. Catastrophe theory provides provocative models, but as of now its applications to bargaining are limited. This situation may occur from a lack of agreement on how to estimate the parameters of catastrophe surfaces. Other theoretical models can be tested through analyses of variance or regressions, but catastrophe models, until recently, have lacked adequate statistical grounding for such tests. Fortunately, the statistical theory of catastrophe models is progressing (Cobb, 1978, 1981), as is the software needed for estimation purposes (Oliva, Desarbo, Day, & Jedidi, 1987).

Finally, researchers need to develop theories that integrate the communication of offers in bargaining with the communication of other strategies and tactics. This undertaking requires two types of research.

First, researchers must assess the relative importance of offer and nonoffer communication. This chapter contends that offers overshadow the impact of any other type of communication in bargaining, but this assumption needs to be tested. Second, and more vitally, researchers need to develop theories that incorporate both offers and nonoffers into their explanatory framework. Dynamic models of nonoffer communication can be developed in a fashion analogous to modeling offers, although more complicated state spaces would substitute for feasible outcome sets. The result, however, will provide a richer description of the bargaining process, one in which offers both influence and are influenced by the entire communication situation.

REFERENCES

Bacharach, S. B., & Lawler, E. J. (1981). Power and tactics in bargaining. *Industrial Labor Relations Review, 34*, 219-233.

Bartos, O. J. (1966). Concession-making in experimental negotiations. In J. Berger, M. Zelditch, Jr., & B. Anderson (Eds.), *Sociological theories in progress* (Vol. 1, pp. 3-28). Boston: Houghton Mifflin.

Bartos, O. J. (1974). *Process and outcome of negotiations.* New York: Columbia University Press.

Cobb, L. (1978). Stochastic catastrophe models and multimodal distributions. *Behavioral Science, 23*, 351-354.

Cobb, L. (1981). Parameter estimation for the cusp catastrophe model. *Behavioral Science, 26*, 75-78.

Druckman, D. (1977). Boundary role conflict: Negotiation as dual responsiveness. *Journal of Conflict Resolution, 21*, 639-662.

Ellis, D. G., Hamilton, M., & Aho, L. (1983). Some issues in conversation coherence. *Human Communication Research, 9*, 267-282.

Gleick, J. (1987). *Chaos: Making a new science.* New York: Penguin.

Harsanyi, J. C., & Selten, R. (1972). A generalized Nash solution for two-person bargaining games with incomplete information. *Management Science, 18*, 80-106.

Hofstadter, D. R. (1986). Mathematical chaos and strange attractors. In D. R. Hofstadter, *Metamagical themas: Questing for the essence of mind and pattern* (pp. 364-395). New York: Bantam Books.

Hopmann, P. T., & Smith, T. C. (1977). An application of a Richardson process model: Soviet-American interactions in the test ban negotiations 1962-1963. *Journal of Conflict Resolution, 21*, 701-726.

Isnard, C. A., & Zeeman, E. C. (1976). Some models from catastrophe theory in the social sciences. In L. Collins (Ed.), *The use of models in the social sciences* (pp. 44-100). Boulder, CO: Westview.

Kelley, H. H., Beckman, L. L., & Fischer, C. S. (1967). Negotiating the division of a reward under incomplete information. *Journal of Experimental Social Psychology, 3*, 361-398.

Livne, Z. (1987). Bargaining over the division of a shrinking pie: An axiomatic approach. *International Journal of Game Theory, 6,* 223-242.

Luce, R. D., & Raiffa, H. (1957). *Games and decisions: Introduction and critical survey.* New York: John Wiley.

May, R. (1976). Simple mathematical models with very complicated dynamics. *Nature, 261,* 459-467.

Oliva, T. A., Desarbo, W. S., Day, D. L., & Jedidi, K. (1987). *GEMCAT:* A General multivariate methodology for estimating *cat*astrophe models. *Behavioral Science, 32,* 121-137.

Oliva, T. A., Peters, M. H., & Murthy, H. S. K. (1981). A preliminary empirical test of a cusp catastrophe model in the social sciences. *Behavioral Science, 26,* 153-162.

Osgood, C. (1962). *An alternative to war or surrender.* Urbana: University of Illinois Press.

Pruitt, D. G. (1981). *Negotiation behavior.* New York: Academic Press.

Putnam, L. L., & Jones, T. S. (1982). The role of communication in bargaining. *Human Communication Research, 8,* 262-280.

Richardson, L. F. (1960). *Arms and insecurity: A mathematical study of the causes and origins of war.* Pittsburgh: Boxwood Press.

Rubin, J. Z., & Brown, B. R. (1975). *The social psychology of bargaining and negotiation.* New York: Academic Press.

Siegel, S., & Fouraker, L. E. (1960). *Bargaining and group decision making: Experiments in bilateral monopoly.* New York: McGraw-Hill.

Thom, R. (1975). *Structural stability and morphogenesis: An outline of a general theory of models* (D. H. Fowler, Trans.). Reading, MA: Benjamin/Cummings. (Original work published 1972)

Tutzauer, F. (1986). Bargaining as a dynamical system. *Behavioral Science, 31,* 65-81.

Tutzauer, F. (1987). Exponential decay and damped harmonic oscillation as models of the bargaining process. In M. L. McLaughlin (Ed.), *Communication yearbook 10* (pp. 217-240). Newbury Park, CA: Sage.

Tutzauer, F. (1991). Bargaining outcome, bargaining process, and the role of communication. In B. Dervin & M. J. Voigt (Eds.), *Progress in communication sciences* (Vol. 10, pp. 257-300). Norwood, NJ: Ablex.

Chapter 4

PHASE STRUCTURES IN NEGOTIATION

Michael E. Holmes

TIME MATTERS in negotiations; a negotiation begins, unfolds, and concludes. Ann Douglas's (1957, 1962) seminal case studies and later work by Gulliver (1979) and Morley and Stephenson (1977) describe negotiation as unfolding in a series of stages or phases. Phase models provide a narrative explanation of negotiation processes; that is, they identify sequences of events that constitute the story of a negotiation. In this approach a *phase* is a coherent period of interaction, characterized by a dominant constellation of communicative acts. This constellation serves a set of related functions in the movement from initiation to resolution of a dispute. Phase models address how and why negotiation behavior changes over time as parties interact.

PHASE STRUCTURES

A phasic view of negotiation is compatible with assumptions widely shared by communication researchers, namely, that negotiation is a process and negotiations are constituted by communication (Putnam & Jones, 1982). Despite this affinity and despite work in small group research (see Fisher, 1970, 1982; Poole, 1981, 1983a, 1983b; Poole & Roth, 1989), communication scholars have devoted little attention to phase models of negotiation. This neglect is unfortunate because phase research enables scholars to explore how interaction changes over time, how the longitudinal structure of negotiation is related to input and outcome variables, and how interventions (such as change of bargainers) influence the development of a negotiation (Holmes & Poole, 1991).

This chapter examines conceptual and methodological issues of phase analysis by casting developmental processes as the central question for communication perspectives on negotiation. First, this chapter positions phase models in relation to dominant approaches to negotiation. Second, representative prescriptive and descriptive phase models of negotiations are reviewed. Third, theoretical and methodological challenges inherent in phase research are explored. The fourth and final section centers on future directions for phase analysis of negotiations.

THE UNEASY PLACE OF PHASE MODELS IN NEGOTIATION RESEARCH

To understand the relative scarcity of phase analysis, this chapter positions phase models in relation to four communication perspectives on negotiation: mechanistic, psychological, interpretive-symbolic, and systems-interaction (Chatman, Putnam, & Sondak, 1991; Putnam & Jones, 1982; Putnam & Poole, 1987). In the negotiation arena, the psychological and systems-interaction approaches are dominant, even though interest in interpretive-symbolic approaches is growing (see Keough, Chapter 5, this volume; Wilson, Chapter 8, this volume; Francis, 1986).

The mechanistic and psychological perspectives are rooted in variance forms of explanation. In mechanistic research on negotiation, the precursor variables of communication channel or opportunity to communicate are associated with bargaining outcomes. Psychological negotiation research focuses on the negotiators, in particular on the variables of attitudes, cognitions, message content, information transmission, and responses to messages. Neither mechanistic nor psychological approaches address process issues or the way sequences of events in time constitute negotiations. Moreover, researchers in these areas do not develop longitudinal or phase models.

The interpretive-symbolic and systems-interaction perspectives typically surface as process theories. The former addresses how "meanings are created, maintained, and modified through interaction" (Chatman et al., 1991; see Putnam & Holmer, Chapter 6, this volume). The interpretive-symbolic perspective includes discourse analytic and rhetorical approaches. Explanation of the social world within the interpretive-symbolic perspective occurs at the level of turn, act, or interact. It is a micro-analytic approach that often neglects larger interaction structures such as phases (Putnam, 1984). For example, Francis (1986) uses conversational analysis to identify a number of collaborative acts that constitute the negotiation work of talking topically and talking as a team. He explains short sequences of turns at talk, but he does not address how these sequences fit together in developing the negotiation over time. Wilson (Chapter 8, this volume) reviews a number of discourse analytic studies that identify face-saving or facework sequences. In each case, a facework episode is framed as an isolated event that can be examined independently of the sequence of events surrounding it.

The systems-interaction perspective is most congruent with phasic approaches, since it examines "the patterns or the sequential development of verbal and nonverbal messages" (Chatman et al., 1991, p. 141). Researchers working within this perspective seek to identify recurring patterns of communication that constitute the negotiators' system of interaction. System-interaction researchers employ categorical coding systems to describe and quantify interaction (e.g., Bales's Interaction Process Analysis, 1950; Morley & Stephenson's Conference Process Analysis, 1977; Walcott & Hoppmann's Bargaining Process Analysis, 1975). Studies typically use the ratios of different categories of negotiation interaction to predict outcomes (Lewis & Fry, 1977; Stern, Sternthal, & Craig, 1975; Theye & Seiler, 1979).

In the study of small group decision making, the systems-interaction approach is closely aligned with phase analysis (see, for example, Fisher, 1982). In the case of negotiation research, however, most systems-interaction researchers neglect phase models or limit themselves to simple tests of the Douglas model. These studies compare category ratios across predetermined intervals of negotiation (usually three or more equal portions) to detect changes over time in patterns of interaction (Bednar & Curington, 1983; Landsberger, 1955; Morley & Stephenson, 1977; Putnam, Wilson, & Turner, 1990). For the most part, these studies have tested Douglas's three-phase model (however, Landsberger, 1955, tests Bales's model of orientation, evaluation, and control phases). Even though they represent an important step toward a phasic approach to negotiation, they are constrained by a method that identifies phases indirectly through changes in act ratios. This approach is fraught with dangers of methodological artifacts and is unable to detect subtleties of phase structure (Poole, 1981).

In summary, phase models are ignored by social psychological approaches less concerned with time and process, and by process-oriented approaches wed to the micro-analytic level of turns, tactics, and conversational structure. However, phasic approaches are not entirely neglected. There is a small body of literature outlining prescriptive phase models for the practice of negotiation, and there are descriptive phase models stimulated by Ann Douglas's (1957, 1962) work.

PRESCRIPTIVE PHASE MODELS

In the case of prescriptive models, phases are coherent periods of activity that center on a particular subgoal or milestone in the negotiation. Prescriptive phase models serve as guides or exemplars for negotiation. These models depict the sequence of events that one party should impose on a negotiation. Negotiators can use the models as yardsticks for gauging progress, predicting what will happen next, and focusing activity at a given time (T. Abbott, 1986). Table 4.1 lays out four prescriptives models for conventional negotiations (i.e., collective bargaining or inter-organizational negotiation) and for crisis negotiation. Other models are available (e.g., Nieuwmeijer, 1988), but these four are representatives of most models and include a variety of negotiating contexts. Atkinson (1980) and Zartman and Berman (1982) are typical collective bargaining models. Carlisle and Leary (1981) offer a model for negotiating groups, and the Michigan State Police (Donohue, Kaufman, Smith, & Ramesh, 1990) model guides the practice of hostage negotiations.

Problem-solving and decision-making events compose the models in Table 4.1. The consistency of these models derives from the practitioner's interest in mastering negotiation as a form of joint decision making. The life of a negotiation is therefore characterized as a sequence of problem-solving or decision-making events, rather than as a conversational structure or a series of proposal exchanges.

Although the number of phases differs across the models, all of them identify three types: initiation, problem solving, and resolution phases. Initiation and early problem-solving phases center on the discovery and definition of incompatible goals. They are marked by each party's efforts to acknowledge the dispute, to specify priorities, to emphasize points of difference between the parties, and to posture for positions. Problem solving and resolution phases seek a settlement for the incompatible goals while managing the parties' interdependence. Problem-solving phases are characterized by debate, information exchange, bartering, and movement toward a joint solution. Resolution phases are constituted by formu-

TABLE 4.1 Prescriptive Phase Models of Negotiation

Atkinson (1980)	Carlisle & Leary (1981)	Zartman & Berman (1982)	Michigan State Police (Donohue, et al., see below)
		INITIATION PHASES	
Exploration	Preliminaries	Diagnostic	Introduction and Relationship Development
		PROBLEM-SOLVING PHASES	
Expectation Structuring	Positioning	Formulation	Problem Clarification and Relationship Development
	Bargaining		
Movement and Solution Development	Exploration		Problem Solving
		RESOLUTION PHASES	
Conclusion	Settlement	Details	Resolution Structuring

NOTE: Prenegotiation phases have been omitted.

lation of agreements and attention to the details and execution of the final agreement (Putnam, 1984).

The difference between the fourth model in Table 4.1 and the other prescriptive models is the context of negotiation. The Michigan State Police model serves as a guide to the practice of hostage negotiation (Donohue, Kaufmann, Smith, & Ramesh, 1990). Hostage negotiation differs from conventional negotiations in the crisis nature of the situation and in the role of the police as negotiating parties who lack prior involvement in the dispute (Donohue, Rogan, Ramesh, & Borchgrevink, 1990). Nevertheless, the phase model for hostage negotiation resembles those already discussed. Specifically, the negotiation begins with an initiation phase that focuses on pre- liminaries to bargaining. Since the parties lack a prior relationship, this phase includes identifying participants and establishing a working relationship. Problem-solving phases begin with problem clarification and relationship building, followed by problem solving. The problem clarification phase is necessary because there is no prior relationship between the parties and because often at the outset of the bargaining the demands are unknown to both parties. In the problem solving phase, the parties work together toward a mutually acceptable outcome to be implemented in the resolution phase.

Prescriptive phase models of negotiation reflect the sequence of goals in a negotiation aimed at a satisfactory result. The phases arise from the accumulated experience of negotiators, rather than from theoretical assumptions about negotiation activity. As such, prescriptive models tend to focus on the activity of one party and to neglect the transactional nature of negotiation. They assume that phases are distinct, discrete, and controllable by the negotiator. Each phase sets the stage for following phases. Since event sequences for unsuccessful negotiations are not determined, prescriptive models implicitly assume that all negotiations are successful.

DESCRIPTIVE PHASE MODELS

Scholarly efforts to identify stages of negotiation date back to Ann Douglas's (1962) in-depth studies of four collective bargaining sessions that culminated in mediation. She characterizes negotiation as a sequence of phases (see Table 4.2) that cannot be telescoped. Since researchers draw heavily on her model, it is outlined in detail.

The Douglas phase model resembles the prescriptive models discussed earlier in describing initiation, problem-solving, and resolution phases. Phase 1, Establishing the Negotiating Range, is a lengthy initiation stage in which the appearance of deep and irreconcilable cleavage between the parties surfaces. The negotiators' speeches are like lengthy public orations. In this period, negotiators seldom interrupt each other or other team members. The style is one of forensic fireworks and dogmatic pronouncements. Vehement demands and counterdemands are made. Efforts are made to discredit the other side, in a hard-hitting critique. Even though there is considerable conflict, it occurs between participants acting as party representatives. At the level of interpersonal relations, there may be warmth and good will. Phase 2, Reconnoitering the Range, shows a shift toward problem solving as negotiators seek out areas of agreement that hold promise. This phase entails extensive interpersonal interaction, tactical maneuvers, and jockeying for position. The parties still hold firm and press the other side to capitulate. Negotiators yield ground only after much reluctance and clear signs of tacit agreement.

Phase 3, Precipitating the Decision-Reaching Crisis, brings the negotiation to an end with the announcement of a formal agreement. As parties converge, three strategies aid in narrowing the options: (1) a yes-no format of questions and answers, in conjunction with careful control of information, (2) forced-choice alternatives, and (3) use of a combined official/unofficial interaction, with official joint meetings "at

TABLE 4.2   Descriptive Phase Models of Negotiation

Douglas (1962)	Gulliver (1979)	Putnam, Wilson, & Turner (1990)	T. Abbott (1986)	Bednar & Curington (1983)
		INITIATION PHASES		
Establishing the Range	Search for Arena	Agenda Definition and Problem Formulation	Introduction	Distributive
	Agenda and Issue Identification			
		PROBLEM-SOLVING PHASES		
Reconnoitering the Range	Exploring the Range	Narrowing Differences	Demands Made, Met, or Refused	Integrative
	Narrowing the Range		Impasse	
	Preliminaries to Final Bargaining		Suicide Threat	
		RESOLUTION PHASES		
Precipitating the Decision- Making Crisis	Final Bargaining	Testing Agreement and Implementation	Surrender	Distributive
	Ritualization			
	Execution			

the table" and unofficial party caucuses or side-bar conferences to test agreement.

The model outlined by Putnam et al. (1990) is a spin-off of the Douglas model used to test for the development of negotiator argument and the selection of argument types at different times during the negotiation. Bargaining sessions defined by natural negotiation breakpoints form the three phases. The study concludes that negotiation phases are effective predictors of argument types, a finding that provides indirect support for the phase model.

Gulliver (1979) is also indebted to the Douglas model, even though his model subdivides the three phases into a more detailed picture of negotiation processes. Gulliver's model stems from case studies of negotiation in a variety of contexts and cultures and thereby applies to a wider range of negotiations than does the Douglas model.

Gulliver divides the initiation period into the search for an arena and agenda formulation, or the identification of issues and demands in the dispute. He identifies three problem-solving phases. The first is an exploration of the range of the dispute in which initial demands are reiterated, clarified, and elaborated. As a more concrete agenda emerges, the phase of narrowing the differences occurs. Since each party has voiced commitment to key issues and demands, negotiators can turn their attention to resolution. This transition from problem solving to resolution is accomplished in preliminaries to final bargaining. These preliminaries include searching for a viable range of alternatives, testing of trading possibilities, and refining a bargaining formula.

Gulliver (1979) describes three resolution phases. Final bargaining is marked by the exchange of specific, substantive proposals, accompanied by concession making when parties converge on points of agreement. If there is a final agreement, it is reached in this phase. The parties may demand a gesture of good faith commitment to the agreement, which typically occurs in the ritualization phase. Finally, the negotiation concludes with execution of the agreement, although this phase may take place in post-negotiation interaction.

The most unusual model in Table 4.2 is a descriptive model of hostage negotiation (T. Abbott, 1986). Unlike the other models, it is the result of T. Abbott's case study of a number of hostage negotiations in California and is independent of the prior work by Douglas. It is similar to prescriptive models in its use as a tool for training and practice. Unlike the earlier prescriptive models, however, it is based on systematic observation of negotiations. The model posits a sequence of phases specific to hostage negotiation instead of a series of generic stages framed in a problem-solving vernacular.

Despite these differences, the model resembles the other descriptive models. Negotiation begins in an introduction phase, proceeds through problem solving in phases dominated by demands, and concludes with agreement in a surrender phase. The primary differences are in the problem-solving phases. The "demands made, met, or refused" phase is analogous to reconnoitering the range of the dispute, but the impasse and suicide threat phases have no direct correlates in the other models. The impasse phase represents the limits of narrowing the range of the dispute. At this point, only core issues remain and no means of resolution are known. A suicide threat often follows impasse. The perpetrator displays commitment to demands and demonstrates unilateral efforts to end the interdependence of the parties. If the suicide threat is not enacted, the perpetrator (in a concluding surrender phase) eventually accepts the need to come to agreement with the police.

The last model in Table 4.2 consists of three phases, but only two phase types. It is a phase model adaptation of Walton and McKersie's (1965) distributive and integrative bargaining. Originally, the model described two orientations: distributive bargaining entails "efforts to maximize gains and minimize losses within a 'win-lose' or self gain orientation" (Putnam, 1990, p. 3) while integrative bargaining "aims to reconcile the interests of both parties, reach joint benefits, or attain 'win-win' goals" (p. 3). However, researchers have employed the orientations to describe interaction processes (see Poole, Shannon, & DeSanctis, Chapter 2, this volume). According to Putnam (1990), distributive processes are "sequences of action that move the negotiation toward rigidity, conflict escalation, and increased potential for win-lose or lose-lose outcomes," and integrative processes are sequences that "move the interaction toward increased flexibility and increased potential to maximize joint benefits" (p. 4).

Models of distributive and integrative bargaining fall into three modes: separate, interdependence, and stage models (Putnam, 1990). The separate models characterize entire negotiations as distributive or integrative; the interdependence models argue for an inseparable intertwining of the two in any negotiation; and the stage models (e.g., Bednar & Curington, 1983) posit a sequential development of distinct phases of distributive and integrative negotiation. The three-stage model in Table 4.2 suggests that negotiations begin distributively as parties seek to identify and differentiate issues in dispute, become integrative as the parties enter into problem solving, and end distributively as parties vie for advantage in the final agreement. In her review of the literature, Putnam (1990) notes empirical support for the initial distributive phase, but mixed support for the second and third phases.

The other models in Table 4.2 describe particular functions or problem-solving events in a negotiation. The Bednar and Curington (1983) model is less specific, insofar as it identifies a set of behaviors that treat interaction independently of its function. That is, parties can engage in integrative or distributive interaction whether accomplishing an agenda, engaging in problem solving, or resolving details of an agreement. For example, Gulliver (1979) describes shifts in dominant orientation (antagonism to coordination) within each phase of his model. This suggests that distributive/integrative models are best subsumed within other phase models, as in the case studies by Douglas (1962).

Iklé's (1964) model of international negotiations is both simpler in structure and more grand in scale than the collective bargaining and interpersonal dispute models displayed in Table 4.2. It describes diplomatic negotiations between friendly nations who, according to Iklé (1964): "first reach agreement on a framework of broad objectives and principles. Then they deduce detailed points of agreement from this framework by applying mutually acceptable methods of reasoning" (p. 215). The framework phase accomplishes both initiation and problem solving. It defines the range of the dispute, the issues that are debatable, and the approximate range of final terms. Next, "deductive methods" of generating specific terms (logical, scientific, or legal reasoning; Iklé, 1964, p. 215) comprise the detail phase. Agreement is foreshadowed long before the resolution phase, which may even be delegated to technical experts instead of professional negotiators. Established and friendly relations be- tween negotiating countries contributes to the simple structure of Iklé's model. The model does not hold for cases of antagonistic relations, since parties may abandon the framework or may seek to distort the methods of deduction in their favor.

The descriptive models depict successful negotiations. Both Douglas (1957, 1962) and Morley and Stephenson (1977) argue that unsuccessful negotiations do not proceed through the orderly stages of phase models. Unsuccessful negotiations are stalled in an intermediate phase, or cycle between phases without advancing toward phases later in the sequence, for example, alternating between exploring and narrowing the range in Gulliver's (1979) model. The assumption of a successful negotiation is apparent in the T. Abbott (1986) model, which labels the final phase surrender, even though not all hostage negotiations reach a negotiated surrender.

In summary, the dominant descriptive model for negotiation is Douglas's three-stage model and its derivatives. Since most descriptive models are not guides for practitioners, they depict the unfolding negotiation itself, rather than the activities of only one party. The models treat negotiation as an orderly sequence of initiation, problem-solving, and resolution phases. Adhering to a unitary sequence, they describe a single sequence of phases merging from one to the next without abrupt transitions. The apparent clarity with which these phase models tell the story of events in negotiations belies the theoretical and methodological complexity inherent in their application. The development and testing of descriptive phase models is hampered by a lack of reflection on the nature of phases and the nature of causal processes that drive movement from phase to phase. Assumptions about these two issues lie at the heart of phase modeling.

THEORETICAL AND METHODOLOGICAL
ISSUES IN PHASE MODELING

The purpose of this chapter is not to present a new phase model for negotiation, but rather to clarify, synthesize, and extend current perspectives on negotiation phases. Hence this discussion addresses a series of issues and questions that researchers confront when undertaking phase modeling and analysis. Phase modeling requires explicit recognition of, and adjustment to, the essential differences between process and variance explanations of the social world.

VARIANCE AND PROCESS
MODELS OF THE SOCIAL WORLD

Social scientific modes of explanation assume variance or process forms. These two approaches make fundamentally different assumptions about the primary elements and relationships that constitute the social world (Mohr, 1982). Variance approaches explain the social world in terms of causal relationships between precursor and outcome variables (i.e., quantified characteristics or attributes of an entity). The central challenge for variance approaches is to operationalize and manipulate variables that represent conceptual constructs. For example, researchers might seek to identify relationships among variables of orientation, aspiration level, and negotiation outcomes. Phase models inherently are at odds with pure variance models that assume input/output forms.

Process approaches describe the social world in terms of histories or stories of occurrences of events ordered in time. The central assumptions are (1) the social world occurs in discrete states and events, and (2) the sequential ordering of events is critical to outcomes (Mohr, 1982). Process approaches base explanations on probabilistic processes and causal factors that generate the order of events. Process researchers are interested in discovering a typical event sequence or a typology of sequences (A. Abbott, 1988). The central challenge for the researcher is *colligation,* the attempt to "section the continuous social process into events and stories" (A. Abbott, 1984, p. 192). Phase modeling is a form of process explanation in that such models parse processes into sequentially ordered stages or phases that constitute a coherent story. The phase models of negotiation discussed earlier assume there is a typical sequence of phases, although the instantiation of the phase sequence may vary from case to case (Gulliver, 1979).

Causality is a more complex construct in process explanations than in variance explanations. In phase modeling, the researcher aims to identify the dynamics that create change over time, that is, what causes the end of one phase and the beginning of the next. The difficult issue for the phase researcher arises from these two forms of social explanation. The move from viewing the world as composed of entities with attributes, to viewing the world as events ordered in time is not trivial. Phase researchers need to grapple at the theoretical level with unconventional definitions of constructs and at the methodological level with novel and unfamiliar tools for identifying those constructs and exploring their relationships.

THEORETICAL ISSUES IN PHASE MODELING

The two key theoretical issues are (1) what constitutes a phase? and (2) what dynamics generate changes in interaction from phase to phase? One of the thorniest issues in phase analysis is defining the phase itself. Phase definitions dictate methodological choices and influence assumptions about causal processes. At least two definitions are available: phases as stages and phases as episodes. A stage definition, used throughout this chapter, treats a phase as a period of interaction dominated by particular communicative acts or negotiation functions. Phases can overlap and shade into one another because exact boundaries between phases are arbitrary. Phase analyses that compare ratios of interaction across portions of a negotiation ultimately employ a stage definition of phases. In the absence of clear natural boundaries between phases, research reveals shifts in interaction by comparing ratios of acts within fixed intervals and arbitrarily defined boundaries.

An episodic view defines phases as clearly identifiable interaction structures within explicit boundaries. Baxter (1982) treats episodes as sets of "sequential utterances with a perceived beginning point and end point" (p. 24). A phase approach within the interpretive-symbolic perspective might use discourse analytic concepts and methods to identify negotiation episodes, ones that are analogous to conversation episodes. A phase, then, is an interaction sequence in which participants jointly accomplish a particular act in the negotiation. For example, a phase might be an opening sequence accomplished by negotiators who signify their willingness to enter into the interaction, or a "demand" sequence in which an issue is identified, a demand made, and a response given. The primary difference between this definition and the previous one is the use of episodic rather than arbitrary boundaries between phases. These boundaries are determined by changes in the interaction rather than researcher fiat. The definition of phases will vary from model to model. What is important for conceptual clarity and methodological choice is that a definition is provided.

Change over time is at the heart of phase modeling, yet most descriptive phase models gloss the question of what causal mechanisms generate movement from phase to phase. It is tempting to assume that each phase sets the stage for the following phase in simple functional causality. Gulliver (1979) notes the enticing clarity of this process dynamic, but argues that it is too simple "both empirically and conceptually" (p. 121).

The traditional Aristotelian typology of material, efficient, formal, and final causes provides a useful framework for phase development in negotiation. Aristotle argues that every object or event involves all four causes (Guthrie, 1981). Material causality reminds us that communication is constitutive of negotiation phases. Efficient causality draws our attention to the local dynamics of the interaction, whether turn to turn or phase to phase. Formal causality encourages attention to larger structures that make up a negotiation. Final causality considers negotiator goals as a motivating force in negotiation development. For this discussion, Gulliver's (1979) model is framed according to each type of cause.

The first cause in Aristotle's typology, material causality, does not directly explain change from phase to phase. It is the classical expression of the notion of constitution. Phases of talk are the material cause of a negotiation in that the phases themselves *are* the negotiation. Without the talk, there is no negotiation. Shifts in the talk, therefore, define the different events in the negotiation. The other forms of causality provide explanations for why the shifts occur.

An explanation based on efficient causality posits that each phase causes its successor. For example, agreement on an agenda would necessarily lead participants to explore the range of the dispute, which in turn would cause the parties to move to narrowing the issues. The behavior of the participants is caused by the events that precede that behavior. For instance, as one party advances an agenda proposal, the other party may agree, disagree, or advance another item for the agenda. As each responds to the other, an agenda phase unfolds. As that phase is concluded, the parties react by moving to discussion of the items placed on the agenda. Events in the current stage determine events in the next.

Formal cause is the "pattern or genus that causes the form a product takes" (Kennedy, 1980, p. 62). Phase structures surface in negotiation because of the form that negotiation takes. Phases are defining characteristics of negotiation. This somewhat circular definition is rooted in culturally shared expectations of the proper form for a negotiation. Negotiators begin by establishing the range of the dispute because they are negotiating, rather than performing a wedding or some other genre of interaction. The defining pattern of negotiation involves progress through a culturally determined series of initiation, problem-solving, and resolution phases. Participants recognize the proper form of a negotiation that guides their behavior to accomplish the elements of the form.

Final cause is "the end, that which a thing is for" (Guthrie, 1981, p. 223). The final cause of a negotiation's phase structure is the negotiation outcome. Negotiators enact the stages of a negotiation in order to achieve the outcome. The phases represent changes necessary to move from a beginning rooted in conflict, interdependence, and incompatible goals to an end in which the interdependence is managed and the incompatible goals resolved. In this sense, phases exist because of negotiation outcomes.

Final cause is a key element in Gulliver's (1979) phase theory:

> The whole process is given persistence and movement by the basic contradiction between the parties' conflict and their need for joint action. This contradiction generates opposing dispositions . . . that give the possibility of continuous impetus toward some final agreement and outcome. (p. 186)

Shifts from phase to phase occur as participants change their behavior to move toward their final cause. Without the need for an outcome, negotiation could consist solely of agenda setting or problem exploration. However, these activities alone will not lead to a negotiated outcome; hence, bargainers move from one activity to the next to identify, define, explore, and resolve their conflict.

The typology of causes indicates that it is not enough to describe the order of events in a negotiation. A full explanation requires a description of the complex and multifaceted dynamics that create and drive the sequence of events. The phase structure of a negotiation arises from three factors: from local processes or efficient cause as parties react to one another and attempt to control what is happening at the moment, from cultural expectations or formal cause as the parties enact what they perceive as the proper form of interaction, and from global processes or final cause as the parties seek to move from conflict to resolution.

An alternative but compatible framework for considering causal mechanisms of phase structures stems from Poole and Doelger's (1986) structurational model of decision development phases. They argue that the surface structure of phases in small group decision making is generated from two underlying structures. One structure entails the participant's task representation, that is, the mental model of the genre of interaction and the emergent shared representation of the task. This structure encompasses the shared model of the process developed in the course of the interaction. The individual and shared representations of the interaction task are analogous to formal cause as defined earlier. The second structure consists of the rules for conversational coherence (e.g., topicality and turn-taking rules). The rules for conversational coherence represent efficient cause, since they define how one behavior shapes or constrains the next one.

Adapted to a negotiation context, the structures are participant representations of the negotiation task and rules for conversational coherence. The phase structure of a negotiation arises from the joint influence of these structures on the interaction. Mental models of the task guide each participant's behavior. For example, parties aim to begin by establishing an agenda and then advance their own position. Each negotiator also must abide by the rules of conversational coherence, which entails departing from the mental model of the task to adapt to the other person's behavior. This creates order as the parties' activities converge around a shared representation of the task. It may also create disorder as local conversational processes override the more global negotiation structure (Wilson & Putnam, 1990).

The structurational model has the advantage of bringing together cognitive aspects with local and global interaction dynamics. Although Poole and Doelger (1986) advance a compelling argument for a structurational view of small group decision development phases, the process has yet to be explored in a negotiation context.

In summary, a fully developed phase model should contain an explicit definition of a phase and an explanation of the causal processes driving movement from phase to phase. Douglas (1962) is unclear on both issues; Gulliver (1979) specifies a stage definition of phases and explores both information exchange and shifts in relationship as efficient causes of progress from phase to phase. Unfortunately, most empirical tests of phase models have neglected these issues by substituting assumptions rooted in methodological choices.

METHODOLOGICAL ISSUES IN PHASE ANALYSIS

Researchers need to address two challenges in testing phase models and relating them to negotiated outcomes: (1) how do we identify phases? and (2) how do we compare phase sequences? The methodological choices that phase researchers have made stem from their answers to the conceptual issues previously outlined. Development of phase models relies on case study observation, with empirical tests of these models conducted from interaction coding and statistical analysis of predefined intervals within negotiations.

The most fully developed scholarly models of negotiation phases emanate from extensive case studies. Douglas's (1962) collective bargaining case studies utilize transcribed recordings of bargaining sessions and caucus meetings, field notes on bargaining activities, and interviews with key individuals. Gulliver (1979) used a historico-ethnographic approach in his cross-cultural case studies of negotiations.

The fine-grained detail of the case study is invaluable for developing phase models. It provides the researcher with intimate knowledge necessary to identify the shifts in interaction and events that characterize different negotiation stages. However, this approach is less suited for testing phase models. For example, Douglas (1962) resorts to an unusual test of the model that emerged in her study. She argues that a shift from an interparty to an interpersonal relationship is associated with movement through the phases. She identifies this shift through the ability of independent judges to discern, from the transcribed talk, negotiator party identity at different points in the negotiation.

The level of description in a case study precludes useful phase sequence comparison. The developmental patterns of individual cases are abstracted in a general model that disregards cross-case differences, as the models of Douglas (1962) and Gulliver (1979) demonstrate. Hence case study approaches conceptualize phases as stages rather than as episodes and posit unitary rather than multiple sequences of phases.

Researchers who use interaction analysis to avoid the limitations of case studies are constrained in other ways. The traditional approach to phase analysis resembles methods used in small group decision development research. Researchers unitize and categorize the talk according to an interaction analysis coding system designed to capture the phase model. The sequence of coded units is divided into three or more equal divisions and the ratio of code category occurrences is compared across divisions. In some cases natural breakpoints such as negotiating sessions are used to divide the interaction (Putnam et al., 1990). Differences in ratios across divisions in the manner predicted constitutes support for the phase model. These studies often use only a single case or a handful of cases (Morley & Stephenson, 1977; Putnam et al., 1990). When a larger number of cases are used, the data are aggregated across cases by computing and comparing the mean ratios for a given category. Case by case sequence comparison is not performed (see Jones, 1988, for an exception).

An interesting consequence of this traditional way of testing for phase structure is that variance assumptions and variable analytic methods are used to test a process model. Instead of identifying events, the method converts the interaction into entities (arbitrary divisions of talk) with attributes (ratios of interaction categories). The attribute profile is used to label the entity as a particular kind of event.

Although this traditional approach provides support for phase models, it suffers from three methodological weaknesses: (1) using a stage definition of phases by dividing the negotiation sessions into an arbitrary number of intervals of equal length, (2) disguising important phase structures of shorter duration than the arbitrary intervals, and (3) precluding detection of between-cases differences by aggregating data across cases (Poole, 1981). These weaknesses limit traditional interaction analysis approaches to tests of unitary sequence models such as the Douglas (1962) three-stage model.

Conceptual and methodological blinders have constrained our use of phase models. This chapter sets forth three uses for phase analysis: to describe how interaction changes over time, to explore how the longitudinal structure of negotiation relates to input and outcome variables, and to examine how interventions (such as a change of negotiators) influence the development of bargaining. Current approaches to phase modeling address the first question but provide limited answers to the second one. To address the second and third questions, researchers need to adopt methods that are not limited to unitary sequence models of negotiation phases.

FUTURE DIRECTIONS FOR PHASE MODELING

Negotiation phase research as currently practiced resembles small group decision development work in the 1970s and early 1980s. The models are unitary sequence and the methods limit discovery of varied sequences and links between phase structure and other negotiation characteristics. Current decision development work has moved beyond unitary models to multiple sequence models and to descriptions of sequence typologies. It is time for negotiation phase research to take this step as well. Alternative methods of phase analysis are not restricted to tests of unitary sequences. These methods are in use in small group studies but are not applied to negotiation research. This discussion briefly reviews three of these tools: flexible phase mapping, gamma analysis, and optimal matching analysis. The first two are used to colligate or map phases in a negotiation; the third is a sequence comparison tool. All three utilize interaction data coded with a suitable coding system.

Flexible phase mapping (Poole, 1983a, 1983b; Poole & Roth, 1989) is a sequence parsing technique used to establish phase boundaries within a sequence of interaction codes. A full description of the method is provided in Holmes and Poole (1991). In brief, it applies researcher-determined parsing rules that define the minimum conditions constituting a phase and define the various conditions indicating a boundary between phases. The following is a simple set of mapping rules: (1) a phase is indicated by the contiguous occurrence of three or more interaction codes of the same phase value and (2) once a phase has been identified by rule 1, the terminal phase boundary is indicated by the contiguous occurrence of more than two codes of a phase value different from the preceding codes.

In actual cases the parsing rules and phase value rules may be more complex. Flexible phase mapping can be adapted to either stage or episodic definitions of phases by varying the rules that identify phase boundaries. In either case, changes in the interaction, rather than dividing the talk into equal portions, dictate where phase boundaries are placed.

Consider a sequence of interaction codes from a hypothetical coding system that consists of categories A, B, and C. The sequence AAAAB ABCABCCCBCCCAAA represents codes for 20 turns at talk. For this discussion, assume that A and B share the same phase value (arbitrarily labeled Type I) while C has a phase value of Type II. An application of the rules to the code sequence yields three phases: an initial Type I phase (AAAABAB), a Type II phase (CCCBCCC), and a concluding Type I phase (AAA).

A phase map of a simulated hostage negotiation (Holmes, 1991) is shown in Figure 4.1. The original data consist of 625 turns at talk, coded according to a system based on Gulliver's phase types. The code sequence is parsed with flexible phase mapping and is normalized to a length of 100 units for comparison with other cases. The map is read as a time-line of the negotiation, from the top left portion to the end at the bottom right. The three tracks of the map display the telephone calls, participant changes, and the sequence of phases constituting the negotiation. Three negotiators bargain with the hostage-taker. Note that changes of negotiators at approximately point 40 and point 60 in the bargaining trigger Gulliver's search for an arena phase, as the hostage-taker contests the changes in participants.

A complex phase map with clear boundaries and repeating phases may not be suitable for testing a unitary stage model of negotiation with overlapping phases that fade into one another. For such models, Pelz's gamma analysis is appropriate. This method uses the Goodman-Kruskal gamma statistic to establish a global description of phase order and the degree of phase overlap (Holmes & Poole, 1991; Pelz, 1985). It can be applied to any sequence of categorical data.

Gamma analysis creates a unitary sequence map in which a phase type can occur only once. Precedence scores, which range from 1.0 to −1.0, indicate the order of the phases. The greater the precedence score, the earlier the phase occurs. Separation scores measure the overlap or relative distinctness of the phases. The more contiguous the codes are in a phase, the higher the separation score. Gamma analysis of the 100-unit phase sequence in Figure 4.1 yields a phase map similar to Gulliver's (1979) phase model. The phases follow the order shown in Table 4.2, but agenda clarification and exploring the range of the dispute overlap, and there is a null or disordered phase between exploring and narrowing the range of the dispute.

Detailed phase maps (such as Figure 4.1) and gamma maps constructed from the same data provide different descriptions of a negotiation's phase structure. The maps embody episodic and stage definitions of phases. The differences between the maps underscore the need to select phase analysis methods congruent with the model tested. The maps are alike, however, in being process oriented and event-driven rather than deriving from conventional variance methods.

Gamma analysis and flexible phase mapping provide important advantages over traditional methods. They preserve case differences by independently mapping each case. The structure of each phase map is

	Contact	Parties	Negotiation Activity		Contact	Parties	Negotiation Activity
	01		ARENA				
			AGENDA				
							EXPLORE NULL EXPLORE
10.			EXPLORE AGENDA	60.			OUTCOME
	02		ARENA		05	N2/H1	AGENDA
			NARROW				ARENA
							AGENDA EXPLORE AGENDA
20.			EXPLORE AGENDA	70.	06		EXPLORE OUTCOME
							AGENDA
			EXPLORE AGENDA				NARROW
30.	03		EXPLORE AGENDA EXPLORE	80.	07		EXPLORE PRELIM
							EXPLORE PRELIM OUTCOME
			AGENDA				
	04	N1/H1	EXPLORE PRELIM AGENDA				EXPLORE PRELIM EXPLORE
40.			ARENA AGENDA	90.			OUTCOME NARROW OUTCOME
			EXPLORE AGENDA EXPLORE PRELIM				
50.				100.	08	N3/H1	RITUAL

Figure 4.1. Phase Map of Telephone Conversations, Participant Changes, and Negotiation Activity for a Simulated Hostage Negotiation
SOURCE: Holmes (1991, p. 186)

dictated by changes in the interaction, rather than by predefined intervals. Preservation of casewise differences allows the researcher to develop sequence typologies and to test for contextual or process influences on phase development. For example, events external to the talk itself may create order or disorder in a negotiation. Change in negotiators, specifically, may require repetition of functions accomplished in a prior phase, such as agenda definition. To test for systematic links between phase structures and other events requires grouping cases by their sequential similarities.

Gamma analysis results for different cases can be grouped and compared by the order, unity, and overlap of phases. Detailed phase maps produced by flexible phase mapping can be compared with optimal matching analysis techniques (A. Abbott & Forrest, 1986). *Optimal matching analysis* is a blanket term for a family of sequence comparison techniques used in a variety of disciplines (Sankoff & Kruskal, 1983). As a test of unitary sequences, optimal matching can be used to rank-order cases by their distance from a model sequence. A dissimilarity matrix from pairwise optimal matching comparisons of a set of maps can be used in cluster analysis or multidimensional scaling to generate a phase sequence typology.

CONCLUSION

Thirty years of phase research have produced a relatively small number of theories and models. The paucity of phase analysis stems not from the lack of potential, but rather from the conceptual and methodological limitations that are currently practiced. New ways of thinking about phase sequences and new methods for testing phase models are available. The ability to capture subtle characteristics and to generate phase sequence typologies allows the researcher to explore the relationship of phase structure to negotiation inputs and outputs and to interventions in the bargaining process.

REFERENCES

Abbott, A. (1984). Event sequence and event duration: Colligation and measurement. *Historical Methods, 17,* 192-204.

Abbott, A. (1988). Transcending general linear reality. *Sociological Theory, 6,* 169-186.

Abbott, A., & Forrest, J. (1986). Optimal matching methods for historical sequences. *Journal of Interdisciplinary History, 16,* 471-494.

Abbott, T. E. (1986). Time-phase model of hostage negotiation. *Police Chief, 53*(4), 34-35.

Atkinson, G. M. (1980). *An introduction to negotiation.* London: Industrial Relations Training Centre.

Bales, R. F. (1950). *Interaction process analysis.* Reading, MA: Addison-Wesley.

Baxter, L. A. (1982). Conflict management: An episodic approach. *Small Group Behavior, 13,* 23-42.

Bednar, D. A., & Curington, W. P. (1983). Interaction analysis: A tool for understanding negotiations. *Industrial and Labor Relations Review, 36,* 389-401.

Carlisle, J., & Leary, M. (1981). Negotiating groups. In R. Payne & C. L. Cooper (Eds.), *Groups at work* (pp. 165-188). New York: John Wiley.

Chatman, J. A., Putnam, L. L., & Sondak, H. (1991). Integrating communication and negotiation research. In M. H. Bazerman, R. J. Lewicki, & B. H. Shepard (Eds.), *Research on negotiation in organizations* (Vol. 3, pp. 139-164). Greenwich, CT: JAI Press.

Donohue, W., Kaufmann, G., Smith, R., & Ramesh, C. (1990, June). *Crisis bargaining: A framework for understanding intense conflict.* Paper presented at the annual conference of the International Communication Association, Dublin, Ireland.

Donohue, W., Rogan, R., Ramesh, C., & Borchgrevink, C. (1990, April). *Crisis bargaining: Verbal immediacy development in hostage negotiations.* Paper presented at the annual conference of the Central States Communication Association, Detroit.

Douglas, A. (1957). The peaceful settlement of industrial and intergroup disputes. *Journal of Conflict Resolution, 1,* 69-81.

Douglas, A. (1962). *Industrial peacemaking.* New York: Columbia University Press.

Fisher, B. A. (1970). Decision emergence: Phases in group decision making. *Speech Monographs, 37,* 53-66.

Fisher, B. A. (1982). *Small group decision making II.* New York: McGraw-Hill.

Francis, D. W. (1986). Some structures of negotiation talk. *Journal of Language and Social Psychology, 15,* 53-80.

Gulliver, P. H. (1979). *Disputes and negotiations: A cross-cultural perspective.* New York: Academic Press.

Guthrie, W. K. C. (1981). *A history of Greek philosophy* (Vol. 6). New York: Cambridge University Press.

Holmes, M. E. (1991). *An interaction analysis of developmental phases in authentic and simulated negotiations between police and hostage-takers and barricaded suspects.* Unpublished doctoral dissertation, University of Minnesota, Minneapolis.

Holmes, M. E., & Poole, M. S. (1991). Longitudinal analysis of interaction. In S. Duck & B. Montgomery (Eds.), *Studying interpersonal interaction* (pp. 286-302). New York: Guilford.

Iklé, F. C. (1964). *How nations negotiate.* New York: Harper & Row.

Jones, T. (1988). Phase structures in agreement and no-agreement mediation. *Communication Research, 15,* 470-495.

Kennedy, G. A. (1980). *Classical rhetoric and its Christian and secular tradition from ancient to modern times.* Chapel Hill: University of North Carolina Press.

Landsberger, H. A. (1955). Interaction process analysis of the mediation of labor-management disputes. *Journal of Abnormal and Social Psychology, 51,* 552-558.

Lewis, S. A., & Fry, R. F. (1977). Effects of visual access and orientation on the discovery of integrative bargaining outcomes. *Organizational Behavior and Human Performance, 20,* 75-92.

Mohr, L. B. (1982). *Explaining organizational behavior.* San Francisco: Jossey-Bass.

Morley, I., & Stephenson, G. (1977). *The social psychology of bargaining.* London: George Allen & Unwin.

Nieuwmeijer, L. (1988). *Negotiation: Methodology and training.* Pinetown, South Africa: Owen Burgess.

Pelz, D. C. (1985). Innovation complexity and the sequence of innovating stages. *Knowledge: Creation, Diffusion, Utilization, 6,* 261-291.

Poole, M. S. (1981). Decision development in small groups: I. A comparison of two models. *Communication Monographs, 48,* 1-24.

Poole, M. S. (1983a). Decision development in small groups: II. A study of multiple sequences in decision making. *Communication Monographs, 50,* 206-232.

Poole, M. S. (1983b). Decision development in small groups: III. A multiple sequence model of group decision development. *Communication Monographs, 50,* 321-341.

Poole, M. S., & Doelger, J. (1986). Developmental processes in group decision-making. In R. Y. Hirokawa & M. S. Poole (Eds.), *Communication in group decision-making* (pp. 35-62). Beverly Hills, CA: Sage.

Poole, M. S., & Roth, J. (1989). Decision development in small groups: IV. A typology of decision paths. *Human Communication Research, 15,* 323-356.

Putnam, L. L. (1984). Bargaining as task and process: Multiple functions of interaction sequences. In R. L. Street & J. N. Cappella (Eds.), *Sequence and pattern in communicative behavior* (pp. 225-242). London: Edward Arnold.

Putnam, L. L. (1990). Reframing integrative and distributive bargaining. In B. H. Shepard, M. H. Bazerman, & R. J. Lewicki (Eds.), *Research on negotiation in organizations* (Vol. 2, pp. 1-30). Greenwich, CT: JAI Press.

Putnam, L. L., & Jones, T. (1982). The role of communication in bargaining. *Human Communication Research, 8,* 262-280.

Putnam, L. L., & Poole, M. S. (1987). Conflict and negotiation. In F. M. Jablin, L. L. Putnam, K. H. Roberts, & L. W. Porter (Eds.), *Handbook of organizational communication* (pp. 549-599). Newbury Park, CA: Sage.

Putnam, L. L., Wilson, S. R., & Turner, D. B. (1990). The evolution of policy arguments in teacher's negotiations. *Argumentation, 4,* 129-152.

Sankoff, D., & Kruskal, J. B. (Eds.). (1983). *Time warps, string edits, and macromolecules: The theory and practice of sequence comparison.* Reading, MA: Addison-Wesley.

Stern, L. W., Sternthal, B., & Craig, S. C. (1975). Strategies for managing inter-organizational conflict: A laboratory paradigm. *Journal of Applied Psychology, 60,* 472-482.

Theye, L. D., & Seiler, W. J. (1979). Interaction analysis in collective bargaining: An alternative approach to the prediction of negotiated outcomes. In D. Nimmo (Ed.), *Communication yearbook* (Vol. 3, pp. 375-392). New Brunswick, NJ: Transaction Press.

Walcott, C., & Hoppmann, P. T. (1975). Interaction analysis and bargaining behavior. *Experimental Study of Politics, 4,* 1-19.

Walton, R. E., & McKersie, R. B. (1965). *A behavioral theory of labor negotiations: An analysis of a social interaction system.* New York: McGraw-Hill.

Wilson, S. R., & Putnam, L. L. (1990). Interaction goals in negotiation. In J. A. Anderson (Ed.), *Communication yearbook 13* (pp. 374-406). Newbury Park, CA: Sage.

Zartman, I. W., & Berman, M. (1982). *The practical negotiator.* New Haven, CT: Yale University Press.

PART II

INTERPRETIVE PROCESSES
AND LANGUAGE ANALYSIS

Chapter 5

BARGAINING ARGUMENTS AND ARGUMENTATIVE BARGAINERS

Colleen M. Keough

ARGUMENTATION RESEARCH is directly relevant to studies of communication in bargaining. Negotiation researchers note that "the core of what is generally taken as the central process of negotiation [is] reciprocal argument and counter-argument, proposal and counter proposal in an attempt to agree upon actions and outcomes mutually perceived as beneficial" (Sawyer & Guetzkow, 1965, p. 479). Similarly, Axelrod (1977) observes, "After all, most of what happens in negotiation is the assertion of arguments by one side, and the response with other arguments by the other side" (p. 177). Although such comments encourage systematic investigation of bargaining arguments, they also perpetuate the use of *argument* as a generic term with a univocal definition, namely, discourse produced to gain adherence from an opponent. This definition reveals a narrow and mechanistic understanding of argumentative discourse and a narrow view of the role of argument in negotiation.

In actuality, argumentation is a dynamic process that functions dialectically and epistemically through human action. That is, "Argument can be seen as a *method* of knowledge . . . [and] arguments in differing ways *produce* knowledge" (Cox & Willard, 1982, p. xli, emphasis in original; cf. Wenzel, 1980, Willard, 1989). As a method, argumentation informs the dialectic exchange of questions and answers. Ehninger and Brockriede (1963) describe argumentative debate as a critical and cooperative process serving an investigative rather than a manipulative purpose. Epistemically, argumentation produces knowledge through (1) reasons offered in support of claims (Fisher, 1978; McKerrow, 1982; Perelman

109

& Olbrechts-Tyteca, 1969; Toulmin, 1958); (2) arguer's cognitive orientation (Hample, 1985); and (3) the joint production of discourse informed by institutionalized rules of interaction (Jackson & Jacobs, 1981). In sharp contrast to economic models that assume "bargainers have perfect knowledge" (Nash, 1950), this chapter argues that negotiation parallels argumentation as a dialectical process that serves an epistemic function. A negotiation involves tensions that are capable of transcending the conflict if the discourse promotes discovery, appraisal, and collaboration of ideas. While all negotiations do not reach this transcendent state, they are still epistemic because knowledge is produced through argumentative deliberation. For example, in labor negotiations reasons offered in defense of proposals serve an interpretive function. Each side learns about problems in contract administration, concerns of the rank-and-file, and extraordinary concessions given in previous negotiations. This interpretive process illustrates how negotiation performs a sense-making role for organizational members (Putnam, 1985) and how it contributes to shaping an organization's culture (Trice & Beyer, 1984).

When negotiation is treated as an interpretive process, both arguments and arguers need to be examined. Bargaining messages are created through human invention; and negotiators, as human agents, vary in their abilities to construct persuasive discourse. To understand the reflexive process between arguer and argumentative discourse, this chapter describes several argumentation theories, reviews and critiques recent developments in bargaining research, and advocates studying "negotiators as arguers" as a new direction for research.

THEORETICAL FOUNDATIONS OF
BARGAINING ARGUMENT RESEARCH

Contemporary argumentation literature offers negotiation scholars several perspectives from which to design and conduct theoretically-grounded studies. Keough (1987) discusses argumentation's function in game theory, mixed-motive bargaining, and social-psychological studies. She concludes that three argumentation perspectives make immediate and powerful contributions to negotiation research: traditional-rhetorical, conversational, and argument fields.

Most bargaining researchers employ the first two perspectives: traditional-rhetorical and conversational. These two senses of argument represent distinct orientations. Traditional theories define *argumentation* as a form of reason-giving. Conversational theory classifies *argument* as a speech act that emerges from communicative interaction. Since each perspective is important to negotiation research, this chapter outlines their fundamental assumptions and applies their research techniques to negotiation discourse.

TRADITIONAL PERSPECTIVE

Informed by rhetorical theory and debate pedagogy, the traditional perspective defines argument as discourse created by a speaker aimed at persuading a listener to accept a particular course of action or way of thinking. Collectively, the argumentation process is "the whole activity of making claims, challenging them, backing them up by producing reasons, criticizing those reasons, [and] rebutting those criticisms" (Toulmin, Rieke, & Janik, 1979, p. 13).

An argument consists of several elements: claim or conclusion, data, warrant, backing, qualifiers, and rebuttals (Toulmin, 1958). The claim is what a speaker is trying to establish. Facts used to defend a claim are the data. Warrants are principles that justify the link between data and claim and may require backing to validate the relationship. Qualifiers (e.g., terms like *probably, perhaps, certainly*) address the strength or weakness of the argument. Rebuttal or reservation words articulate conditions that would negate the argument as originally stated. In the following example *unless* functions as a reservation word: "A 5% wage increase will satisfy the union, *unless* medical benefits are reduced." Coding systems exist for each element and are developed in the writings of Ehninger and Brockriede (1963), Freeley (1971), Patterson and Zarefsky (1983), and Toulmin et al. (1979).

Because claims and reasons are not always stated explicitly, researchers report difficulties in distinguishing arguments from informative statements (Keough, 1984; Putnam & Jones, 1982). O'Keefe (1977, 1982) provides criteria to assist researchers in selecting and coding argumentative discourse. He distinguishes between the argumentative utterance (an argument) and the making of an argumentative utterance (argument-making). An argument contains implied reasons supporting an explicit or implied claim, whereas argument-making involves the overt expression of reasons. The following excerpt from a teacher-school board negotiation illustrates each type:

Management: Present Article XXI is nonnegotiable.

   Labor: Present Article XXI is negotiable. . . . [It] has already been deemed a negotiable article by both parties, it's grandfathered under the law and we will negotiate it, either with your cooperation or without.

Because the negotiability of Article XXI is a disputed topic, management's statement is an argument and not just an informative sentence. The claim is explicit, "The article is not negotiable," and the reasons are implied to the union negotiator. Because the union negotiator supports her claim with explicit reasons, she engages in argument-making.

Argument-making is easier to code because explicit reasons are required and because operational definitions are possible for coders who are not familiar with the context in which the discourse is produced. If, however, coders are familiar with the negotiation situation and can explicate implied claims and reasons, then the argumentative utterance approach can be used.

Finally, the transcript of teacher negotiations demonstrates that although arguments can be isolated for analysis, they still function collectively in the argumentation process. Thus argumentation needs to be analyzed not only as isolated statements, but also as statements offered within a context of dissensus.

CONVERSATIONAL ARGUMENT PERSPECTIVE

Grounded in speech act theory, conversational argument emphasizes the interactive nature of argument production. Based on a research program developed by Jacobs and Jackson, conversational argument offers a theoretical framework for analyzing how disagreement is managed in interaction (Jackson & Jacobs, 1980, 1981; Jackson, Jacobs, Burrell, & Allen, 1986; Jacobs & Jackson, 1982; Kline, 1979; cf. Trapp, 1986b). In contrast to traditional argumentation theories, this perspective locates the origin of argument in speech acts rather than claims and reasons; thus, an argument is a disagreement episode jointly produced by speakers and listeners. As Jackson and Jacobs (1981) note: "Conversational argument and influence are collaborative activities: influence is not something that a speaker does to an addressee, nor is a line of argument developed from the plan of a single speaker. These speech events are transpersonal structures that persons jointly produce" (p. 79). More specifically, this perspective considers arguers as conversationalists constrained by rules that are produced through human interaction.

Conversations have four structural features that are instrumental in producing arguments: adjacency pairs, preference for agreement, turn taking, and expansion sequences. Adjacency pairs are the basic organizational unit of a conversation and refer to pragmatically linked conversational sequences (e.g., questions-answers, requests-grants/refusals). Each adjacency pair has felicity conditions that identify socially acceptable features of a speech act. Because adjacency pairs have a preference for agreement between their first pair parts (FPP) and second pair part (SPP), an argument is produced when the preferred SPP is not given. Through turn taking, an argument occurs and continues until an appropriately structured adjacency pair resolves the disagreement.

Jackson and Jacobs (1980) explain how a turn is arguable if either its *performative* or *propositional* properties are inappropriate. These properties refer to argument execution and substance, respectively. When the illocutionary properties of an adjacency pair are inappropriate an argument develops on the performative level. That is, the performative level of argumentation focuses on "how" FPPs and SPPs are exchanged. In the following example, management's bargainer asks why his requests for information annoy the union's bargainer.

Management: Here is a proposed change, and all I ask you is, "What's the rationale?" And you seem offended by that and I fail to understand why you're offended.

Union: I'm not offended by your request. I am offended by the length of time you are taking to go over something that really in the end result is not going to make one bit of difference.

The union negotiator argues about the performance properties of the request, not its context. That is, she perceives the information request as time-consuming and unwarranted, regardless of the content.

On the propositional level, an argument emerges because "the truth and consistency of what is said may be treated by the hearer as obstacles to agreement, prompting argument" (Jackson & Jacobs, 1980, p. 255). Propositional argument is illustrated below as the parties dispute the calculation of salary costs.

Union: Well one of the large factors that you're not taking into account is that when teachers retire, leave, whatever, the new teachers are hired at a much lower salary at a considerable savings in all of these areas.

Management: Except that in fact, it doesn't have any appreciable effect on our costs.

Union: It should!

The previous example also shows how argumentative statements are produced throughout the conversation. But in contrast to traditional argumentation approaches, conversational argument contends that people strategically structure arguments through their responses; thus argument development is still a collaborative rather than a monologic process.

In summary, this section describes two theoretical frameworks for argumentation research. The traditional and the conversational perspectives differ in their location of the origins of argument. In the traditional perspective, arguments are invented by the speaker and consist of claims with reasons. In contrast, conversational argument originates when a respondent gives an undesirable SPP. Both perspectives occur in negotiation. In formal contexts (e.g., labor-management, foreign policy), negotiators present preplanned arguments that become redefined through emergent arguments. In other contexts (e.g., roommate conflicts), a person may be drawn into a dispute with no opportunity to preplan his or her discourse. The next section reviews negotiation research guided by these perspectives.

FUNCTIONS OF BARGAINING ARGUMENTS

In most negotiations, messages serve information and exchange functions. They allow bargainers to communicate offers and counteroffers, reveal aspiration levels, and execute tactical moves such as concessions, threats, and promises. Bargaining arguments are a subset of this discourse and do more than simply exchange information. Two essays discuss how bargaining arguments function during negotiations.

Bacharach and Lawler (1981) claim that argument functions to define issues, offer justifications, and influence power relationships. Wilson and Putnam (1990) draw from interpersonal, group dynamics, and organizational bargaining literature to discuss argumentation's instrumental, relational, and identity management functions. Unfortunately, very few of the ideas in these two essays have been tested using theoretically grounded argumentation perspectives. The studies reviewed in this section, in general, are the exceptions. They employ traditional-rhetorical or conversational theories to guide empirical analyses of these functions. In this sense, they serve as models for other research programs.

INSTRUMENTAL FUNCTIONS

Arguments serve instrumental functions because they assist bargainers in reaching a negotiated settlement. Instrumental functions include persuasion and information exchange, issue definition, and joint decision making. These functions inherently overlap, but separate discussions of each highlight their contributions to the negotiation process.

Persuasion and Information Exchange. In social-psychological studies, persuasive arguments generally are operationalized as competitive tactics. For example, Pruitt (1983, p. 170) defines persuasive argument as a type of contentious behavior "aimed at convincing the other [party] that concessions are in his or her own best interests." Kniveton (1989) considers argumentation's function to be the modification of an opponent's target and resistant points.

Putnam, Wilson, and Turner (1990), however, suggest that the link between persuasive arguments and distributive outcomes may be a methodological artifact. They note that typologies typically fail "to distinguish between persuasive arguments used to attack the opponent, to defend one's own position, and to support the other party's ideas" (Putnam et al., 1990, p. 131). Studies that fail to code an argument's target (self or other) and purpose (attack or defend) indicate that persuasive arguments lead to impasses, lower joint benefits, and lower levels of negotiator satisfaction. In contrast, studies that employ comprehensive coding systems find that a balance of competitive and cooperative arguments buffer against escalating conflict spirals (Putnam & Jones, 1982).

Issue Definition. When researchers analyze bargainers' discourse, issue definition is a critical factor. Bacharach and Lawler (1981) comment, "The definition of bargaining issues is neither a simple nor unimportant task in bargaining. . . . The nature of each party's definition and its consequences for the bargaining outcome should be a major concern for both scholars and practitioners" (p. 158). Putnam, Wilson, Waltman, and Turner (1986) concur, "Argument about issue definition is as important as argument about the substance or content of the issue" (p. 79).

Bacharach and Lawler (1981) offer one of the most extensive discussions of argumentation and issue definition in the social-psychological literature. Although they define argumentation as reason-giving, their issue definition model suggests a mechanistic and linear conception of argumentation. Their model includes three dichotomous dimensions of issue definition: scope (specific or broad); number of issues (single or multiple); and prospective payoff (distributive or integrative). These dimensions are used to prescribe one of several different types of argumentation. Thus Bacharach and Lawler's (1981) model presumes that argumentative form and function remain constant throughout the negotiation process. Studies of teacher-school board negotiations challenge this assumption. Argumentative form (i.e., types of claims, reasons, and qualifiers) change as issues are dropped, modified, or retained (Putnam & Geist, 1985). The evolving arguments function as frames of reference for interpreting previous positions.

Contrary to Bacharach and Lawler's model, issue definition is circular and erratic rather than linear. Putnam et al. (1990) find no uniform pattern of argument selection for either bargaining party or bargaining phase (see Holmes, Chapter 4, this volume). Nor is a linear, phase-type pattern evident when arguments for and against issues are analyzed collectively as an argumentative case. "Issue definition surfaces throughout the bargaining whenever both sides clash directly on the nature and support for their bargaining proposals" (Putnam et al., 1986, p. 79).

Issue definition also affects outcomes. When negotiators concur on the definition of an issue, trade-off or compromise bargaining occurs (Putnam et al., 1990). That is, bargainers exchange offers and counteroffers until they reach a satisfactory midpoint. Bacharach and Lawler (1981) suggest divergent definitions may lead to redefinition that promotes reaching an agreement. On the one hand, when the parties define an issue differently, they may develop their cases more fully and may search for alternatives that collectively reframe an issue (Putnam et al., 1986). On the other hand, when the parties simply defend rather than develop their positions impasse may occur (Roloff, Tutzauer, & Dailey, 1989).

Joint Decision Making. Small group decision-making studies support the collaborative function of argumentative discourse. In decision-making groups, argumentation's instrumental functions of advocacy, discovery, and clarification of reason giving influence group outcomes (Hirokawa

& Scheerhorn, 1985). Effective groups critically assess arguments, whereas ineffective groups accept arguments and make decisions with minimal supporting evidence (Hirokawa & Pace, 1983). Consensus groups differ from dissensus groups in their use of convergent arguments. Convergent arguments, created from the positions of other group members, serve a collaborative function. "It appears that the joint construction of an argument is persuasive to others as it presents a unified view of what supporters consider reasonable" (Canary, Brossmann, & Seibold, 1987, p. 33). This finding supports Putnam et al.'s (1986) results that collaborative problem solving emerges from diverse perspectives on issues.

Overall, studies on the instrumental functions of negotiation arguments focus on bargaining outcomes and the processes that produce them. The integrative and distributive effects of argumentation seem influenced by research design. Coding systems that treat persuasive arguments as competitive tactics report that argumentation leads to competitive solutions. Whereas the use of comprehensive coding systems demonstrates that argumentation has both cooperative and competitive possibilities. The potential of argument to create innovative outcomes is most powerful when negotiators use reason giving as an exploratory technique rather than as a tactic to defend their positions.

RELATIONAL AND IDENTITY MANAGEMENT FUNCTIONS

Bargaining arguments serve relational functions as they build trust, promote unity, and manage power relations (see Donohue & Ramesh, Chapter 9, this volume). Negotiator identity is managed by meeting role expectations and maintaining face (see Wilson, Chapter 8, this volume; Wilson & Putnam, 1990). Although numerous studies address these functions, little research focuses on the role of argumentation in these processes. One type of argumentative discourse that conveys relational and identity functions is prenegotiation accounts. This literature is presented as an arena for future research on bargaining arguments.

Prenegotiation Accounts. Bies's (1989) work on the use of accounts to manage prenegotiation interactions has implications for the study of bargaining arguments. Specifically, research on prenegotiation accounts expands the context traditionally studied in negotiation, facilitates investigation of how unsuccessful argumentative statements generate conversational argument, and illustrates both relational and identity functions. An *account* is an explanation that justifies a decision (i.e., reasons given in support of a claim). Its purpose is to manage conflict before it happens (i.e., prevent the development of conversational argument). Its effectiveness depends on the timing of delivery, the perceived adequacy of the account, and the perceived sincerity of the account giver. Bies identifies three types of accounts that managers use to de-escalate subordinates' reactions to unfavorable resource allocation: causal, referential, and ideological.

Causal accounts are explanations or excuses that attempt to mitigate one's responsibility for an unfavorable outcome. A labor negotiator might offer such an account to management if the rank-and-file rejected a contract settlement and negotiations were reopened. Referential accounts attempt to reframe the consequences of an undesirable outcome through the use of three types of references: social, temporal, and aspirational. A social reference contends that other bargaining units have not received favorable offers. Temporal references suggest that favorable outcomes come at different times. Aspirational references attempt to recalculate a target's expectations; thus they function to manipulate an opponent's perceptions of his or her alternatives.

Finally, ideological accounts appeal to shared values, basic belief systems, or joint goals. These accounts function normatively to sanction a person's decision by associating it with higher-order motives. Strategically, an ideological account could be used to increase common ground and to decrease differences. While not disputing the potential positive benefits of ideological accounts, Keough and Lake (1991) conclude that value arguments in contract negotiations are very complex because (1) values may or may not be stated explicitly; (2) espoused values may contradict values-in-practice; and (3) there may be multiple value hierarchies (see Donohue & Ramesh, Chapter 9, this volume). Quite simply, the search for shared values is laudable but not always plausible.

Bies (1989) suggests future research should investigate reciprocal use of accounts between managers and employees. Other authors note that a singular account is rarely sufficient to stop subsequent dialogue; hence, accounting is often a multiple step process (McLaughlin, Cody, & Rosenstein, 1983). Second, accounting occurs in informal negotiation contexts and centers on the tacit agreements that shape the rules and policies for "getting things accomplished" in complex organizations (Strauss, 1979).

In summary, researchers employ both traditional-rhetorical and conversational argument as perspectives for investigating the instrumental, relational, and identity functions of bargaining. Although these functions are discussed separately, argumentation is multifunctional. By definition the purpose of argumentation is to gain adherence, which also entails information exchange. Movement toward a joint settlement requires issues to be defined and discussed. Relational issues such as trust and power are inherently linked to argument production and bargaining arguments influence perceptions of self and others. The major conclusion from this review is that linear, mechanistic, and univocal conceptions of argument unnecessarily limit research findings. When argumentation is theoretically grounded and clearly defined, its cooperative and competitive functions are evident. Moreover, under proper conditions, arguments can function dialectically to create transcendent positions that facilitate collaborative outcomes.

THE NEGOTIATOR AS ARGUER

Just as social-psychological theories directed conflict research away from mathematical formulas toward person variables (Druckman, 1977), recent developments in argumentation guide studies of bargainer characteristics. These theories de-emphasize verbal messages and center on the people who engage in argumentation. Source characteristics are worthy of investigation because the quality of argumentative discourse cannot be judged independent of its producers. "The worth of any decision which may emerge from an argumentation exchange is to a considerable extent dependent upon the good sense and acumen of the individuals who make it" (Ehninger, 1970, p. 106).

Concepts for studying the characteristics of arguers include traits of argumentativeness and verbal aggression (Infante & Rancer, 1982), cognitive editing (Dallinger & Hample, 1989), and argumentative competence (Trapp, 1986a). These concepts represent psychological, cognitive, and behavioral orientations, respectively. This section introduces each concept, integrates it with established negotiation research, and suggests future scholarly and pragmatic research.

PSYCHOLOGICAL ORIENTATION

Argumentativeness is a psychological trait that predisposes a person to recognize controversial issues and to advocate and refute positions

(Infante & Rancer, 1982). Despite the pejorative use of this term, a high degree of argumentativeness is a positive trait linked to higher grades in college (Infante, 1982), higher subordinate job satisfaction (Infante & Gordon, 1985), greater superior satisfaction with subordinate performance (Infante & Gordon, 1988), and greater communication satisfaction (Infante & Rancer, 1982), than is a low degree of argumentativeness. Onyekwere, Rubin, and Infante (1991) posit that a high degree of argumentativeness contributes to negotiator and mediator competence. However, Roloff et al. (1989) suggest that an argumentative nature may be a liability for integrative negotiation because the need to win will prevent collaborative problem solving. Keough (1990) reports argumentativeness does not lead to deadlocks in a simulated, integrative negotiation, but her study is limited; hence the results should be interpreted cautiously.

Roloff et al.'s (1989) concern may apply to verbal aggression rather than to argumentativeness. *Verbal aggression* is the predisposition to attack an opponent's self-concept instead of, or in addition to, his or her position. It correlates positively with measures of verbal hostility, assault, and communication apprehension (Infante & Wigley, 1986). For example, abused spouses score low in argumentativeness and perceive their spouses as high in verbal aggression. The inability to argue constructively may cause spouses to become verbally aggressive and violent (Infante, Chandler, & Rudd, 1989; Infante, Sabourin, Rudd, & Shannon, 1990). Consistent with research on conflict spirals, Lim (1990) reports that verbal aggressiveness increases when a receiver is unfriendly. In addition, rejecting a proposal increases verbal aggressiveness faster than does offering a counterproposal.

Argumentativeness and verbal aggression scales are strong research tools for investigating bargainer characteristics. The scales are reliable, valid, and easy to administer. Furthermore, they allow scholars to examine the relationship between psychological traits, negotiator performance, and bargaining outcomes. For example, in combination with conversational argument and discourse analytic techniques, researchers could examine the relationship between argumentativeness, verbal aggression, and performative or propositional turns. The literature suggests that verbally aggressive people would argue on a performative level, while argumentative people would argue on a propositional level. Results from these studies would be valuable for conflict intervention training.

COGNITIVE ARGUMENT
AND NEGOTIATOR COGNITION RESEARCH

Recent interest in negotiator cognition melds economic with industrial relations and psychological models of bargainer behavior and treats negotiation as a decision-making or an information-processing activity. Studies that investigate negotiator cognition examine judgment accuracy, negotiator frames, the decision to negotiate, the rationality of matching processes, negotiator role, and bargainer experience (also see Putnam & Holmer, Chapter 6, this volume; Neale, Northcraft, & Bazerman, 1989). Missing from this research is the cognitive assessment of communication tactics prior to their enactment in negotiation strategies (for an exception to this claim, see Roloff & Jordon, Chapter 1, this volume). Hample (1985) offers an information-processing perspective on argumentation. Because it describes the mental processes preceding verbalization, cognitive argument is an addition, not a replacement, to traditional-rhetorical and conversational argument perspectives. Cognitive argument includes:

> Everything involved in "thinking out" an argument or the need for one; the memorial processes of storage, retrieval, and reconstruction of pertinent cognitive elements; the information processing that is applied to the argument and its potential parts; the creative energies that generate new arguments or responses to them; and the productive abilities that give form to utterance. (Hample, 1985, p. 2)

Cognitive argument involves an editing process in which a person mentally evaluates an argument prior to verbalization. Dallinger and Hample (1989) identify three criteria for editing an argument: (1) effectiveness —will the argument work and not be inappropriate or too negative? (2) person-centered criteria—will the argument harm one or both parties or their relationship? (3) discourse competence—is the argument untrue or irrelevant for this situation? Hample and Dallinger (1987a, 1987b, 1987c, 1987d, 1987e) examine how arguments are edited in compliance-gaining situations. Even though situational influences have not been studied systematically, preliminary personality profiles have emerged for the effectiveness and the person-centered criteria. Namely, people who are high in verbal aggression, low in interpersonal orientation, and high in self-reported argumentative effectiveness use these criteria to reject arguments. In contrast, person-centered criteria are used by people who are low in verbal aggression, high in interpersonal orientation, and low in self-reported argumentative effectiveness. Cognitive argument theory could enhance negotiator cognition research. Much of this research identifies judgmental deficiencies such as overconfidence, nonrational escalation, assuming a fixed-pie perspective, overreliance on salient information, and inappropriate frames of reference (Neale et al., 1989). This work focuses on outcomes rather than on the processes used to produce these outcomes. Cognitive editing criteria facilitate the analysis of decision-making processes. By employing a verbal protocol technique (Bazerman & Carroll, 1987), it is possible to· record both the production and editing of argumentative discourse. This information would be useful in determining whether judgmental deficiencies originate from creation or selection errors. Admittedly, verbal protocols are difficult to use in field research, but they can be used in laboratory experiments and in evaluating negotiators during training sessions.

ARGUMENTATIVE COMPETENCE
AND NEGOTIATION EFFECTIVENESS

An issue that has yet to be discussed is the relationship between a person's argumentation skills and his or her effectiveness as a negotiator. That is, are good arguers also effective negotiators? This very pragmatic question can be tested via a behavioral measure of a speaker's argumentative competence (Trapp, 1986a; Trapp, Yingling, & Wanner, 1987). Developed from traditional argumentation theory, the Argumentative Competence Instrument (ACI) assesses a speaker's discourse on two dimensions: effectiveness and appropriateness. Effectiveness items measure "good" argumentation skills: being logical, providing sufficient evidence, making clear connections, changing the opponent's mind, explaining ideas clearly, and using persuasive techniques. The appropriateness scale employs negatively worded items that assess such inappropriate behaviors as belittling, insulting, interrupting, misquoting the opponent, being arrogant and overbearing, and twisting facts to fit one's own position. An overall argumentative competence score is calculated by subtracting the appropriateness score from the effectiveness score.

The ACI has self-assessment and opponent-assessment forms. The dual instruments enable scholars to examine both source and receiver perceptions of argumentative skills. To date, only one study employs the ACI in a negotiation setting (Keough, 1990). Because of its small subject pool, this study serves as a pilot test of the relationship between argumentative competence, negotiator gender, and outcomes.

Results indicate that neither negotiator gender nor outcome affect self-assessment scores. However, gender and outcome produce significant main effects for the opponent-effectiveness subscale. Regardless of opponent's gender, males rate their opponents more effective than do females. This counter-intuitive finding is a positive sign that the sex-role stereotype of a female's inability to argue rationally is fading. As expected, perceived winners rate their opponents as less effective than do perceived losers. More importantly, negotiators in win-win dyads give their opponents higher effectiveness scores than do perceived losers or perceived winners in win-lose dyads. These results suggest that competent arguers bring out the best in each other.

In summary, research on negotiators as arguers offers exciting new directions for dispute resolution scholars. The development of instruments to measure characteristics of arguers facilitates this line of study. Pragmatic benefits from this work might appear in negotiator and mediator selection and training. Theoretical gains might stem from discovering how psychological traits, cognitive processes, and skills affect message production, negotiation process, and bargaining outcomes. As noted in the introduction, studying both arguers and argument is critical for understanding the dialectical and epistemic nature of negotiation.

SUMMARY

Argumentation represents a distinguished tradition in speech communication. From its origins in Ancient Greece to contemporary perspectives, argumentation theorists have studied the management of disagreement through human discourse. Clearly, argumentation theory applies to negotiation research. This research may be descriptive, evaluative, or normative. It may look at reason giving, emergent arguments, or source characteristics.

A fundamental purpose of this chapter is to discourage misconceived and atheoretical use of the term *argument*. Generic or univocal use of this concept thwarts critical investigations of argument in negotiation by confounding research designs, impeding theory-building, and hampering comparative analyses. This chapter reviews and critiques several argumentation perspectives as alternatives to these problems. Hopefully, these perspectives will expand research on argument in negotiation by offering theoretical grounding, by aiding interpretation of data and findings, and by opening up new areas of inquiry.

REFERENCES

Axelrod, R. (1977). Argumentation in foreign policy settings: Britain in 1918, Munich in 1938, and Japan in 1970. In I. W. Zartman (Ed.), *The negotiation process* (pp. 175-192). Beverly Hills, CA: Sage.

Bacharach, S. B., & Lawler, E. J. (1981). *Bargaining: Power, tactics, and outcomes.* San Francisco: Jossey-Bass.

Bazerman, M. H., & Carroll, J. S. (1987). Negotiator cognition. In B. M. Staw & L. L. Cummings (Eds.), *Research in organizational behavior* (Vol. 9, pp. 247-288). Greenwich, CT: JAI Press.

Bies, R. J. (1989). Managing conflict before it happens: The role of accounts. In M. A. Rahim (Ed.), *Managing conflict: An interdisciplinary approach* (pp. 83-91). New York: Praeger.

Canary, D. J., Brossmann, B. G., & Seibold, D. R. (1987). Argument structures in decision-making groups. *Southern Speech Communication Journal, 53,* 18-37.

Cox, J. R., & Willard, C. A. (1982). Introduction: The field of argumentation. In J. R. Cox & C. A. Willard (Eds.), *Advances in argumentation theory & research* (pp. xiii-xlvii). Carbondale: Southern Illinois University Press.

Dallinger, J. M., & Hample, D. (1989). Biological and psychological gender effects upon cognitive editing of arguments. In B. E. Gronbeck (Ed.), *Spheres of argument: Proceedings of the Sixth SCA/AFA Conference on Argumentation* (pp. 563-568). Annandale, VA: Speech Communication Association.

Druckman, D. (Ed.) (1977). *Negotiations: Social-psychological perspectives.* Beverly Hills, CA: Sage.

Ehninger, D. (1970). Argument as method: Its nature, its limitations and its uses. *Speech Monographs, 37,* 101-110.

Ehninger, D., & Brockriede, W. (1963). *Decision by debate.* New York: Dodd, Mead & Company.

Fisher, W. R. (1978). Toward a logic of good reasons. *Quarterly Journal of Speech, 64,* 376-384.

Freeley, A. J. (1971). *Argumentation and debate: Rational decision making* (3rd ed.). Belmont, CA: Wadsworth.

Hample, D. (1985). A third perspective on argument. *Philosophy and Rhetoric, 18,* 1-22.

Hample, D., & Dallinger, J. M. (1987a). Argument editing choices and argumentative competence. In J. W. Wenzel (Ed.), *Argument and critical practices* (pp. 455-464). Annandale, VA: Speech Communication Association.

Hample, D., & Dallinger, J. M. (1987b). *The effects of Machiavellianism, social desirability, gender, and grade point average on cognitive editing of arguments.* Paper presented at the annual meeting of the Speech Communication Association, Boston.

Hample, D., & Dallinger, J. M. (1987c). Individual differences in cognitive editing standards. *Human Communication Research, 14,* 123-144.

Hample, D., & Dallinger, J. M. (1987d). The judgment phase of invention. In F. H. van
Eemeren, R. Grootendorst, J. A. Blair, & C. A. Willard (Eds.), *Argumentation: Perspectives and approaches* (pp. 225-234). Dordrecht, Holland: Foris.

Hample, D., & Dallinger, J. M. (1987e). Self-monitoring and the cognitive editing of
arguments. *Central States Communication Journal, 38,* 152-165.

Hirokawa, R. Y., & Pace, R. (1983). A descriptive investigation of the possible communication-based reasons for effective and ineffective group decision making. *Communication Monographs, 50,* 363-379.

Hirokawa, R. Y., & Scheerhorn, D. R. (1985). Argumentation and negotiation. In J. R.
Cox, M. Sillars, & G. Walker (Eds.), *Argument and social practice: Proceedings of
the Fourth SCA/AFA Conference on Argumentation* (pp. 737-746). Annandale, VA:
Speech Communication Association.

Infante, D. A. (1982). The argumentative student in the speech communication classroom: An investigation and implications. *Communication Education, 31,* 141-148.

Infante, D. A., Chandler, T. A., & Rudd, J. E. (1989). Test of an argumentative skill deficiency model of interspousal violence. *Communication Monographs, 56,* 163-177.

Infante, D. A., & Gordon, W. I. (1985). Superiors' argumentativeness and verbal aggressiveness as predictors of subordinates' satisfaction. *Human Communication Research,
12,* 117-125.

Infante, D. A., & Gordon, W. I. (1988). Argumentativeness and affirming communicator
style as predictors of satisfaction/dissatisfaction with subordinates. *Communication Quarterly, 37,* 81-90.

Infante, D. A., & Rancer, A. S. (1982). A conceptualization and measure of argumentativeness. *Journal of Personality Assessment, 46,* 72-80.

Infante, D. A., Sabourin, T. A., Rudd, J. E., & Shannon, E. A. (1990). Verbal aggression
in violent and nonviolent marital disputes. *Communication Quarterly, 38,* 361-371.

Infante, D. A., & Wigley, C. J., III. (1986). Verbal aggressiveness: An interpersonal model
and measure. *Communication Monographs, 53,* 61-69.

Jackson, S., & Jacobs, S. (1980). Structure of conversational argument: Pragmatic bases
for the enthymeme. *Quarterly Journal of Speech, 66,* 251-265.

Jackson, S., & Jacobs, S. (1981). The collaborative production of proposals in conversational argument and persuasion: A study in disagreement regulation. *Journal of the
American Forensic Association, 18,* 77-90.

Jackson, S., Jacobs, S., Burrell, N., & Allen, M. (1986). Characterizing ordinary argument: Substantive and methodological issues. *Journal of the American Forensic
Association, 23,* 42-57.

Jacobs, S., & Jackson, S. (1982). Conversational argument: A discourse analytic approach.
In J. R. Cox & C. A. Willard (Eds.), *Advances in argumentation theory and research*
(pp. 205-237). Carbondale: Southern Illinois University Press.

Keough, C. M. (1984, May). *Bargaining argument analysis: Presentation and critique of
a coding system.* Paper presented at the annual meeting of the International Communication Association, San Francisco.

Keough, C. M. (1987). The nature and function of argument in organizational bargaining
research. *Southern Speech Communication Journal, 50,* 1-17.

Keough, C. M. (1990, June). *The relationship between argumentativeness and argumentative competence in integrative negotiations as influenced by negotiator sex and
perceived winner.* Paper presented at the Second International Society for the Study
of Argumentation Convention, Amsterdam, The Netherlands.

Keough, C. M., & Lake, R. A. (1991). Values as structuring properties of contract negotiations. In C. Conrad (Ed.), *The ethical nexus: Values, communication, and organizational decisions* (pp. 171-189). Norwood, NJ: Ablex.

Kline, S. L. (1979). Toward a contemporary linguistic interpretation of the concept of stasis. *Journal of the American Forensic Association, 16,* 95-103.

Kniveton, B. (1989). *The psychology of bargaining.* Brookfield, VT: Gower.

Lim, T. (1990). The influences of receivers' resistance on persuaders' verbal aggressiveness. *Communication Quarterly, 38,* 170-188.

McKerrow, R. E. (1982). Rationality and reasonableness in a theory of argument. In J. R. Cox & C. A. Willard (Eds.), *Advances in argumentation theory and research* (pp. 105-122). Carbondale: Southern Illinois University Press.

McLaughlin, M. L., Cody, M. J., & Rosenstein, N. E. (1983). Account sequences in conversations between strangers. *Communication Monographs, 50,* 102-125.

Nash, J. F., Jr. (1950). The bargaining problem. *Econometrica, 18,* 155-162.

Neale, M. A., Northcraft, G. B., & Bazerman, M. H. (1989). Cognitive aspects of negotiation: New perspectives on dyadic decision making. In M. A. Rahim (Ed.), *Managing conflict: An interdisciplinary approach* (pp. 149-160). New York: Praeger.

O'Keefe, D. J. (1977). Two concepts of arguing. *Journal of the American Forensic Association, 13,* 121-128.

O'Keefe, D. J. (1982). The concepts of argument and arguing. In J. R. Cox & C. A. Willard (Eds.), *Advances in argumentation theory and research* (pp. 3-23). Carbondale: Southern Illinois University Press.

Onyekwere, E. O., Rubin, R. B., & Infante, D. A. (1991). Interpersonal perception and communication satisfaction as a function of argumentativeness and ego-involvement. *Communication Quarterly, 39,* 35-47.

Patterson, J. W., & Zarefsky, D. (1983). *Contemporary debate.* Boston: Houghton Mifflin.

Perelman, C., & Olbrechts-Tyteca, L. (1969). *The new rhetoric: A treatise on argumentation.* Notre Dame, IN: University of Notre Dame Press.

Pruitt, D. G. (1983). Strategic choice in negotiation. *American Behavioral Scientist, 27,* 167-194.

Putnam, L. L. (1985). Bargaining as organizational communication. In R. D. McPhee & P. K. Tompkins (Eds.), *Organizational communication: Traditional themes and new directions* (pp. 129-148). Beverly Hills, CA: Sage.

Putnam, L. L., & Geist, P. (1985). Argument in bargaining: An analysis of the reasoning process. *Southern Speech Communication Journal, 50,* 225-245.

Putnam, L. L., & Jones, T. S. (1982). Reciprocity in negotiations: An analysis of bargaining interaction. *Communication Monographs, 49,* 171-191.

Putnam, L. L., Wilson, S. R., & Turner, D. B. (1990). The evolution of policy arguments in teachers' negotiation. *Argumentation, 4,* 129-152.

Putnam, L. L., Wilson, S. R., Waltman, M. S., & Turner, D. (1986). The evolution of case arguments in teachers' bargaining. *Journal of American Forensic Association, 23,* 63-81.

Roloff, M. E., Tutzauer, F. E., & Dailey, W. O. (1989). The role of argumentation in distributive and integrative bargaining contexts: Seeking relative advantage but at what cost? In M. A. Rahim (Ed.), *Managing conflict: An interdisciplinary approach* (pp. 109-119). New York: Praeger.

Sawyer, J., & Guetzkow, H. (1965). Bargaining and negotiation in international relations. In H. C. Kelman (Ed.), *International behavior: A social-psychological analysis* (pp. 466-520). New York: Holt, Rinehart & Winston.

Strauss, A. (1979). *Negotiations: Varieties, contexts, processes, and social order.* San Francisco: Jossey-Bass.

Toulmin, S. E. (1958). *The uses of argument.* Cambridge, UK: Cambridge University Press.

Toulmin, S. E., Rieke, R., & Janik, A. (1979). *An introduction to reasoning.* New York: Macmillan.

Trapp, R. (1986a, November). *The concept of argumentative competence.* Paper presented at the annual meeting of the Speech Communication Association, Chicago.

Trapp, R. (1986b). The role of disagreement in interactional argument. *Journal of the American Forensic Association, 23,* 23-41.

Trapp, R., Yingling, J. M., & Wanner, J. (1987). Measuring argumentative competence. In F. H. van Eemeren, R. Grootendorst, J. A. Blair, & C. A. Willard (Eds.), *Argumentation: Across the lines of discipline* (pp. 253-261). Dordrecht, Holland: Foris.

Trice, H. M., & Beyer, J. M. (1984). Studying organizational cultures through rites and ceremonials. *Academy of Management Review, 9,* 653-669.

Wenzel, J. W. (1980). Perspectives on argument. In J. Rhodes & S. Newell (Eds.), *Proceedings of the Summer Conference on Argumentation* (pp. 112-133). Annandale, VA: Speech Communication Association.

Willard, C. A. (1989). *A theory of argumentation.* Tuscaloosa: University of Alabama Press.

Wilson, S. R., & Putnam, L. L. (1990). Interaction goals in negotiation. In J. A. Anderson (Ed.), *Communication yearbook 13* (pp. 374-406). Newbury Park, CA: Sage.

Chapter 6

FRAMING, REFRAMING, AND ISSUE DEVELOPMENT

Linda L. Putnam and Majia Holmer

A MAJOR CONCERN in negotiation is how to reach a settlement in which both parties share joint gains. Both popular and academic texts spend considerable effort prescribing effective ways to reach joint agreements (Fisher & Ury, 1981; Jandt, 1985; Lewicki & Litterer, 1985). These recommendations include concentrating on interests rather than positions (Fisher & Ury, 1981), engaging in problem solving (Lewicki & Litterer, 1985), avoiding conflict escalation (Pruitt & Rubin, 1986), and building trust and motivation to work together (Lewicki & Litterer, 1985). One of the first advocates of joint agreements, Mary Parker Follett (1942), claims that integration brings differences into the open and leads to a process of *revaluation* in which both parties reframe their stances on an issue. For Follett, integration is a circular process in which differences are juxtaposed in a spontaneous flowing together of interests and desires. Unity surfaces not from giving in [compromise] but from "getting the desires of each side into one field of vision" (Follett, 1942, p. 39).

The "field of vision" that Follett describes resembles what has become an important concept in the negotiation literature, *bargaining frame*. Each bargainer enters the negotiation with fields of vision or frames of reference that help him or her construct meaning or make sense of the situation. Revaluation parallels *reframing* by altering fields of vision to reveal a different vantage point (Bolman & Deal, 1991). Although scholars differ in their exact definitions of *frame* and of *reframing*, both concepts refer to the way negotiators come to understand their situation.

Framing and reframing are important concepts in the study of negotiation. First, framing is a key to deciphering how bargainers conceive of
ongoing sets of events in light of past experiences (Bartlett, 1932). In
negotiation, bargainers must react to momentary changes in behaviors, not
as blank receptacles, but as individuals who interpret and make sense of
their world (Tannen, 1979). Frames, then, are linked to such concepts as
cooperative-competitive orientations (Rubin & Brown, 1975), expectations for a settlement (Gulliver, 1979), biases of bargainers (Neale &
Bazerman, 1985), choice of dispute resolution modes (Merry & Silbey,
1984), approaches to third-party intervention in formal and informal disputes (Donohue, 1991; Sheppard, Blumenfeld-Jones, & Roth, 1989), and
interpretive schemes (Gray & Donnellon, 1989). Frames and reframing
are also related to the way bargainers conceive of the scope, definition,
and relationship among issues in the negotiation (Bacharach & Lawler,
1981; Putnam, 1990; Putnam, Wilson, Waltman, & Turner, 1986). Even
though researchers typically treat frames as cognitive devices such as
schema, scripts, prototypes, and categories, framing and reframing are
tied to the ongoing activity of bargaining, the escalation and de-escala-
tion of conflict, and negotiated outcomes (Bazerman, 1983; Neale &
Bazerman, 1985, 1991).

Framing and reframing are also salient concepts for communication
research, even though only a few negotiation scholars incorporate communication variables into their studies (Carroll & Payne, 1991; De Dreu,
Emans, & Van de Vliert, 1991; Gray & Donnellon, 1989; Thompson &
Hastie, 1990). Information seeking and interactions between bargainers
play a key role in the process of framing. Moreover, framing entails the
construction of shared meanings that typify social and cultural contexts
(McLeod, Pan, & Rucinski, 1989). In effect, framing and reframing are
vital to the negotiation process and are tied to information processing,
messages patterns, linguistic cues, and socially constructed meanings.

This chapter reviews and critiques the way that researchers have studied
framing in negotiation through focusing on three different approaches:
cognitive heuristics, frame categories, and issue development. Because
these approaches differ in theoretical underpinnings, past research has
not merged these divergent literatures. This review concentrates on the
concept of framing rather than on detailed summaries of research findings.
After reviewing and critiquing the negotiation literature, we introduce
two alternative models, Bateson's (1972) psychological model of framing and Goffman's (1974) frame analysis. Finally, we set forth ways to

improve the study of framing in bargaining through adopting concepts from Bateson and Goffman.

APPROACHES TO RESEARCH ON FRAMING IN NEGOTIATION

The study of frames in bargaining is a fairly recent phenomenon, even though this work falls into the larger rubric of negotiator orientations and predispositions. Frames, however, differ from cooperative and competitive orientations in the early Prisoner's Dilemma literature and from the study of cognitive complexity by centering on cognition and interaction rather than on motivations, attitudes, and personality traits (Rubin & Brown, 1975). Approaches to the study of framing in negotiation differ in their theoretical foundations and assumptions. The three approaches that surface in the negotiation literature—cognitive heuristics, frame categories, and issue development—will be reviewed and critiqued in light of their theoretical roots, definitions, characteristics, research findings, role of communication, and underlying assumptions. This section concludes with an assessment of the strengths and weaknesses of each approach for research on communication and negotiation.

COGNITIVE HEURISTICS

The cognitive heuristics approach is rooted in behavioral decision theory and prospect theory of human judgment (Bazerman, 1983; Raiffa, 1982; Tversky & Kahneman, 1981). Behavioral decision theory posits that bargainers may share a zone of agreement or overlap in their target and resistant points, yet they are unable to reach mutual agreement (Lewicki & Litterer, 1985; Raiffa, 1982). Neale and Bazerman (1985, 1991) treat this problem as a deviation from rationality that stems from negotiator judgment. Drawing from cognitive models of decision making, Neale and Bazerman (1985, 1991) identify the decision frames that introduce systematic bias in negotiation and discuss ways to reduce these biases.

Theory and Definitions. Their treatment of decision frames draws heavily from Kahneman & Tversky's (1979) Prospect Theory. A *frame* is defined as "a decision maker's conception of the acts, outcomes, and contingencies associated with a particular choice" (Tversky & Kahneman,

1981, p. 453). Framing emanates from the way an individual formulates a problem through his or her norms, habits, and personal characteristics. Frames also reflect the way that individuals employ cognitive heuristics or simple rules of thumb for making choices (Neale & Bazerman, 1991). That is, decision makers *satisfice* or select an acceptable or reasonable solution rather than strive for the best alternative.

Characteristics. The key characteristics of framing in this approach are perceptions of loss-gain, risk aversion and risk seeking, anchoring or reference points for frames, overconfidence, availability, negotiator judgments, and the isolation effect. Prospect theory holds that in selecting a decision option in situations of certainty, a person's response to a loss is more extreme than his or her reaction to a gain (Kahneman & Tversky, 1979). Individuals frame or evaluate potential gains and losses as positive or negative. The theory purports that individuals are more likely to accept a settlement when faced with a potential gain and hold out for future concessions when faced with a potential loss (Neale & Bazerman, 1991). The frame, then, encompasses the potential of losses and gains in light of the perceived certainty of a given outcome.

Neale and Bazerman (1985) translate framing heuristics into biases in negotiation through manipulating *perceptions of losses and gains* and observing *risk seeking and risk aversion* behaviors.[1] Individuals who view an outcome as a potential gain make more concessions and see the negotiated outcome as more fair than do those who hold a negative frame or see their trade-offs as losses (Neale & Bazerman, 1985). Moreover, negotiators with positive frames complete more transactions and attain higher overall profits than those who view outcomes as losses (Bazerman, Magliozzi, & Neale, 1985; Neale & Northcraft, 1986; Schurr, 1987). Further studies show that negative frames are linked to escalation of conflict (Bazerman, 1984), potential impasse (Bazerman & Neale, 1982, 1983), and strike and third-party intervention (Farber & Katz, 1979).

In these studies framing centers primarily on the negotiation task. Relational and context elements also impinge on negotiator frames. Specifically, positive affect in integrative bargaining may reverse the predictions of decision frames. Hollingshead and Carnevale (1990) observe that when negotiators exchange positive affect, bargainers with positive frames are more risk seeking, more likely to risk nonagreement, and less likely to make concessions than are negotiators with negative frames. Single- versus multi-issue agendas also influence the predictions of a loss-gain frame. Bontempo (1990) reports that in the positive frame, a one-issue agenda leads to greater agreement, higher satisfaction with outcomes, and more perceived fairness than does a multi-item agenda. In contrast, in the negative frame, a multi-item agenda results in a more satisfactory outcome than does a single-item agenda. In both studies, the introduction of relational and context variables reverses the frame effect. Finally, framing shaped by a bargainer's assigned role as a buyer or a seller also influences negotiated outcomes and becomes a source of decision bias (McAlister, Bazerman, & Fader, 1986; Neale, Huber, & Northcraft, 1987).

A positive or negative frame for negotiation stems from the selection of a reference point or an anchor. For example, in a contract negotiation between union and management, the union's reference point or anchor might be last year's contract or the union's publicly announced position or even management's initial offer (Neale & Bazerman, 1991). *Anchors* refer to the designated starting point for assessing whether an offer or settlement option is a gain or a loss. They are easily available and provide ready framing of targets, goals, and initial offers. Anchors, however, may also lead to biases in decision making when bargainers perceive outcomes as losses and fail to adjust reference points in light of the negotiation process. Negotiators who remain committed to initial offers or who hold to their target points in the face of concessions may be unable to reach agreement, even if a positive bargaining range exists (Neale & Bazerman, 1991). Neale (1984) and Huber and Neale (1986) illustrate that the setting of initial goals, whether difficult or easy, has a significant effect on aspirations and expectations for future performance.

Anchoring also establishes a range of confidence for making a judgment. A bias of *overconfidence*, then, also affects an individual's cognitive frame. In situations of uncertainty or moderate-to-extreme difficulty, individuals overestimate their confidence in their judgments (Neale & Bazerman, 1991). In framing the contingencies associated with uncertain outcomes, individuals rarely use disconfirming evidence to test their judgments and they rely on initial estimates to anchor their confidence (Einhorn & Hogarth, 1978). Both patterns lead to a bias of overconfidence in an individual's cognitive frame.

Overconfidence surfaces when bargainers estimate the likelihood that an arbitrator will accept their team's final offer (Bazerman & Neale, 1982; Neale & Bazerman, 1983). Moreover, negotiators who consistently believe that an arbitrator will rule in their favor are unwilling to compromise at the table (Farber, 1981; Farber & Bazerman, 1986). An overconfidence bias in judgment also leads to a reduction in the number of concessionary activities and to a high proportion of impasse outcomes (Neale & Bazerman, 1985). In effect, overconfidence, as a bias in cognitive framing, leads to fewer compromises and more impasses than do judgments based on accurate levels of confidence.

Overconfidence as a bias in cognitive framing may relate to the *availability* bias or the ease of recalling unlikely events (Tversky & Kahneman, 1973). The ease in imagining an event, retrievability of instances, and similarity of association promote quick recall of events from memory and bias a negotiator's frame. In applying the availability heuristic to negotiation, Neale (1984) compares the vividness or ease of imagining perceived costs of negotiating versus the monetary and time costs of arbitration. When personal costs such as dissatisfaction with constituents are salient, bargainers are less likely to settle at the table. In contrast, when the cost of going to arbitration is salient, negotiators are likely to reach agreement through compromise. Moreover, presenting information in a vivid and colorful rather than a pallid manner makes options more available or salient in a negotiator's frame (Taylor & Thompson, 1982; Wilson, Northcraft, & Neale, 1989).

Finally, information that is concrete or readily available is more easily retrieved than events that are not perceived as concrete (Tversky & Kahneman, 1974). In negotiation, Northcraft and Neale (1986) observe that because out-of-pocket costs are more concrete, they are more likely to be included in financial decision making than are opportunity costs. Since negotiators see out-of-pocket costs as more concrete, they seem more numerous that, in turn, influences a bargainer's judgment. In addition to biases of overconfidence and availability, *judgments that are particular to negotiation situations* also affect cognitive frames. Such biases as the mythical fixed pie, nonrational escalation of conflict, and devaluing the other party's concessions (see Neale & Bazerman, 1991 for an explanation of these biases).

A final heuristic that affects a negotiator's frame is the *isolation effect* (Tversky & Kahneman, 1974, 1981). This effect applies to the way individuals evaluate a set of potential options in decision making. Making choices among options typically follows a "sequential-process-of-elimination" (Tversky, 1972) in which individuals choose the most important attribute of an option and eliminate alternatives that do not include this attribute. Similar strategies include a lexicographic procedure in which negotiators weigh some issues as more important than others or determine if each alternative meets a predetermined cutoff level (Carroll & Payne, 1991). This bias is similar to the isolation effect, but the elimination of alternatives is based on priority rather than sequence. Although negotiation researchers have not tested the isolation effect directly, Thompson and Hastie (1990) use the lexicographic procedure to find that bargainers stress their most important options and fail to make gains on alternatives that do not meet their cutoff levels. Both the isolation and the lexicographic effects may influence the way bargainers evaluate alternatives and engage in logrolling and splintering of multiple alternatives.

Role of Communication. As a whole, research supports the relevance of Tversky and Kahneman's (1974) theory for negotiations. The literature on cognitive heuristics represents an extensive body of research on framing and cognitive biases in negotiation. Although most of this work centers on inputs to the bargaining process, this approach has implications for communication studies. Within Tversky and Kahneman's (1974) model, communication is the key to understanding how colorful and emotional information functions in the availability heuristic and how feedback alters negotiator overconfidence (Neale & Northcraft, 1990). It is also critical in determining how relational and context factors such as affect and role credibility impinge on positive and negative frames.

In addition, information search, sequencing, and amount are directly related to cognitive frames and to communication processes during the negotiation (Carroll & Payne, 1991). Specifically, bargainers who provide more information about their own interests make fewer judgment errors than do those who do not give information (Thompson & Hastie, 1990). Since information giving and seeking are positively reciprocated, the role of information exchange is critical to a bargainer's judgments. Reciprocity is also linked to the explicit or implicit communication of decision frames. De Dreu et al. (1991) observe that negotiators rely on their opponents' decision frames to direct subsequent negotiation behaviors more often than they depend on their own frames. Specifically, when bargainers send messages that convey a loss or a gain frame, approximately 40% of the opponents reciprocate with the same language. Moreover, negotiators are more cooperative when their opponents employ positive as opposed to negative frames.

Frames, schema, and scripts also shape the use of strategies, tactics, and persuasive appeals in bargaining. Carroll and Payne (1991) point out how tough versus soft stances in negotiation reflect distributive and integrative scripts and how direct and indirect forms of persuasion reveal schema that negotiators have for their opponents and their bargaining situation. Adding communication to research on cognitive framing is important. However, these additions limit the role of communication by treating it as transmission or as an exchange. Integrating communication into the cognitive heuristics approach alters the concept of framing from a static to a dynamic model. As Carroll and Payne (1991) observe, negotiators

> must develop a strategy or plan, pay close attention to one's own preferences, seek out information for the opponent's preferences, figure out what to say or do next, pay attention to what the opponent is saying or doing, and be aware of the implications of all of this for revising the strategy and even revising basic beliefs and preferences. (p. 23)

What is needed in the cognitive heuristics approach is an infusion of theoretical models that move framing from a static to a dynamic process, provide a link between framing and reframing, broaden the locus of frames from the individual to the larger social context, and treat frames as being developed collectively rather than originating solely from perceptual and mental activities.

FRAME CATEGORIES

Theory and Definitions. A second approach to the study of framing in negotiation is not well developed nor well researched. It aims to merge cognitive views of framing with linguistic analysis. In Gray and Donnellon's (1989) work, *frames* consist of categories of bargaining experiences derived from the literature (Bacharach & Lawler, 1981; Bazerman et al., 1985; Fisher & Ury, 1981; Putnam & Geist, 1985; Rubin & Brown, 1975). They initially posit six types of categories: (1) *substantive frames* define what the conflict is about, (2) *loss-gain frames* provide interpretations associated with the risk or benefits of various outcomes, (3) *characterization frames* are expectations and evaluations of the other disputants' behaviors and attitudes, (4) *process frames* are expectations about how the negotiation will or should proceed, (5) *aspiration frames* express the disputants' underlying interests and needs, and (6) *outcome frames* are the disputants' preferred positions or solutions (Gray, Purdy, & Bouwen, 1990). Drawing from Fillmore (1975) and Tannen (1979), Gray and Donnellon (1989) use linguistic patterns to index types of cognitive frames and past experiences of bargainers. Hence, they combine a top-down view of frames, informed by research from the bargaining literature, with a bottom-up notion of frames as linguistic cues. *Reframing* refers to the way frame categories shift throughout the negotiation and to the way ambiguity contributes to these shifts and to subsequent changes in interpreting the conflict.

Characteristics. Frames exist at multiple levels of analysis, namely, type, content, pattern, range, and level of abstraction. To investigate the role of framing in negotiation, researchers determine what frames disputants are evoking in interpreting the conflict, the content of those interpretations, and the extent to which negotiators change their frames and interpretations. Gray and Donnellon (1989) analyze transcripts from the Sheridan Chemical negotiation case and find that bargainers use multiple frames simultaneously during the negotiation, but that these frames are salient at different times during the interaction. The bargainers may hold similar or disparate frames that influence their interpretations. Mismatches in framing are sources of conflict (Gray, 1991, p. 12). Mismatches arise in three ways: (1) the use of different types of frames, (2) different content for the same frame, (3) inferences that negotiators make at different levels of abstraction (Gray, 1991; Gray et al., 1990). Ambiguity that stems from these mismatches creates misunderstanding that may lead to escalation and stalemate or, conversely, may promote reframing. Adjustment of understanding through reframing, or frame alignment, leads to conflict resolution.

In a subsequent study, Gray et al. (1990) analyze episodes of contract negotiations between a performer and an opera company, role played by MBA students. They employ discourse analysis to draw inferences of frame categories based on lexical, syntactical, and social data; the content of the talk; and the function of messages in the interaction. They report two major changes in the typology of frames from their analysis. First, they add an evidentiary frame to encompass facts and supporting evidence for outcome or loss-gain frames and second they develop their category system into a hierarchy with substantive and process categories acting as metaframes to classify text into the remaining frames. The researchers then develop subcategories for characterization and loss-gain frames and divide the transcript into content issues, such as salary discussion and career concerns. Their findings reveal that integrative agreements stem from discussing a large number of issues and from using aspirations frames. Moreover, a specific frame appears to dominate discussion of separate issues. Outcome frames depict discussions of salary concerns while characterization frames typify interaction on career issues.

Role of Communication. Communication plays a central role in the frame categories approach. Language choice reflects a bargainer's experiences, systems of beliefs, and perception of the negotiation. Thus communication serves a constitutive role by revealing the frame categories in use, by determining the ambiguity and overlapping nature of frames, and by tracking instances of reframing. Moreover, in this approach, frames reside in the meanings or interpretive schemes reflected in the interaction of negotiators rather than in their mental states.

Although this approach is communicative in nature and represents a noble effort to integrate frames with social interaction, it inadvertently conflates mutual understanding with agreement. Mutual understanding may be a necessary but not a sufficient condition for conflict or for agreement. Negotiators could conceivably use the same frame, identical frame content, or parallel levels of abstraction, and remain fundamentally opposed. Conversely, in the absence of mutual understanding, bargainers may reach integrative agreements through logrolling and cost compensation. Another problem with this approach is using a priori categories to generate a typology of frames in use. Pre-selected or a priori categories may not be consistent with the interpretive underpinnings of this research. Furthermore, the Gray et al. (1990) study lacks clarity methodologically in identifying the beginning and ending of coded units and in making inferences from categories and their interrelationships. Finally, the results of the Gray et al. study indicate that modifications of other approaches such as issue development (Putnam, 1990), issue transformation (Mather & Yngvesson, 1980-1981), and issue management (Donohue, 1991) may yield the same findings. Nonetheless, Gray and Donnellon (1989) should be commended for their dynamic view of frames, routed in disputants' interpretations.

ISSUE DEVELOPMENT

A third approach to framing, issue development, also adopts a communication perspective to negotiation. This approach centers on the task or agenda by focusing on the way issues change during the negotiation process. As an area of research, it is typically associated with the transformation of disputes rather than with negotiator frames (Felstiner, Abel, & Sarat, 1980-1981; Mather & Yngvesson, 1980-1981; Putnam, 1985, 1990). It operates from the assumption that disputes are transformed through shifting frames or altering the way problems are conceptualized.

The framing of a dispute determines the importance and relevance of available facts in a case (Mather & Yngvesson, 1980-1981; Pinkley, 1990). In this approach, then, a *frame* refers to the definition, meaning, and conceptualization of an issue. Issues correspond to agenda items or topics of concern in a dispute. They differ from positions, which refer to alternatives for reaching agreements and from interests or the needs and desires that underlie positions (Fisher & Ury, 1981). In comparison with cognitive heuristics, issue development focuses on the way bargainers assess alternatives, but it differs from the isolation effect in linking assessments to social interaction. Although issue development encompasses substantive, solution, and outcome frames, it differs from frame categories in centering on the argument or clash of issues as the basis of framing and reframing. Thus argumentation embodies referents that provide a cognitive picture of bargaining events and the way these events should be interpreted (Comaroff & Roberts, 1977). Issue development, then, differs from the other two perspectives on framing in its theoretical roots, its definition of framing and reframing, and the role of context in negotiation.

Theory and Definitions. The theoretical roots of issue development reside in the literatures on dispute resolution, argumentation, and policy deliberations. Frames or the conceptualizing of issues are co-constructed or determined collectively through the way individuals make sense of their situation (Eden, Jones, Sims, & Smithin, 1981). That is, issues are not objective agenda items; rather they undergo a process of naming, blaming, and claiming through the way that people talk or argue about them (Felstiner et al., 1980-1981). Naming occurs when disputants label a situation as a problem. Disputants, then, negotiate blame by discussing who or what caused the problem. Claiming takes place when the person or side with the grievance confronts the individual or organization that they think caused the problem. Although each side enters the negotiation with some conception or interpretation of an agenda item, the way people talk about a problem influences the way they define it. Frames, then, are not simply features of individual cognition, they are co-constructed in the ways that bargainers define problems and courses of action jointly through their talk.

In negotiation, argumentation and debate are means of co-constructing the scope, interrelatedness, and breadth of bargaining issues (Bacharach & Lawler, 1981). That is, arguments are epistemic in that they produce knowledge about the issues under deliberation, the other party's preferences and interests, and the institutionalized rules produced through interaction (see Keough, Chapter 5, this volume). That is, the pro and con attacks on agenda items aim to recast the opponent's definition of an issue. Issue development, then, becomes "a continual process of assessing and reassessing agenda items in light of attacking arguments, information exchanged, and interpretations that bargainers give to these activities" (Putnam, 1990, p. 10).

Characteristics. Characteristics of frames in this approach include the bargaining context, the process of shaping issues, and reframing or generating novel solutions to issues. *Bargaining context* impinges on the way both sides define issues. A particular agenda item is framed within a context of recurring problems between labor and management and the relationships among constituent groups (Derber, Chalmers, Stagner, & Edelman, 1961; Friedman & Gal, 1990; Mather & Yngvesson, 1980-1981; Putnam, 1985). For example, negotiation issues often arise from organizational practices, past grievances, and bargaining history (Derber, Chalmers, & Edelman, 1965).

Framing occurs through the *process of shaping issues.* Although each side typically begins with a conceptualization of the problem, this definition shifts through interactions with the other party. Three types of interactions reveal how framing is jointly shaped. First, arguments between bargainers attack the significance, the stability of problems, the disadvantages of proposals, and the perceived workability of solutions (Putnam & Wilson, 1989; Putnam, Wilson, & Turner, 1990). As each side raises concerns about the importance of an agenda item, its scope, its harms, both parties engage in shaping or framing a problem. Certain items become *stock issues* that recur from one negotiation to the next. For the union, wages as an agenda item may always be too low. Hence, labor argues for the salience of this problem in light of management's conception of the issue and in relationship to particular historic and economic conditions.

Second, framing of issues occurs jointly through the way both sides clash on their arguments or make *cases* to convince the other party. A case is an overall justification that one side constructs in support of its position. Cases resemble a lawyer's brief for defining a problem. When one side presents a case to change the current structure, and the other side disagrees with this need, both sides may "talk past each other" or "talk around an issue" until they find common ground or a new way to conceive of the problem. Each side's case, however, shifts in light of the other party's objections.

Finally, the way bargainers work together to shape issues also emerges from multiple agenda items. That is, each issue in a negotiation contains subissues or segments of the proposal. For instance, although the major issue in purchasing a car might be the price, other issues such as financing, trade-ins, and accessories are embedded in the buyer-seller exchange. These subissues may not be on the agenda when the price negotiation begins. However, as they surface in the bargaining, they influence how the issue becomes defined. Thus multiple agenda items and the splintering, merging, and dropping of issues influence the ways that problems are framed (Putnam & Geist, 1985).

In issue development, *reframing* refers to the transformation of a problem or the way each party develops a qualitatively different field of vision for understanding an agenda item. Drawing from work in organizational development, reframing is *unfreezing* past definitions of issues and reformulating new ones (Bartunek, 1984, 1988; Osiek, 1986). It represents more than a change in the nuance of understanding; reframing is the development of a novel or entirely different view, a *double-loop shift* in understanding a problem (Argyris & Schon, 1974). Reframing, then, corresponds to Follett's (1942) notion of revaluation or integrative solutions and to Pruitt's (1983) techniques of bridging and expanding the pie.

Reframing occurs through challenging the way a party conceives of an issue or through demonstrating that a current frame is ineffectual. A form of reframing that issue development addresses is promoting Janusian thinking or ways to conceive of two or more antithetical positions as simultaneously compatible (Rothenberg, 1979). The pro and con arguments in negotiation provide a forum for juxtaposing opposite positions and for creating multiple interpretations of issues. Negotiation, then, resembles the *dialectical inquiry process* used in reframing managerial decision making (Mason & Mitroff, 1981). In this technique, managers in group sessions generate novel solutions through debating the underlying assumptions on different conceptions of a problem.

Reframing also occurs through employing new metaphors or analogies to present a qualitatively different story about a problem (Schon, 1979). The captivating analogy that transformed traditional cold war frames in the Cuban missile crisis illustrates this type of reframing (Jonsson, 1990). Narratives conveyed during teachers' negotiations also show how bargainers reframe issues through shifting heroes and villains and altering the themes of stories linked to key agenda items (Putnam, Van Hoeven, & Bullis, 1991).

Role of Communication. Communication plays a primary role in the issue development approach. Social interaction is the critical instigator of changes in frames. These changes occur through argumentation, language use, and symbolic forms such as metaphors and stories. Frames or the ways negotiators conceive of problems are co-constructed through interaction as both parties adjust and react to each other's arguments. In effect, frames are not stable entities, rather they are processes that shape and are shaped by pro and con arguments, case making, and social meanings revealed through interaction.

Issue development as an approach to understanding frames in negotiation is limited, however, in its failure to incorporate framing prior to bargaining and in treating issues or problems as the lens to frames and to the social context. Bargainers do not enter negotiation as blank templates. The work on cognitive heuristics underscores the importance of frames that each side holds as they enter the process. Issue development draws from bargainer predispositions in analyzing initial arguments and the origin of issues (Putnam & Geist, 1985; Putnam et al., 1986); however, as a perspective on framing, issue development does not assess these predispositions directly.

Also, as the other perspectives on framing suggest, frames encompass negotiator relationships, stereotypes about bargaining as a social phenomena, and aspirations and goals that extend beyond the agenda. Issue development uses the bargaining agenda as a lens to other aspects of the conflict situation. Since this lens relies on the substantive discussion of issues, this approach is limited in what it can reveal about other aspects of negotiation. Moreover, the larger organizational and economic context enters into issue development through references to past practices. The framing of social situations, however, consists of multiple layers of frames tied to organizational life and to the social context of bargaining.

COMPARISON OF THE THREE APPROACHES

This review and critique indicates that all three perspectives, cognitive heuristics, frame categories, and issue development, offer promise but fail to provide a comprehensive and adequate representation of frames in negotiation. A comparison of the three approaches reveals different strengths and weaknesses. Moreover, the three approaches differ in their notions of what frames are, where they reside, how meanings relate to frames, what reframing is, and the role of frames in the negotiation process (see Figure 6.1).

In the cognitive heuristic perspective, frames are the conceptions of activities linked to choices. This definition differs from focusing on interpretive schemes (frame categories) and from examining the way problems become conceptualized (issue development). The three definitions are similar in that they focus on the way particular negotiation activities are conceptualized.

However, the major differences in the treatment of frames stem from their characteristics rather than their definitions. That is, framing is a stable or static feature in the cognitive perspective while the other two approaches treat it as dynamic. The dynamic element in the frame category approach is the shifting of the form, content, and abstraction of frames revealed through language. In the issue development perspective, however, framing is enacted in and revealed through argumentative discourse. Although all three approaches see frames as constructing negotiator experiences, the cognitive heuristic approach reifies this process by making frames into mental fixtures while the frame category approach reifies frame typologies into a priori categories.

In the cognitive heuristic approach, framing resides in the perceptual biases of negotiators, while the second approach locates frames in interpretive schemes housed in language and frame categories. In issue development, framing resides in each side's interpretation of the conflict as revealed through their talk. Meanings are in people in the first perspective, in the bargainers' levels of interpretation in the second approach, and in the bargaining interaction that constitutes definitions of the problem in the third perspective. The three approaches differ in their treatments of reframing with cognitive heuristics viewing it as feedback to correct biases, the frame category approach treating it as shifts in interpretations over time, and issue development viewing it as a qualitatively different definition of the problem. Each perspective links framing to strategies, outcomes, and conflict escalation. However, the cognitive heuristic approach treats frames as determinants of bargaining behaviors and outcomes while the other two perspectives view frames as explanatory devices for understanding how strategies and outcomes evolve.

All three perspectives refine the elusive concepts of bargaining expectations and predispositions; and all three present alternatives for understanding how each side makes sense of the bargaining situation. However, all three approaches share several key limitations including, namely, their omission of nonverbal communication, reflexivity of frames, and

Comparison of Three Approaches to Framing

	Cognitive Heuristics	Frame Categories	Issue Development
Definition	Perception of biases associated with choice	Categories and interpretive schemes	Conceptualization of a problem
Nature	Stable perceptual biases	Hierarchically arranged categories	Dynamic interaction processes
Location	Cognition	Superimposed and constitutive of discourse	Meanings that arise from discourse
Meanings	Reside in people	Frame categories, content, and levels of abstraction	Understandings of problems
Reframing	Correction of biases	Shifts in frame categories and meanings	Transformation of understandings
Role in Negotiation	To identify and overcome barriers to rationality	To develop identical frames	To further joint problem solving

Figure 6.1. Comparison of Three Approaches to Framing

the production and reproduction of frames in social context. Two theoretical approaches, used widely in communication but not in the bargaining literature, present options for addressing these weaknesses.

ALTERNATIVE MODELS
OF FRAMING AND REFRAMING

Two alternative models also treat frames as interpretive schemes. Both Bateson's (1972) theory of psychological frames and Goffman's (1974) model of frame analysis focus on interpretive schemes, but they differ in focus, scope, and breadth from the three approaches reviewed in this chapter. Unlike the cognitive heuristic perspective, frames do more than shape the biases in negotiator judgments and unlike the frame category approach, frames are not a priori typologies of interpretations. Unlike issue development, frames arise covertly through unstated rules, complex links between verbal and nonverbal behaviors, and messages that reflect back on the negotiation.

THEORY OF PSYCHOLOGICAL FRAMES

For Bateson (1972), frames are *classes or sets of messages* deemed as meaningful actions. These messages entail verbal statements, nonverbal expressions, and interpretations that contextualize relationships and situations. These messages perform *metacommunication* functions in that they provide implicit and explicit cues about how to interpret a frame. Metacommunication is communication about communication, or the way that language provides cues for interpreting both the content or substance of talk as well as the relationship between communicators (see Donohue & Ramesh, Chapter 9, this volume).

For example, the same words in a message can be said in different ways to evoke different meanings. If a negotiator says, "We've conceded all we can at this point. You need to compromise on this issue," the other negotiator must frame this message in a set of categories and react to this command. He or she can detect nonverbal cues, read the ambiguity in the words, observe the low-power language style, and conclude that the message is a bluff (see Gibbons, Bradac, & Busch, Chapter 7, this volume). However, he or she might observe a firm and rigid vocal pattern, stiff nonverbal cues, past negotiator behaviors, and the timing of the message and decide to avoid potential escalation by conceding.

Frames, then, are sets of messages that occur in a psychological context shaped by loops or patterns of metacommunication. They are fluid and reflect back upon the messages that constitute them. Frames are reflexive in that sets of messages are nested within cues that signal how to interpret messages and that reflect back upon ongoing interaction (Rawlins, 1987). Thus a posturing frame in negotiation calls for extreme offers, firm positions, and emotional outbursts as ways of signaling the opponent how to interpret these remarks. If the opponent interprets the message cues as posturing, these patterns reflect back on the posturing frame that constitutes meaning for this class of messages.

Frames are situated in social contexts through premises of communication, cues that signal the beginning and ending of events, and patterns of behavior. Both the learning process and the social context, however, are dynamic and are therefore revised through interpretations of ongoing interactions. In particular, bargaining is a type of social context in which ambiguous messages and evasive behaviors are enacted in complex ways. Negotiators learn how explicit statements, nonverbal cues, and the exchange of offers signal the other bargainer's interests, priorities, and needs. These signals change and may alter the frames of messages and the social context. Messages that explore options may alter the frame from posturing to problem solving and change the social context to collective decision making. Another set of messages, however, may alter the frame to win-lose competition and change the social context to conflict cycles.

Reframing, in Bateson's (1972) theory, centers on changes in framing. It is the process of learning new premises for communication and new cues for altering the social context. Reframing is adopting a qualitatively different frame or class of messages, similar to reframing in the issue development approach. The frame of competition or win-lose at the beginning of negotiation might be reframed through interpreting messages as posturing or play. Reframing might also occur if a negotiator conceives of a set of ambiguous messages as an attack or aggressive move rather than as ignorance or neutrality. As negotiators communicate about how to interpret their messages, they may change old habits and adopt qualitatively different frames or classes of messages for interacting.

MODEL OF FRAME ANALYSIS

For Goffman (1974), frames are definitions of the situation. They are similar to what Bateson (1972) calls the social context; but they relate to individual intentions, cultural and historical understandings, and natural forces. Frames, then, embody the past and present, including prior negotiations, work relationships, current aspirations, and substantive expectations. Goffman, like Bateson, centers on how frames are modified or transformed. In this way, both theories are similar to the frame categories and issue development approaches. However, Goffman argues against a categorical model of reframing in which small-scale shifts in understanding are identical to macro-level reframing.

Since many elements make up social situations, individuals render some of them as figure and others as ground. This figure-ground relationship forms the *primary framework* for a given situation. For example, in a teacher-school board negotiation, each team enters the situation with their own primary frameworks or sets of interests and aspirations that stem from their life situations. An issue like classroom size may become figure for the teachers framed within a backdrop of school policies, teacher-administrative relationships, student-teacher interaction, educational philosophy, and economic and demographic features of the school district. Negotiation juxtaposes alternative primary frameworks against one another. Reaching a settlement may require transforming these frameworks.

Reframing in Goffman's (1974) theory occurs through two processes: *keying* and *fabrication*. At the macro or social context level, keying brings into focus particular dimensions of everyday life, when past events are recreated in current interactions. Thus negotiating the issue of teacher evaluation in a union contract relives past teacher assessment experiences. Negotiators could key this issue in a number of ways, but both parties need a shared understanding of when and how negotiations will occur. Primary frameworks are rarely keyed in their entirety due to their complexity and inclusiveness. Rather keyed issues are *anchored* or rooted in everyday life. Anchoring indicates how an issue like teacher evaluation is rooted in larger struggles over autonomy and control. Thus negotiation brings key aspects into question in examining primary frameworks. Anchoring locates a keyed issue in background experiences and in deeper frames of meaning.

At the micro-level, interaction processes *channel* or shape the way keyed issues are perceived. At any point in time, multiple *tracks* of activity take place in negotiation. Each activity comprises a separate track. Thus tracks in negotiations may include the issue under immediate discussion, the anchoring of it in daily activities, communication within a team, secret signals and gestures, and complex interests of both sides.

Thus framing in bargaining is multidimensional. Each side strives to control framing, that is, to shape how issues are keyed and what dimensions are channeled for discussion. If neither is fully successful, interactions may reframe issues through separating or interlocking multiple tracks of activity. Splintering and logrolling are examples of channeling processes that modify and expand upon keyed issues.

Micro processes of interaction also impinge on primary frameworks through *embedding* or nesting frames within frames. Embedding examines the keying within each of the multiple tracks. For example, class size as an issue is embedded in a union track of work load and in an administrative track of cost accounting. Discussion of class size during negotiation may also key quality of education. The teachers might claim that larger class size jeopardizes quality of education and warrants additional compensation to maintain high standards. Hence, the expansion of class size shapes the work-load issue in which it is framed. Reframing may occur if the administration introduces quality of education into its cost-accounting track as a way of defining the class size situation. The dynamics and outcome of negotiations on class size could lead to redefining *work load,* which may ultimately transform the primary framework of working conditions.

Reframing also occurs through *fabrication.* Fabrication is similar to keying in that it recasts some dimensions of everyday life that are salient in primary frameworks. In keying, however, both parties are cognizant of how discussion of an issue defines a situation. Fabrication, in contrast, involves deceit. One team may define the situation deceitfully to shape the way the other side perceives it. For example, the school board may claim near bankruptcy, yet, in fact, possess reserves hidden in other accounts. The teachers may fabricate anger and stage a walkout to pressure the school board to move on issues. Both sides may fabricate allegiance to such issues as quality of education to veil deeper agenda items. The track of a fabricated issue forms an ostensive frame that is merely a prop for an unspoken but genuine track. Moreover, negotiators may enact a fabrication that is actually genuine. For instance, they may find it useful to pretend to bluff when, in fact, they are serious.

For Goffman (1974), then, framing is the way people define situations. Issues and activities that are rooted in past experiences, social relationships, and historical context are keyed for deliberation. Keyed issues, then, exist in multiple tracks of activity that are channeled or shaped through interaction. Embedding refers to how issues are keyed within specific tracks. Discussion of issues, in turn, may reflect back on and alter primary frameworks or the way individuals conceive figure-ground relationships.

Communication is a critical aspect of framing in both theories. For Bateson, communication is the essence of framing through sets of messages, metacommunication, and premises of interaction. For Goffman, communication shapes the way bargainers perceive keyed issues, invoke and integrate tracks of activity, and embed frames within frames. In both theories, interaction is central to reframing through keying and fabrication and through adopting different classes of messages and new habits of communication.

Thus Bateson (1972) reminds us that frames are dynamic, reflexive, and intertwined with implicit as well as explicit messages. Goffman (1974) orients framing to ways of defining the social situation. He centers on the multidimensional, multilayered nature of frames anchored in past experiences. Moreover, Goffman contributes the concept of *primary framework,* which links framing to a larger social context.[2]

Because both theories of framing are comprehensive and complex, it would be difficult to test or even apply them as complete theoretical perspectives. However, researchers could employ elements of each theory to improve on the shortcomings of the other approaches to framing in negotiations.

IMPROVING RESEARCH ON FRAMING IN NEGOTIATIONS

Each approach to the study of framing in negotiation has particular strengths and weaknesses. Concepts drawn from Bateson and Goffman provide ways of enriching these approaches without altering their theoretical roots. The study of framing in the cognitive heuristic perspective could be broadened by treating frames as dynamic processes. In fact, the need to study the dynamic quality of framing surfaces in Thompson and Hastie's (1990) findings. They report that judgment errors change within the first five minutes of bargaining and that these changes are strong predictors of negotiated outcomes. To test the dynamic nature of framing, researchers could employ time-series measures to detect variations in positive and negative frames at different intervals during the bargaining (Monge, Farace, Eisenberg, Miller, & White, 1984). Also, researchers could alter anchors or reference points to examine the effects of these changes on loss-gain frames and on bargaining concessions.

Manipulating messages and models of communication that extend beyond information processing could show how the types and characteristics of interaction enter into the framing process. For example, how do bargainers phrase messages that convey positive and negative frames? Are there differences in the characteristics of frame messages, such as language intensity, immediacy, or diversity? (see Gibbons et al., Chapter 7, this volume). Finally, researchers could employ verbal protocols and account analysis to test variations in bargainer expectations or confidence levels during the negotiation. In effect, treating framing as a dynamic process centers on how bargainers change expectations and preferences (Druckman, 1977; Gulliver, 1979).

Another way to broaden the scope of the cognitive heuristic perspective is to examine sources of biases in the primary frameworks of negotiators. By using verbal protocols or other interview techniques, researchers could ascertain how and why certain availability heuristics are present. They could seek out how these heuristics relate to societal views of bargaining, buyer- seller relationships, and organizational goals. Researchers could also employ scenarios to manipulate primary frameworks and to determine how different figure-ground arrangements might influence loss-gain frames, anchoring, or overconfidence. For example, does a loss-gain frame operate differently if the goal of pushing a certain product line becomes keyed and the goal of overall profit moves to the background?

The frame category approach does not adequately explain how subtle nuances of meaning recontextualize the larger issues in negotiation. Rather than applying a priori categories, Gray et al. (1990) could generate frame categories from the way interaction keys bargaining content and relationships. These categories, as Goffman suggests, could be contextually embedded rather than hierarchically imposed. Researchers could also generate frame categories inductively by asking bargainers about their expectations, aspirations, and interpretations of key issues (Pinkley, 1990).

Issue development treats framing as the way bargainers conceptualize problems or agenda items. Explicit messages about bargaining issues function as a lens to reveal relationships, constituent roles, and sources of agenda items. By centering on the framing of issues, this approach ignores metacommunication, implicit messages, and the larger social context of negotiation.

Incorporating Goffman's notion of primary frameworks and Bateson's work on metacommunication could enhance the contributions of issue development. Placing issues in primary frameworks shifts the focus of framing to experiences prior to the negotiation. Researchers could tie discourse to primary frameworks through illuminating various tracks of activities such as explicit discussion of issues, implicit references to intentions and motives, and intrateam communication. Insights gleaned from account analysis could reveal how, for example, intentions or constraints imposed by constituents function as tracks to regulate explicit issues. Researchers might employ discourse analysis to sort out the different tracks of activity in negotiation. Implicit references also function as metamessages that signal how to interpret explicit communication. Using Goffman's elements of framing makes it possible for bargainers to reframe without having a clear preconception of the problem. That is, Goffman's model allows for ambiguity and ambivalence to emerge as a viable frame for negotiation (Gulliver, 1979).

CONCLUSION

Although only a few negotiation texts include sections on framing, interpretive schemes, or meaning (Jonsson, 1990; Neale & Bazerman, 1991), the way disputants conceive of their situation directly influences bargaining processes and outcomes. Framing is not only the key to examining such constructs as preferences and orientations, it is also the lens for deciphering how past experiences, social context, and message reflexivity influence bargaining. Framing is also critical for understanding reframing or the way alternative definitions of a situation emerge from bargaining interaction. If we could explain how negotiators alter primary frameworks and reclassify messages, we could help bargainers learn from their situation, generate new metaphors for their experience, and produce novel solutions for reaching settlements.

Research on framing and reframing in negotiation is in its infancy. The three approaches reviewed in this chapter make inroads to the study of interpretive schemes in negotiation. Each approach, however, presents only a myopic view of this complex process. By integrating concepts from two alternative models of framing, each approach could broaden its scope, enrich its explanatory power, and find ways to merge micro and macro aspects of negotiation.

NOTES

1. In applying Tversky and Kahneman's (1981) prospect theory, Neale and Bazerman (1991) drop the role that certainty plays in mediating risk aversion and risk seeking be-

haviors. In its original formulation, prospect theory predicts that in situations of high certainty individuals will be "risk averse in choices involving *sure* gains and risk seeking in choices involving *sure* losses" (Tversky & Kahneman, 1981, p. 263; emphasis added).

In Neale and Bazerman's (1985) predictions the relationship between overconfidence and risk behaviors may not hold if certainty is incorporated into the links between positive framing and risk avoidance and between negative framing and risk seeking.

2. Bateson provides a microtheory of framing governed by the interpersonal dynamics of the situation while Goffman presents a macro-micro theory of frames centered on primary frameworks in social situations. Both Bateson and Goffman examine framing through sets of messages, the shaping of issues, and multiple embedded tracks of activity. Bateson's concepts of metacommunication and reflexivity of messages would subsume Goffman's notions of tracks of activity, channeling, and fabrication.

Reframing for both theorists represents adopting qualitatively different classes of messages or primary frameworks. Hence, both theorists view reframing as radical changes rather than minor modifications in defining the situation. Unlike Goffman, however, Bateson locates frames at the interpersonal level with messages linked to interpretive schemes. Goffman's theory, in contrast, centers upon macroframes or primary frameworks embodied in social, economic, and political processes. Thus a primary framework exists for labor-management relationships, for bargaining as an activity, and for organizational practices that aid in defining situations.

REFERENCES

Argyris, C., & Schon, D. A. (1974). *Theory in practice: Increasing professional effectiveness*. San Francisco: Jossey-Bass.

Bacharach, S. B., & Lawler, E. J. (1981). *Bargaining: Power, tactics, and outcomes*. San Francisco: Jossey-Bass.

Bartlett, F. C. (1932). *Remembering: A study in experimental and social psychology*. Cambridge, UK: Cambridge University Press.

Bartunek, J. M. (1984). Changing interpretive schemes and organizational restructuring: The example of a religious order. *Administrative Science Quarterly, 29*, 355-372.

Bartunek, J. M. (1988). The dynamics of personal and organizational reframing. In R. E. Quinn & K. S. Cameron (Eds.), *Paradox and transformation* (pp. 137-162). Cambridge, MA: Ballinger.

Bateson, G. (1972). *Steps to an ecology of mind*. New York: Ballantine.

Bazerman, M. H. (1983). A critical look at the rationality of negotiator judgment. *American Behavioral Scientist, 27*, 211-228.

Bazerman, M. H. (1984). The relevance of Kahneman and Tversky's prospect theory on organizational behavior. *Journal of Management, 10*, 333-343.

Bazerman, M. H., Magliozzi, T., & Neale, M. A. (1985). Integrative bargaining in a competitive market. *Organizational Behavior and Human Decision Processes, 35*, 294-313.

Bazerman, M. H., & Neale, M. A. (1982). Improving negotiation effectiveness under final offer arbitration: The role of selection and training. *Journal of Applied Psychology, 67*, 543-548.

Bazerman, M. H., & Neale, M. A. (1983). Heuristics in negotiation: Limitations to dispute resolution effectiveness. In M. H. Bazerman & R. J. Lewicki (Eds.), *Negotiating in organizations* (pp. 51-67). Beverly Hills, CA: Sage.

Bolman, L. G., & Deal, T. E. (1991). *Reframing organizations.* San Francisco: Jossey-Bass.

Bontempo, R. N. (1990, August). *Heuristics and negotiations: Effects of frame and agenda.* Paper presented at the annual meeting of the Academy of Management Association, San Francisco.

Carroll, J. S., & Payne, J. W. (1991). An information processing approach to two-party negotiations. In M. H. Bazerman, R. J. Lewicki, & B. H. Sheppard (Eds.), *Research on negotiation in organizations: Handbook of negotiation research* (Vol. 3, pp. 3-34). Greenwich, CT: JAI Press.

Comaroff, J. L., & Roberts, S. A. (1977). The invocation of norms in dispute settlement. In I. Hamnett (Ed.), *Social anthropology and law* (pp. 77- 112). New York: Academic Press.

De Dreu, C. K. W., Emans, B. J. M., & Van de Vliert, E. (1991, June). *Other's decision frame in negotiation behavior: An exploration of frame-exchange.* Paper presented at the annual conference of the International Association for Conflict Management, Den Dolder, The Netherlands.

Derber, M., Chalmers, W. E., & Edelman, M. T. (1965). *Plant union-management relations: From practice to theory.* Urbana: University of Illinois Press.

Derber, M., Chalmers, W. E., Stagner, R., & Edelman, M. (1961). Communication: Union-management relations research. *Industrial and Labor Relations Review, 14,* 446-453.

Donohue, W. A. (1991). *Communication, marital dispute, and divorce mediation.* Hillsdale, NJ: Lawrence Erlbaum.

Druckman, D. (1977). Social-psychological approaches to the study of negotiation. In D. Druckman (Ed.), *Negotiations: Social-psychological perspectives* (pp. 15-44). Beverly Hills, CA: Sage.

Eden, C., Jones, S., Sims, D., & Smithin, T. (1981). The intersubjectivity of issues and the issues of intersubjectivity. *Journal of Management Studies, 18,* 37-47.

Einhorn, H. J., & Hogarth, R. M. (1978). Confidence in judgment: Persistence illusion of validity. *Psychological Reports, 85,* 395-416.

Farber, H. S. (1981). Splitting-the-difference in interest arbitration. *Industrial and Labor Relations Review, 35,* 70-77.

Farber, H. S., & Bazerman, M. H. (1986). The general basis of arbitrator behavior: An empirical analysis of conventional and final offer arbitration. *Econometrica, 54,* 1503-1528.

Farber, H. S., & Katz, H. C. (1979). Interest arbitration, outcomes, and the incentive to bargain. *Industrial and Labor Relations Review, 33,* 55-63.

Felstiner, W. L. F., Abel, R. L., & Sarat, A. (1980-1981). The emergence and transformation of disputes: Naming, blaming, claiming. *Law and Society Review, 15,* 631-654.

Fillmore, C. J. (1975). An alternative to checklist theories of meaning. *Proceedings of the First Annual Meeting of the Berkeley Linguistics Society* (pp. 123-131). Berkeley, CA: Institute of Human Learning.

Fisher, R., & Ury, W. (1981). *Getting to yes: Negotiating agreement without giving in.* Boston: Houghton Mifflin.

Follett, M. P. (1942). Constructive conflict. In H. C. Metcalf & L. Urwick (Eds.), *Dynamic administration: The collected papers of Mary Parker Follett* (pp. 30-49). New York: Harper & Brothers.

Friedman, R. A., & Gal, S. (1990). *Managing around roles: Building groups in labor negotiations.* Unpublished manuscript. Harvard University, Graduate School of Business Administration.

Goffman, E. (1974). *Frame analysis: An essay on the organization of experience.* New York: Harper & Row.

Gray, B. (1991, June). *The framing of disputes: Patterns, processes, and outcomes in different contexts.* Paper presented at the annual conference of the International Association of Conflict Management, Den Dolder, The Netherlands.

Gray, B., & Donnellon, A. (1989). *An interactive theory of reframing in negotiation.* Unpublished manuscript. Pennsylvania State University, College of Business Administration.

Gray, B., Purdy, J. M., & Bouwen, R. (1990, June). *Comparing dispositional and interactional approaches to negotiating.* Paper presented to the annual conference of the International Association for Conflict Management, Vancouver, Canada.

Gulliver, P. H. (1979). *Disputes and negotiations: A cross-cultural perspective.* New York: Academic Press.

Hollingshead, A. B., & Carnevale, P. (1990). Positive affect and decision frame in integrative bargaining: A reversal of the frame effect. In L. R. Jauch & J. L. Wall (Eds.), *Best Paper Proceedings of the Fiftieth Annual Meeting of the Academy of Management Association* (pp. 385-389). San Francisco: Academy of Management.

Huber, V. L., & Neale, M. A. (1986). Effects of cognitive heuristics and goals on negotiator performance and subsequent goal setting. *Organizational Behavior and Human Decision Processes, 38,* 342-365.

Jandt, F. E. (1985). *Win-win negotiating: Turning conflict into agreement.* New York: John Wiley.

Jonsson, C. (1990). *Communication in international bargaining.* New York: St. Martin's.

Kahneman, D., & Tversky, A. (1979). Prospect theory: An analysis of decision under risk. *Econometrica, 47,* 263-291.

Lewicki, R. J., & Litterer, J. A. (1985). *Negotiation.* Homewood, IL: Irwin.

Mason, R. O., & Mitroff, I. I. (1981). *Challenging strategic planning assumptions.* New York: John Wiley.

Mather, L., & Yngvesson, B. (1980-1981). Language, audience, and the transformation of disputes. *Law and Society Review, 15,* 775-821.

McAlister, L., Bazerman, M. H., & Fader, P. (1986). Power and goal setting in channel negotiation. *Journal of Marketing Research, 23,* 228-237.

McLeod, J. M., Pan, Z., & Rucinski, D. M. (1989, May). *Framing a complex issue: A case of social construction of meaning.* Paper presented at the annual meeting of the International Communication Association, San Francisco.

Merry, S. E., & Silbey, S. (1984). What do plaintiffs want? Reexamining the concept of dispute. *Justice System Journal, 9,* 151-177.

Monge, P. R., Farace, R. V., Eisenberg, E. M., Miller, K. I., & White, L. L. (1984). The process of studying process in organizational communication. *Journal of Communication, 34,* 22-43.

Neale, M. A. (1984). The effect of negotiation and arbitration cost salience on bargainer behavior: The role of arbitrator and constituency in negotiator judgment. *Organizational Behavior and Human Performance, 34,* 97-111.

Neale, M. A., & Bazerman, M. H. (1983). The role of perspective-taking ability in negotiating under different forms of arbitration. *Industrial and Labor Relations Review, 36,* 378-388.

Neale, M. A., & Bazerman, M. H. (1985). The effects of framing and negotiator overconfidence on bargainer behavior. *Academy of Management Journal, 28,* 34-49.

Neale, M. A., & Bazerman, M. H. (1991). *Cognition and rationality in negotiation.* New York: Free Press.

Neale, M. A., Huber, V. L., & Northcraft, G. B. (1987). The framing of negotiations: Context versus task frames. *Organizational Behavior and Human Decision Processes, 39,* 228-241.

Neale, M. A., & Northcraft, G. B. (1986). Experts, amateurs, and refrigerators: Comparing expert and amateur decision making on a novel task. *Organizational Behavior and Human Decision Processes, 38,* 305-317.

Neale, M. A., & Northcraft, G. B. (1990). Experience, expertise, and decision bias in negotiation: The role of strategic conceptualization. In B. H. Sheppard, M. H. Bazerman, & R. J. Lewicki (Eds.), *Research on negotiation in organizations* (Vol. 2, pp. 55-75). Greenwich, CT: JAI Press.

Northcraft, G. B., & Neale, M. A. (1986). Opportunity costs and the framing of resource allocation decisions. *Organizational Behavior and Human Decision Processes, 37,* 348-356.

Osiek, C. (1986). *Beyond anger.* Boston: Paulist Press.

Pinkley, R. L. (1990). Dimensions of conflict frame: Disputant interpretations of conflict. *Journal of Applied Psychology, 75,* 117-126.

Pruitt, D. G. (1983). Integrative agreements: Nature and antecedents. In M. H. Bazerman & R. J. Lewicki (Eds.), *Negotiation in organizations* (pp. 35-50). Beverly Hills, CA: Sage.

Pruitt, D. G., & Rubin, J. Z. (1986). *Social conflict: Escalation, stalemate, and settlement.* New York: Random House.

Putnam, L. L. (1985). Bargaining as task and process: Multiple functions of interaction sequences. In R. L. Street & J. N. Cappella (Eds.), *Sequence and pattern in communicative behavior* (pp. 225-242). London: Edward Arnold.

Putnam, L. L. (1990). Reframing integrative and distributive bargaining: A process perspective. In B. H. Sheppard, M. H. Bazerman, & R. J. Lewicki (Eds.), *Research on negotiation in organizations* (Vol. 2, pp. 3-30). Greenwich, CT: JAI Press.

Putnam, L. L., & Geist, P. (1985). Argument in bargaining: An analysis of the reasoning process. *Southern Speech Communication Journal, 50,* 225-245.

Putnam, L. L., Van Hoeven, S. A., & Bullis, C. A. (1991). The role of rituals and fantasy themes in teachers' bargaining. *Western Journal of Speech Communication, 55,* 85-103.

Putnam, L. L., & Wilson, S. R. (1989). Argumentation and bargaining strategies as discriminators of integrative outcomes. In M. A. Rahim (Ed.), *Managing conflict: An interdisciplinary approach* (pp. 121-141). New York: Praeger.

Putnam, L. L., Wilson, S. R., & Turner, D. B. (1990). The evolution of policy arguments in teachers' bargaining. *Argumentation, 4,* 129-152.

Putnam, L. L., Wilson, S. R., Waltman, M. S., & Turner, D. (1986). The evolution of case arguments in teachers' bargaining. *Journal of the American Forensic Association, 23,* 63-81.

Raiffa, H. (1982). *The art and science of negotiation.* Cambridge, MA: Belknap.

Rawlins, W. K. (1987). Gregory Bateson and the composition of human communication. *Research on Language and Social Interaction, 20,* 53-77.

Rothenberg, A. (1979). *The emerging goddess.* Chicago: University of Chicago Press.

Rubin, J. Z., & Brown, B. R. (1975). *The social psychology of bargaining and negotiation.* New York: Academic Press.

Schon, D. A. (1979). Generative metaphor: A perspective on problem-setting in social policy. In A. Ortony (Ed.), *Metaphor and thought* (pp. 254-283). Cambridge, UK: Cambridge University Press.

Schurr, P. H. (1987). Effects of gain and loss decision frames on risky purchase negotiations. *Journal of Applied Psychology, 72,* 351-358.

Sheppard, B. H., Blumenfeld-Jones, K., & Roth, J. (1989). Informal thirdpartyship: Studies of everyday conflict intervention. In K. Kressel, Dean G. Pruitt, and Associates (Eds.), *Mediation Research* (pp. 166-189). San Francisco: Jossey-Bass.

Tannen, D. (1979). What's in a frame? Surface evidence for underlying expectations. In R. Freedle (Ed.), *New directions in discourse processes* (pp. 137-181). Norwood, NJ: Ablex.

Taylor, S. E., & Thompson, S. (1982). Stalking the elusive "vividness" effect. *Psychological Review, 89,* 155-181.

Thompson, L. L., & Hastie, R. M. (1990). Social perception in negotiation. *Organizational Behavior and Human Decision Processes, 47,* 98-123.

Tversky, A. (1972). Elimination-by-aspects: A theory of choice. *Psychological Review, 79,* 281-299.

Tversky, A., & Kahneman, D. (1973). Availability: A heuristic for judging frequency and probability. *Cognitive Psychology, 5,* 207-232.

Tversky, A., & Kahneman, D. (1974). Judgment under uncertainty: Heuristics and biases. *Science, 185,* 1124-1131.

Tversky, A., & Kahneman, D. (1981). The framing of decisions and the psychology of choice. *Science, 211,* 453-458.

Wilson, M. G., Northcraft, G. B., & Neale, M. A. (1989). Information competition and vividness effects in on-line judgments. *Organizational Behavior and Human Decision Processes, 44,* 132-139.

Chapter 7

THE ROLE OF LANGUAGE
IN NEGOTIATIONS:
THREATS AND PROMISES

Pamela Gibbons, James J. Bradac, and Jon D. Busch

IN EVERYDAY TALK, a person might say, "The truck negotiated the curve." This statement implies an interaction between the vehicle and the curve that allows the truck to remain road-bound as long as the driver is attentive and responsive. The interaction is purely nonverbal: driver vision and muscle movement interact with road contour and condition of the road. This phrase, however, is a metaphorical use of the term *negotiated*. It maps particular features of an essentially linguistic concept upon a nonverbal domain. That is, the curve communicates to the driver the proposition: "Be attentive and responsive and you can remain on the road."

Negotiation in a nonmetaphorical sense entails the communication of propositions between participants. Propositions are the relationships between agency and action that find expression in language. In this sense, negotiation is essentially linguistic. Negotiation represents the exchange of information through language that coordinates and manages meaning. In most cases, this process involves using language to evoke similar meanings between the speaker's intentions and the hearer's perceptions. As such, language is the primary mechanism through which bargaining is conducted; hence, it should become a central construct for negotiation research.

Our basic claim is that language has its own unique force in the negotiation process and that understanding the role of language is critical to a complete understanding of negotiation. In this chapter, *negotiation* is defined as a method of social decision making, one that is accomplished through persuasion and haggling (Druckman, 1977). Since persuasion entails the use of message tactics, this chapter also employs threats and promises as exemplars for understanding how language functions as speech acts and as linguistic and paralinguistic cues. In addition, this chapter addresses the issues of intentionality and control that underlie a linguistic focus on negotiation.

Negotiators use both linguistic and perceptual evidence to create and manage the negotiation context. Although some researchers are beginning to examine how language functions in everyday business negotiations (Graham, 1987), theory development lags behind in understanding the complex role that language plays in this process.

LANGUAGE IN NEGOTIATION:
A RESEARCH REVIEW

Although most social psychological research on bargaining centers on strategies and tactics, some recent studies examine the general role that language plays in negotiation in general and in strategies and tactics in particular. Work outside the field of communication typically emanates from a sociolinguistic perspective and uses a variety of discourse analytic methods. Cicourel (1988) advocates paying attention to the various cognitive, linguistic, and organizational contexts that shape language use in negotiations. He recommends an ethnographic approach in which understanding the speech community (for instance, management of XYZ company and labor union Local 155) and the specific speech event (for example, contract negotiations that occur every three years) can influence the participants' or the analyst's expectations about the language that is produced. Cicourel argues for studying the setting, participants, functions, and topics that influence language choices, in a way reminiscent of Ervin-Tripp's (1966) context-driven model of linguistic variation.

Francis (1986) provides an analysis of an ongoing, multiphased labor negotiation that uses conversational analysis. His approach demonstrates that conversational analysis, a method that is usually applied to a single segment of an informal conversation, might also apply to a formal planned negotiation that occurs over an extended time frame. As in most conversational analyses, the analyst selects certain segments of talk to highlight his or her points. Francis's analysis is particularly interesting in revealing the amount of interpersonal negotiation that goes on within the larger, formal, and structured labor negotiation process.

Neu (1988) uses the conversational analytic techniques developed by Sacks, Schlegloff, and Jefferson (1974) to uncover the structure of negotiations that take place in the laboratory. She codes transcripts of 22 structural (e.g., pauses, rate, and volume) and functional (e.g., requests for information, self-disclosure, and recommendations) linguistic and paralinguistic variables. Although her assignment of some variables to either structural or functional categories is problematic, a factor analysis reveals that certain language features are linked to particular negotiation processes. For example, requests for information, soft tone of voice, and acknowledgments facilitate bargaining interaction. Her work is important because it considers the effects of specific language variables on negotiation processes and outcomes.

In a different setting, Lauerbach (1989) uses speech act theory (Searle, 1969) and interaction rules (Goffman, 1967; Grice, 1975; Habermas, 1981) to analyze the public communication of President Reagan at a press conference on Nicaragua. This study has implications for negotiation because it focuses on issues of conflict and war in international relations. Lauerbach's painstaking effort shows how a close and detailed linguistic analysis reveals the ways in which communicators accomplish difficult and sometimes competing tasks. She uses specific speech act schemata to uncover how the conflicting demands for politeness, which often require vagueness and obscurity (Brown & Levinson, 1978), are integrated with the demands for clarity, which often sacrifice politeness (Grice, 1975). Lauerbach's work is particularly applicable to everyday negotiations that take place between partners in an ongoing relationship. These negotiations must achieve particular outcomes for one or both partners as well as preserve the partners' relationship—two goals that are not always compatible.

Other studies on language in negotiation center on cross-cultural differences in turn-taking, back-channeling, and initiative-response patterns of Spanish and Swedish business negotiations (Fant, 1989); in the use of disclaimers, positive and negative affect displays, and consensus markers in Danish and Spanish negotiations (Grindsted, 1989); and in speaker-hearer references, topic allocation, and conversational sequencing of Danish and Spanish negotiations (Grindsted, 1990a, 1990b). Cross-cultural negotiations provide a unique arena for comparing issues of power and social distance that shape the use of politeness strategies and face management (Villemoes, 1991; see Wilson, Chapter 8, this volume).

SPEECH ACTS, THREATS, AND PROMISES

To understand the role of language in negotiation, analysts need to explore the linguistic elements that comprise propositions. In the classic negotiation situation in which two parties (A and B) hold mutually relevant but competing goals (X and not X) and dissimilar reward and punishment potentials (Y and Z), language operates at two levels: proposals at the logical level and semantics, syntax, and phonetics (words and sounds that constitute style) at the pragmatic level. Each of these levels is explored in the negotiation context and then illustrated by focusing on threats and promises in bargaining. Threats and promises are selected as exemplars because of their significance as key coercive moves, their historical treatment as tactics rather than linguistic acts, and their centrality in understanding the linguistic features of other types of coercive strategies.

TWO LEVELS OF LANGUAGE IN NEGOTIATION

The mutual acknowledgment of goal incompatibility ("We have a difference here") is a linguistic act or set of acts invoked through interaction of agencies who hold opposing interests. The linguistic act takes the form of a proposal that combines two abstract concepts ("we" and "difference") and becomes a grammatical utterance. The first level of language in negotiation, then, is the proposal that functions logically in an agent-action relationship.

The second level or surface form moves from speech acts to smaller units of analysis: phonetics, semantics, and syntax. Phonetics entails the acoustical representation of syllables, words, and sentences while semantics focuses on word choice or the lexical nature of language. Syntax is sentence structure that joins semantics to form the high order elements in a language hierarchy. Phonetics linked to word choice and clauses via normative rules for language use. Hence, language is a rule-governed, hierarchical system in which concepts are linked to other concepts and represented phonetically (Bradac, Bowers, & Courtright, 1979).

This hierarchical system is unique in its capacity to formulate and convey propositions. Propositions are expressed in particular syntactic forms that often imply other proposals to recipients. For example, "It's cold in here" may imply "The window needs to be closed." People often imply more information in a proposition than their words suggest or than the surface forms of their utterances denote. Thus language has both logical and pragmatic levels that correspond to an utterance's proposal, its surface form, and the force of this form (Searle, 1969). The effect of an utterance upon a hearer is a complex function of language form, situational perception, cultural assumption, attributed understanding, and attributed intention (Bradac, Hopper, & Wiemann, 1989).

THREATS AND PROMISES IN NEGOTIATION

Beyond acknowledging differences, negotiators must deal with competing goals and indicate what will happen if proposals are not adopted. These needs might be codified in two forms, "if x, then y" or "if not x, then z." A familiar speech act that represents the first form is a promise ("If you work hard, I will give you a raise") while the second form is a threat ("If you do not work hard, I will fire you"). Bowers (1974) indicates that negotiators often use a hybrid form of these speech acts, one that is simultaneously a promise and a threat, a *thromise* (for example, "Stay with me and prosper; leave me and die"). Threats, promises, and thromises are quintessentially linguistic acts.

Generally speaking, three broad perspectives frame research on the role of threats and promises in negotiation. The first approach, adhering to a social psychological perspective, focuses on such factors as costs, rewards, and effectiveness of threats and promises (Tedeschi & Bonoma, 1977; Tedeschi, Bonoma, & Schlenker, 1972; Tedeschi, Gaes, & Rivera, 1977). Research questions from this tradition center on the "why, when, how and against whom coercive means will be employed" (Tedeschi, Gaes, & Rivera, 1977, p. 104). *Coercion* is defined as the exercise of power through the use of particular tactics that aim to reward or punish the opponent. Analysis of threats and promises in this tradition indicates that the use of coercive tactics is a measure of last resort (Tedeschi & Bonoma, 1977).

As a second perspective, Bacharach and Lawler (1981) examine the relative power that bargainers bring to and use in negotiation. Similar to the first approach, Bacharach and Lawler focus on the way facets of power affect the uses of and responses to tactics in bargaining situations. Deriving their hypotheses from power dependence theory, they report that negotiators rely on their own power rather than on their opponents' in selecting bargaining tactics.

The third perspective emanates from Deutsch's (1973) classical work on competition and coercion. In this approach, threats are treated as unattractive alternatives that are not as effective in obtaining joint profits as are other strategies. Although the sharing of open and honest information may be more socially acceptable than the use of coercion, the observation that threats occur in bargaining situations suggests their potential efficacy for resolving conflict. While these three perspectives appear diverse, all of them treat threats and promises as strategic constructs linked to negotiated outcomes. These perspectives then emphasize what types of threats are used and what effects these types have on the bargaining outcome. The strategic level of analysis, however, explains very little about the way language distinguishes among coercive strategies, the linguistic dimensions of threats, and the role of intentionality and control in using threats and promises in negotiations.

Language and Related Coercive Strategies. At the proposal level, threats typically link a specific request with a proposed punishment whereas promises tie a request to a conditional reward (Putnam & Jones, 1982b). Threats and promises may be explicit or implied. Implied threats and promises often omit the conditional punishment or reward, respectively. Another form of implication is the expression of a promise that implies a threat or vice versa (e.g., "Work hard and succeed" implies "Slack off and fail"). Threatening through implication conveys a desired action while allowing negotiators to save face and to avoid potential damage to a relationship (Bowers, 1974; Brown & Levinson, 1978). Implied threats and promises also enable bargainers to remain flexible and to avoid premature commitment to an explicitly codified position. They are particularly effective when negotiators have considerable common ground or mutual knowledge of each other's positions (Bowers, 1974).

A critical aspect that distinguishes threats and promises from other coercive strategies is intentionality. This chapter treats intentions as a particular kind of belief (e.g., "I believe that I will perform this particular action"). A *lie* is an utterance that the speaker intends to convey to the listener ("speaker believes W") when in fact the speaker believes the opposite ("speaker actually believes not W") (Bradac, Friedman, & Giles, 1986). In a negotiation, bluffing is an example of a lie. Bluffing occurs when negotiator A wants negotiator B to believe that A has the capacity to implement a threat when, in fact, this capacity does not exist and A knows it. A bluff can become a devious message when its phonetic or pragmatic form makes the speaker unaccountable for the hearer's belief that the threat was genuine when indeed it was not (Bowers, Elliot, & Desmond, 1977). The devious bluffer, for instance, may produce a logically ambiguous utterance in which the speaker presents both "W" and "not W" as plausible and credible propositions. The bluffer believes that some feature of the hearer's context, for instance, cognitive tendencies or past bargaining, favor the "W" inference and "W" is the inference that the bluffer wants the listener to believe.

Evasion, another coercive strategy, is important in situations of goal incompatibility. An *evasion* is an utterance that maintains or even increases the hearer's uncertainty about the speaker's intentions and specifically about his or her willingness to follow through on a threat or a promise. The speaker produces an utterance that influences the hearer not to form a belief about whether the speaker intends "W" or "not W." When a negotiator lacks resources to support a threat or does not want to lie, he or she may use evasion to forestall the opponent's actions and to maintain uncertainty. Thus bargainers use language to evade as well as to confront their negotiation-relevant intentions.

Variations in coercive strategies also take place at the level of syntax or the sentence structure of a threat. This structure contributes to the effectiveness of threats and promises. For example, Donohue and Diez (1985) and Jordan and Roloff (1990) report that requests that use a question-imperative form ("Could you restate your position?") obligate the opponent to respond and produce more verbal compliance than do demands, imperative requests, need statements, or resource inquiries. The question-imperative syntax leads to a sequence of questions and answers that facilitates verbal responsiveness, especially when the negotiators know each other and the procedures are flexible. Relatedly, Murdock, Bradac, and Bowers (1984) report that explicit threats, promises, and thromises that contain outcome statements encoded in a null form ("If you perform normally, I won't penalize you") are less likely to produce compliance than parallel threats in which the preferred outcomes are coded positively ("If you don't perform normally, I will penalize you").

Linguistic Dimensions of Threats. A closer examination of the surface level of language indicates two purposes that phonetics, semantics (lexicon), and syntax perform. These purposes are embodied in language use through five dimensions: polarization, immediacy, intensity, lexical diversity, and high-power language style. First, surface forms of language reveal to the hearer information about the speaker's feelings or evaluations of topics or issues (affect revelation). Second, surface forms of language provide inferences about the speaker's traits and abilities (impression formation). Negotiator A's language style will influence negotiator B's judgments about A's intellectual competence, power, status, group affiliation, and social attractiveness. Thus a bargainer's verbal proposition, often expressed in an implicit form, carries a certain force in the negotiation process. Semantic and syntactical choices reveal a bargainer's feelings about these propositions and the inferences derived from propositions and language style affects B's reactions to A's threats and promises.

The first language dimension, *polarized language,* surfaces when a bargainer uses a positive lexicon to depict his or her own position and a negative one to characterize the opponent's stance. Polarized language is an explicit way in which speakers reveal their feelings. This type of semantics or word choice typify threats made in the heat of the moment that employ extreme evaluative terms (for instance, "Look, we're the *good* guys here. If you *jerks* can't come up with a *measly* $.25 an hour raise, you won't see us back on the job for *100 years!*"). Since a bargainer's use of polarized language reinforces his or her existing attitudes (Eisner & Pancer, 1979), the more negotiators rely on this dimension, the more difficult it is to move away from rigid positions and to move toward agreement.

More subtly, bargainers disclose their positive and negative feelings through the second dimension of language, *high and low immediacy* (Mehrabian, 1967; Weiner & Mehrabian, 1968). *Verbal immediacy* is language use that reflects a bargainer's desire to move close to a person who is positively evaluated or to move away from an individual who is disliked (see Donohue & Ramesh, Chapter 9, this volume). High immediacy language embraces its referents while low immediacy language is indirect, avoiding, or noncommittal. Immediacy indicators typically assume one of five forms: (1) spatio-temporal markers that indicate displacement across time and space; the more displacement, the less immediate (for example, "*There* is the proposal" rather than "*Here* is the proposal"); (2) denotative specificity that shows the less specific, the less immediate (for instance, "I work because I need the money" versus "One works because one needs the money"); (3) selective emphasis markers that refer to the order of items in an utterance; first order is more immediate than subsequent order (for example, "The wage changes and the increased benefits" versus "The increased benefits and the wage changes"); (4) agent-action-object markers that indicate the degree a speaker associates with the referent (e.g., "We *want* to reach an agreement" versus "We *should* reach an agreement"); and (5) modification indicators that signal a speaker's uncertainty (for example, "You're wrong" versus "You're wrong, I think").

The use of high or low immediacy is an unconscious process in which a speaker's affective states influence his or her lexical and syntactic choices. By using "there" and "he and I" rather than "here" and "we," respectively, a negotiator decreases immediacy and lowers positive affect with his or her opponent (Mehrabian, 1967). Negotiation, however, is a complex arena in which immediacy may function paradoxically. That is, research reveals that high verbal immediacy and direct communication may increase the psychological distance between partners and lower positive affect (Donohue, Weider-Hatfield, Hamilton, & Diez, 1985; Donohue, Ramesh, & Borchgrevink, 1991). Yet, immediacy may be a more informative aspect of language than is a bargainer's expressed position, especially when a negotiator is trying to keep his or her ultimate goal hidden. Bargainers may be less likely to carry out threats and promises that are expressed in low rather than high immediacy language.

A third language dimension that reveals speaker affect is *language intensity*. Intensity refers to the strength of affect while immediacy signals its positive or negative direction. A negotiator may have a positive attitude toward a position and this attitude may be strong or weak, depending on his or her level of commitment. Thus, high intensity language indicates a strong feeling whereas language low in intensity signals a weak affect. For example, the statement, "Your plan is an outstanding one" is more intense than "Your plan is a good one." High language intensity may also consist of repeated uses of profanity, sex, and death metaphors (Bowers, 1963). In divorce mediation, couples who reach impasse increase their use of intense language (Donohue, 1991; see also Donohue & Ramesh, Chapter 9, this volume). Similarly, bargainers in hostage negotiations use intense language to issue their demands and to make the situation confrontive (Rogan & Donohue, 1991). Language intensity seems particularly salient for conveying the credibility of a threat or promise and for assessing the intentionality of threats in negotiations. Since language intensity is codified culturally, bargainers from a similar culture should have the same descriptors of what constitutes high and low intensity, especially when situational context is known and understood.

The fourth dimension, verbal fluency, or technically, *lexical diversity*, also conveys a speaker's attitudes. Lexical diversity refers to the range and richness of the vocabulary that a speaker uses. Researchers measure it by calculating a ratio of the number of novel words used in an utterance with the total number of words uttered. Speakers who display high levels of lexical diversity are generally rated as more competent, more effective, and less anxious than are those who demonstrate low levels of diversity (Bradac et al., 1979). Low levels of diversity are linked to anxiety (Howeler, 1972) and may occur when a speaker stutters or repeats him- or herself, especially when this stuttering deviates from a speaker's normal patterns.

In a negotiation, however, repetition of a bargainer's position produces low language diversity but may communicate firm commitment or toughness rather than anxiety. In a threat situation, high language diversity may enhance a bargainer's credibility. Also, researchers can draw inferences about a negotiator's response to a threat by evaluating the lexical diversity of his or her subsequent speech. Negotiators may view a decrease in lexical diversity as a positive sign if it matches the diversity level of the partner (Bradac, Mulac, & House, 1988). These changes in diversity levels may provide clues for assessing how lexical diversity functions in bargaining.

The fifth and final dimension of language that influences a bargainer's attitudes is *high-power language style.* High-power language is the reverse of a low-power style that is characterized by the use of hedges ("It's *sort of* an important issue"), hesitations ("er," "um"), tag questions ("It's a good price, isn't it?"), polite forms ("Yes, ma'am"), and intensifiers ("It's an *extremely* good deal"). Speakers with high social status in legal settings typically employ a high-power linguistic style (O'Barr, 1982). Consequently, language style may indicate which negotiator has greater interpersonal power or more social resources than his or her opponent. This strength in a threat situation may enhance credibility and reinforce that a bargainer intends to adhere to his or her commitment. In this case, high-power language may also indicate certainty as well as create an impression of strength (Berger & Bradac, 1982).

For example, imagine the efficacy of a threat expressed in the following manner: "Look, sir, if . . . um . . . you don't really meet our demands, we'll have to sort of, you know, not really show up for work next week" versus "If you don't meet our demands, we won't show up for work next week." The first statement, which employs a low-power style, infers that the bargainer is uncertain about his or her commitment to the threatened course of action. It creates the impression that he or she is ineffectual in carrying out the threat or that his or her constituents do not support this position. The second statement, however, if supported with the warrants accorded to an official negotiator, implies certainty and firm commitment.

In some instances, however, a low-power style may serve a negotiator's purpose, particularly if he or she wants to lack decision control. Bargainers may desire a position of "limited authority" to forestall premature commitment to a proposal (Karrass, 1970; Kennedy, 1987). Negotiators may rely on a low- power style to reduce or to minimize the strength of their own positions. Moreover, when the goal is persuasion rather than coercion, strong arguments that are directly relevant to an issue may play a more critical role in the negotiation than does language style (Gibbons, Busch, & Bradac, in press).

The tactics of "limited authority" and "my hands are tied" suggest that bargaining entails teams and constituent groups who monitor a negotiator's actions (see Turner, Chapter 10, this volume). Groups in conflict also develop characteristic styles of interacting that influence a negotiator's high- or low-power styles.

The Linguistic Category Model is a relatively new tool for analyzing subtle changes in the way in-groups and out-groups describe their own and the other group's behaviors (Fiedler & Semin, 1988; Semin & Fiedler, 1988). The model consists of four categories: (1) descriptive action verbs such as *walk, hit, lift,* and *tell* that index behavioral acts, (2) interpretive action verbs such as *help, hurt,* and *intimidate* that contain an evaluative component and describe a class of behaviors; (3) state verbs such as *hate, love, admire,* and *envy* that depict affective or mental states; and (4) adjectives such as *honest, reliable,* and *intelligent* that reveal an individual's dispositions. These four semantic areas increase in level of abstraction from the first to the last category. Research with this model reveals that in-group members use abstract terms to describe prosocial behaviors of other in-group members and antisocial behaviors of out-group members. Conversely, members use specific verbs from the first two categories to describe their own antisocial behaviors and the out-group's prosocial behaviors (Hamilton, Gibbons, Stroessner, & Sherman, in press; Maass, Salvi, Arcuri, & Semin, 1989).

Since language differences reinforce positive stereotypes of the in-group and negative images of the out-group, this model could be useful in analyzing the degree to which groups are polarized and attitudes and beliefs are entrenched. Threats and promises as coercive or antisocial behaviors may emanate from deep-seated group attitudes rather than from a bargainer's choice (Ancona, Friedman, & Kolb, 1991). Researchers might predict the onset of coercive behavior by examining the abstractness patterns in in-group and out-group interactions. Also, by analyzing level of abstractness in a negotiation, researchers might uncover positive or negative attitudes that are expressed indirectly because of group norms and that may hinder goal agreement.

INTENTIONALITY AND CONTROL IN USING THREATS

This overview of the types and the linguistic dimensions of threats and promises raises several critical issues on the intentionality of communicative behaviors, a speaker's awareness of language use, and the degree that bargainers can control their language styles. Intentionality and speech acts are intertwined in four ways: (1) they both distinguish between propositional statements and the force of these acts; (2) they both must convey the appropriate direction of fit (for example, assertions must match the current state of affairs but directives cannot match since they are designed to bring about change); (3) with the exception of lying, the expression of a proposition also conveys an intention; and (4) the conditions that satisfy a speech act also satisfy intentional states (Searle, 1983).

Although propositional statements and intentionality are strongly linked, speakers may regret utterances and be unaware of the consequences of their actions. A negotiator who is caught up in the heat of the moment may make promises or threats that he or she regrets later or even moments after uttering them. No doubt, conflicting intentions can result in misspoken threats and promises. For example, a bargainer may issue a promise so that negotiations might reach a mutual settlement and later decide that the promise incurs too high a price. Similarly, the desire to gain a concession through issuing a threat may conflict with the intention to preserve a bargaining relationship. Thus, conflicting intentions or minimal intentionality exists and may account for regrets and shifts in a speaker's initial positions.

The use of threats and promises may also evoke different levels of consciousness of actions. Most bargainers are fully aware of uttering a threat and of the intentions expressed in the threat. However, negotiators may not be aware of their motivations for producing threats and of the consequences of issuing them. Moreover, individuals may function with certain heuristics that invoke threats and promises without conscious regard. For example, when threatened by the opponent, a bargainer may automatically and mindlessly reciprocate with a similar threat. Regardless of how mindful a negotiator is of using a threat or of its motivation and consequences, the recipient typically perceives a threat as fully intended and made in complete awareness. However, negotiation history or past relationships might make an opponent suspicious of promise givers and threat makers.

Knowing that bargainers can regret making a threat, even as it is uttered, raises questions about the control of language. Although research and folklore purport that language is the cue over which we exert the most control, conflicting intentions may make full control problematic. Comparisons of verbal and nonverbal messages and studies on detection of lying claim that nonverbal cues reveal the "true" intentions better than do verbal cues (deTurck & Miller, 1990, discuss this claim). In contrast, studies of messages that produce a sense of regret in speakers indicate that in 77% of the cases, speakers immediately realize that they spoke regrettable messages (Knapp, Stafford, & Daly, 1986). The reason that individuals regret a prior utterance is because it hurt someone's feelings. In negotiation, regret may also stem from issuing costly threats and promises that ultimately damage a bargainer's own interests. These findings raise additional questions about the link between intentionality and speech acts and imply that negotiators can lose control of their language patterns.

Issues of intentionality, awareness, and control also apply to language style. For example, a negotiator may use high-power language to give the impression of having control over resources, being the decision maker, and being willing to respond to reason. Yet, the strategy of creating impressions through language works only if a speaker can control his or her style. Can a bargainer who typically uses a low-power style and low lexical diversity change the way he or she speaks? Research in the areas of communication accommodation, language diversity, and self-awareness in information processing offer different responses to this query. Communication Accommodation Theory (Giles, Mulac, Bradac, & Johnson, 1987) posits that communicators adopt a speech style that converges to or diverges from their partner's style. Thus, speakers can control specific dimensions of their language beyond the content of their messages. A convergent move toward similarity of style often indicates a desire for association while a divergent move reflects a desire for differentiation from the partner. Since speakers can adapt to their partners, they can also change their styles to provide their opponents with specific impressions.

Research on language diversity, however, suggests that a speaker's control of his or her linguistic style is minimal. For example, when speakers want to produce high diversity messages such as in an interview situation, the stress level of this situation often leads to the opposite behavior (Howeler, 1972). Other researchers contend that linguistic immediacy is by definition an unconscious indicator of attitudes toward a person or an issue (Wiener & Mehrabian, 1968). In effect, these arenas suggest that speakers have minimal control over their language styles. The literature on information processing and self-awareness supports this claim by noting that individuals are not generally aware of their own or their partner's linguistic behaviors (Carver & Scheier, 1981; Kitayama & Burnstein, 1988; Snyder, 1974). Other studies indicate that naive listeners may be aware of differences in language immediacy, intensity, diversity, polarization, and power of style, but they cannot list specific language features that comprise these dimensions (Gibbons et al., in press). Research on gender differences in language also suggests that although recipients evaluate speakers differently, listeners cannot specify how they do it or even whether males or females produce the messages (Mulac, Incontro, & James, 1985).

Thus the evidence is inconclusive as to whether speech acts and speech style occur without intention or beyond an individual's awareness and control. The critical factor for negotiation is what the circumstances are in which bargainers vary their language patterns to accomplish their goals and to determine factors that might hinder goal achievement. The context and the bargaining relationship may significantly influence perceptions of intentionality and control. For instance, threats within the context of a long-term relationship may function differently than they do in a buyer-seller situation with relative strangers. Thus, information on why a bargainer makes a threat or a promise and whether he or she can uphold it depends on the bargaining relationship and the negotiation situation.

Context and relationship also influence linguistic variation. For example, low-power language may evoke responses of confidence and control in informal negotiations between close friends because the situation fits the use of hesitations for self-disclosure, tag questions to include the other person, and intensifiers to convey commitment. In such a setting, the close friend may view low lexical diversity as a positive rather than a negative feature of language. Relationship may also be a factor in determining change and the effects of change in language style.

FUTURE RESEARCH ON LANGUAGE IN NEGOTIATION

This chapter examines language use in negotiations. Specifically, it centers on the role of speech acts and stylistic variation in threats and promises. By exploring levels of language, linguistic features of different types of threats, and the language dimensions of threats and promises, this chapter demonstrates that coercive tactics should be studied as speech acts characterized by immediacy, intensity, diversity, polarization, and power of style. Moreover, issues of intentionality and control govern the link between speech acts and the meanings of threats and promises. The negotiation context and bargaining relationship play important roles in determining what a threat means, the motivation behind it, a bargainer's awareness of issuing it, and the potential consequences of this utterance for subsequent interaction.

Additional research is needed to examine many of the issues raised in this chapter. More importantly, this work needs to move beyond the well-established effects of language on impression formation (Bradac, 1990) and concentrate on the influence of language on negotiation processes and outcomes. The coding schemes that communication scholars have developed aid in understanding the effects of messages on negotiation processes, particularly at the level of speech acts. For example, Putnam and Jones (1982a, 1982b) employ a modified version of the Bargaining Process Analysis (BPA) to examine the reciprocity of such speech acts as threats, promises, acceptances, accommodations, clarifications, requests for information, and affect expressions. Another coding system used in formal negotiation, Donohue's (1981a, 1981b) Cue-Response Negotiation Coding System (CNCS) includes such speech acts as offers, self-support messages, concession making, disconfirming, and initiating. Also, Hinkle, Stiles, and Taylor (1988) provide a general framework for coding different types of negotiation in their Verbal Response Mode (VRM). This taxonomy features such categories as edifications, disclosures, confirmations, questions, and interpretations. Other coding systems exist with slightly different purposes and categories. Although researchers can employ these systems to study many types of negotiations, their proliferation makes cross-study comparisons difficult. Other methods such as discourse analysis yield rich, detailed descriptions of language behavior in negotiations, but these studies encounter problems in generalization.

Overall, researchers have given little consideration to the effects of language on negotiation processes and outcomes. In particular, future investigations need to take a microscopic look at the impact of phonological, semantic, and syntactic variation on formal and informal bargaining. Neu (1988) begins this process with a system that includes speech acts and language variables, especially filled pauses, volume, speech rate, and hedges. Moreover, since she aims to understand the effects of linguistic structure on bargaining, Neu's study shows how certain language variables relate to negotiated outcomes. The variables that she selects in combination with the language dimensions discussed in this chapter could be used to address the following questions: What language features characterize threats and promises? Why are some threats or promises perceived as more credible than are others, especially when both parties have equal reward-punishment power? Can negotiators manipulate their language patterns to achieve their goals and to manage impressions of their behaviors? How does language convey commitment to a proposal, the likelihood of a settlement, or a change in a bargainer's position? What role does linguistic variation play in formal versus informal negotiations?

CONCLUSION

The five sentences that follow illustrate how language alters the nature of a threat: "Cook dinner or suffer my wrath." "Cook dinner, please or like I'll get mad." "If you cook dinner, I will wash the car." "If you don't cook dinner, I won't wash the car." "If like you . . . well . . . cook dinner, you know . . . I will kind of wash the car." These sentences illustrate that the way a speaker gives a threat or a promise extends beyond content features such as specificity, negative and positive wording, and inclusion of an explicit ultimatum. Bargainers issue threats and promises with a particular language style, using words that signal verbal immediacy and language intensity. Other stylistic features such as lexical diversity and polarized language also influence the context in which bargainers interact. This context impinges on both the expression and the interpretation of threats, promises, and other speech acts in bargaining.

The use of particular speech acts and their language dimensions has consequences for impression formation, mutual affect revelation, judgments of satisfaction, and perceptions of victory or defeat. These consequences are shaped by mutual knowledge, in-group versus out-group status, and the bargaining relationship.

Finally, most of the studies cited in this chapter deal primarily with negotiation or with language research. Very few of them center on the intersection of language research with the use of threats and promises in bargaining. Investigators need to focus their studies on the merger of these research domains. An especially fruitful avenue would be investigations aimed at teasing out the tangled connections among negotiation, intentionality, awareness, and language performance. Research on language use in negotiation has the potential to yield high rewards for theorists as well as for negotiation practitioners who function in the crucible of everyday life.

REFERENCES

Ancona, D. G., Friedman, R. A., & Kolb, D. M. (1991). The group and what happens on the way to "yes." *Negotiation Journal, 7*, 155-173.

Bacharach, S. B., & Lawler, E. J. (1981). Power and tactics in bargaining. *Industrial and Labor Review, 34*, 219-233.

Berger, C. R., & Bradac, J. J. (1982). *Language and social knowledge: Uncertainty in interpersonal relations.* London: Edward Arnold.

Bowers, J. W. (1963). Language intensity, social introversion, and attitude change. *Speech Monographs, 30*, 345-352.

Bowers, J. W. (1974). Guest editor's introduction: Beyond threats and promises. *Speech Monographs, 41*, ix-xi.

Bowers, J. W., Elliot, N., & Desmond, R. (1977). Exploiting pragmatic rules: Devious messages. *Human Communication Research, 3*, 235-242.

Bradac, J. J. (1990). Language attitudes and impression formation. In H. Giles & W. P. Robinson (Eds.), *Handbook of language and social psychology* (pp. 387-412). New York: John Wiley.

Bradac, J. J., Bowers, J. W., & Courtright, J. A. (1979). Three language variables in communication research: Intensity, immediacy, and diversity. *Human Communication Research, 5*, 257-269.

Bradac, J. J., Friedman, E., & Giles, H. (1986). A social approach to propositional communication: Speakers lie to hearers. In G. McGregor (Ed.), *Language for hearers* (pp. 127-152). Oxford: Pergamon.

Bradac, J. J., Hopper, R., & Wiemann, J. M. (1989). Message effects: Retrospect and prospect. In J. J. Bradac (Ed.), *Message effects in communication science* (pp. 294-317). Newbury Park, CA: Sage.

Bradac, J. J., Mulac, A., & House, A. (1988). Lexical diversity level and magnitude of convergent versus divergent style shifting: Perceptual and evaluative consequences. *Language and Communication, 8*, 213-228.

Brown, P., & Levinson, S. (1978). Universals in language usage: Politeness phenomena. In E. N. Goody (Ed.), *Questions and politeness: Strategies in social interaction* (pp. 56-289). Cambridge, UK: Cambridge University Press.

Carver, C. S., & Scheier, M. F. (1981). *Attention and self-regulation: A control-theory approach to human behavior.* New York: Springer.

Cicourel, A. V. (1988). Text and context: Cognitive, linguistic, and organizational dimensions in international negotiations. *Negotiation Journal, 4,* 257-266.

deTurck, M. A., & Miller, G. R. (1990). Training observers to detect deception: Effects of self-monitoring and rehearsal. *Human Communication Research, 16,* 603-620.

Deutsch, M. (1973). *The resolution of conflict.* New Haven, CT: Yale University Press.

Donohue, W. A. (1981a). Analyzing negotiation tactics: Development of a negotiation interact system. *Human Communication Research, 7,* 273-287.

Donohue, W. A. (1981b). Development of a model of rule use in negotiation interaction. *Communication Monographs, 48,* 106-120.

Donohue, W. A. (1991). *Communication, marital dispute and divorce mediation.* Hillsdale, NJ: Lawrence Erlbaum.

Donohue, W. A., & Diez, M. E. (1985). Directive use in negotiation interaction. *Communication Monographs, 48,* 106-120.

Donohue, W. A., Ramesh, C., & Borchgrevink, C. (1991). Crisis bargaining: Tracking relational paradox in hostage negotiation. *The International Journal of Conflict Management, 2,* 257-273.

Donohue, W. A., Weider-Hatfield, D., Hamilton, M., & Diez, M.E. (1985). Relational distance in managing conflict. *Human Communication Research, 11,* 387-406.

Druckman, D. (1977). Social-psychological approaches to the study of negotiation. In D. Druckman (Ed.), *Negotiation: Social-psychological perspectives* (pp. 15-44). Beverly Hills, CA: Sage.

Eisner, J. R., & Pancer, S. M. (1979). Attitudinal effects of the evaluatively biased language. *European Journal of Social Psychology, 9,* 39-47.

Ervin-Tripp, S. M. (1969). Sociolinguistics. In L. Berkowitz (Ed.), *Advances in experimental social psychology* (Vol. 4, pp. 91-165). New York: Academic Press.

Fant, L. (1989). Cultural mismatch in conversation: Spanish and Scandinavian communicative behaviour in negotiation settings. *Hermes, Journal of Linguistics, 3,* 247-265.

Fiedler, K., & Semin, G. R. (1988). On the causal information conveyed by different interpersonal verbs: The role of implicit sentence context. *Social Cognition, 6,* 21-39.

Francis, D. W. (1986). Some structures of negotiation talk. *Language in Society, 15,* 53-79.

Gibbons, P. A., Busch, J., & Bradac, J. J. (in press). Power of style in persuasion and impression formation: A cognitive response analysis. *Journal of Language and Social Psychology.*

Giles, H., Mulac, A., Bradac, J. J., & Johnson, P. (1987). Speech accommodation theory: The first decade and beyond. In M. McLaughlin (Ed.), *Communication yearbook 10* (pp. 13-48). Newbury Park, CA: Sage.

Goffman, E. (1967). *Interaction ritual: Essays on face-to-face behavior.* Garden City, NY: Doubleday.

Graham, J. D. (1987). A theory of interorganizational negotiations. In J. N. Sheth (Ed.), *Research in marketing: A research annual* (pp. 163-183). Greenwich, CT: JAI Press.

Grice, H. P. (1975). Logic and conversation. In P. Cole, & J. Morgan (Eds.), *Syntax and semantics* (Vol. 3, pp. 41-58). New York: Academic Press.

Grindsted, A. (1989). Distributive communicative behaviour in Danish and Spanish negotiation interaction. *Hermes, Journal of Linguistics, 3,* 267-279.

Grindsted, A. (1990a). *How conversation is organized in Spanish and Danish negotiation interaction* (Merino, 7). Odense, Denmark: Odense University, Institute for Commercial Languages.

Grindsted, A. (1990b). *Polyadic sequencing patterns in Spanish and Danish negotiation and their implications for the interrelationship between the negotiators* (Merino, 5). Odense, Denmark: Odense University, Institute for Commercial Languages.

Habermas, J. (1981). *Theorie des kommunikativen Handelns* (Vols. 1-2). Frankfurt am Main: Suhrkamp.

Hamilton, D. L., Gibbons, P. A., Stroessner, S., & Sherman, J. (in press). Stereotypes and language use. In G. R. Semin & K. Fiedler (Eds.), *Language and social cognition.* Newbury Park, CA: Sage.

Hinkle, S., Stiles, W. B., & Taylor, L. A. (1988). Verbal processes in a labour/management negotiation. *Journal of Language and Social Psychology, 7,* 123-136.

Howeler, M. (1972). Diversity of word usage as a stress indicator in an interview situation. *Journal of Psycholinguistic Research, 1,* 243-248.

Jordan, J. M., & Roloff, M. E. (1990). Acquiring assistance from others: The effect of indirect requests and relational intimacy on verbal compliance. *Human Communication Research, 16,* 519-555.

Karrass, C. L. (1970). *The negotiation game.* New York: Thomas Y. Crowell.

Kennedy, G. (1987). *Pocket negotiator.* New York: Blackwell.

Kitayama, S., & Burnstein, E. (1988). Automaticity in conversations: A reexamination of the mindlessness hypothesis. *Journal of Personality and Social Psychology, 54,* 219-224.

Knapp, M. L., Stafford, L., & Daly, J. A. (1986). Regrettable messages: Things people wish they hadn't said. *Journal of Communication, 36,* 40-58.

Lauerbach, G. E. (1989). "We don't want war, but . . ." Speech act schemata and inter-schema-inference transfer. *Journal of Pragmatics, 13,* 25-51.

Maass, A., Salvi, D., Arcuri, L., & Semin, G. (1989). Language use in intergroup contexts: The linguistic intergroup bias. *Journal of Personality and Social Psychology, 57,* 981-993.

Mehrabian, A. (1967). Attitudes inferred from nonimmediacy of verbal communication. *Journal of Verbal Learning and Verbal Behavior, 6,* 294-295.

Mulac, A., Incontro, C. R., & James, M. R. (1985). A comparison of the gender-linked language effect and sex-role stereotypes. *Journal of Personality and Social Psychology, 49,* 1099-1110.

Murdock, J. I., Bradac, J. J., & Bowers, J. W. (1984). Effects of power on the perception of explicit threats, promises, and thromises: A rule-governed perspective. *Western Journal of Speech Communication, 50,* 208-213.

Neu, J. (1988). Conversation structure: An explanation of bargaining behaviors in negotiations. *Management Communication Quarterly, 2,* 23-45.

O'Barr, W. M. (1982). *Linguistic evidence: Language, power, and strategy in the courtroom.* New York: Academic Press.

Putnam, L. L., & Jones, T. S. (1982a). Reciprocity in negotiations: An analysis of bargaining interaction. *Communication Monographs, 49,* 171-191.

Putnam, L. L., & Jones, T. S. (1982b). The role of communication in bargaining. *Human Communication Research, 8,* 262-280.

Rogan, R. G., & Donohue, W. A. (1991, May). *Validation of a message content-based measure of language intensity in naturalistic conflict discourse.* Paper presented at the annual convention of the International Communication Association, Chicago.

Sacks, H., Schegloff, E., & Jefferson, G. (1974). A simplest systematics for the organization of turn-taking for conversation. *Language, 50,* 696-735.

Searle, J.R. (1969). *Speech acts.* Cambridge, UK: Cambridge University Press.

Searle, J.R. (1983). *Intentionality: An essay in the philosophy of mind.* Cambridge: Cambridge University Press.

Semin, G. R., & Fiedler, K. (1988). The cognitive functions of linguistic categories in describing person: Social cognition and language. *Journal of Personality and Social Psychology, 54,* 590-598.

Snyder, M. (1974). The self-monitoring of expressive behavior. *Journal of Personality and Social Psychology, 30,* 526-537.

Tedeschi, J. T., & Bonoma, T. V. (1977). Measures of last resort: Coercion and aggression in bargaining. In D. Druckman (Ed.), *Negotiation: Social-psychological perspectives* (pp. 213-242). Beverly Hills, CA: Sage.

Tedeschi, J. T., Bonoma, T. V., & Schlenker, B. R. (1972). Influence, decision, and compliance. In J. T. Tedeschi (Ed.), *The social influence processes* (pp. 346-418). Chicago: Aldine.

Tedeschi, J. T., Gaes, C. G., & Rivera, A. N. (1977). Aggression and the use of coercive power. *Journal of Social Issues, 33,* 101-125.

Wiener, M., & Mehrabian, A. (1968). *Language within language: Immediacy, a channel in verbal-communication.* New York: Appleton-Century-Crofts.

Villemoes, A. (1991). *Culturally determined strategy preferences in Danish and Spanish business negotiation.* Unpublished manuscript. Copenhagen Business School, Copenhagen, Denmark.

Chapter 8

FACE AND FACEWORK IN NEGOTIATION

Steven R. Wilson

IMAGE MAY NOT BE everything, but for negotiators it is a major concern. Although they haggle over substantive issues, negotiators also claim desired images and identities during interaction and worry about "losing face" and "saving face." During the Persian Gulf crisis, these concerns about face may have been partially responsible for Saddam Hussein's unwillingness to withdraw unconditionally from Kuwait, as well as for the Bush administration's repeated insistence that the United States was not "negotiating" with Iraq.[1] As this example suggests, parties may choose to forgo negotiations when their identities are called in question. When negotiations get underway, concerns about face influence how the parties structure their opening moves, how they respond to their opponent's tactics, and whether they make concessions in order to reach agreement. Many popular texts emphasize the importance of managing concerns about face during conflict and negotiation (e.g., Bach & Wyden, 1968; Fisher & Ury, 1981, Graham & Sano, 1984; Zimmerman, 1985).

This chapter reviews research that explores relationships among concerns about face, negotiation interaction, and outcomes. Within the last 10 years two distinct literatures have emerged concerning the role of face in negotiation. Scholars who work within a *social-psychological tradition* employ experimental studies to investigate how communication (i.e., bargaining tactics) mediates the relationship between face-saving concerns and destructive negotiation outcomes. Researchers who work within a *discourse-interactional tradition* employ quasi-experimental or case studies to examine how communication (i.e., interaction patterns) serves as a vehicle by which participants constantly hammer out a "working consensus" regarding each party's identity. To date, little "cross-fertilization" has occurred between these traditions. After discussing the terms *face* and *facework*, this chapter reviews assumptions and representative investigations from each tradition, and then explores how both traditions can expand our understanding of the role of face in negotiation.

DEFINITIONS AND OVERVIEW

FACE IN NEGOTIATION

Although the concept of *face* dates back at least 2,000 years to Chinese culture (Hu, 1944), most contemporary discussions emanate from Goffman's (1967) article "On Face-Work." Goffman, by describing *face* as the positive value that individuals attach to their situated identities, highlights two important qualities (Tracy, 1990). First, face is a social commodity. Negotiators worry about losing face when their actions or events discredit a desired identity *in the eyes of significant others,* such as their opponent or own constituents. Goffman (1967) writes that although an individual's face "may be his [sic] most personal possession . . . it is only on loan to him from society" (p. 10) and that a "person's face is not lodged in or on his body, but . . . is diffusely located in the flow of events in the encounter" (p. 7).

Second, face is situated, in the sense that different identities arise from the context. Negotiators hope to be seen as "firm" or "tough" advocates who will resist unjust intimidation (B. Brown, 1968; Carnevale, Pruitt, & Britton, 1979). Tjosvold (1983) even equates "social face" and "the image of strength persons want to project in conflict" (p. 50). Although his definition emphasizes an important identity for negotiators, it is too restrictive. Negotiators also can loose face if they do not appear trustworthy, fair, or competent (Pruitt & Smith, 1981; Wilson, Meischke, & Kim, 1990).

At times negotiators project identities that seem undesirable. Friedland (1983) explores a paradoxical "weakness as strength" strategy in which negotiators refuse to make concessions because their "hands are tied" by their constituents. Deutsch (1990) suggests that negotiators claim identities such as being "ignorant" or "belligerent" during distributive bargaining. When enacting other roles, such as teacher or parent, individuals may not desire these latter identities. Hence, negotiators can lose face by acting inconsistently with a range of identities, depending on the institutional and interactional contexts.

There are several reasons why concerns about face are prominent during negotiation. Participants must manage a dilemma concerning concession making and face (B. Brown, 1977). They must make concessions or risk being charged with failure to "bargain in good faith." Yet they also take risks by making concessions, including "image loss" or appearing weak and exploitable to the opponent (Hiltrop & Rubin, 1981).

In addition, bargainers often begin with a differentiation phase, in which they engage in "lengthy public orations characterized by dogmatic pronouncements, vehement demands, and spirited critiques of the other side's position" (Putnam, 1984, p. 234). Although participants clarify issues and priorities through differentiation, they may hesitate later about moving away from publicly defended positions (Folger & Poole, 1984). Finally, bargainers may resist an opponent's contentious tactics simply because they perceive that "to allow oneself to be intimidated . . . is to suffer a loss of social face" (Deutsch, 1961, p. 888). Due to these factors, participants often employ facework during negotiation.

FACEWORK IN NEGOTIATION

Goffman (1967) defines *facework* as "the actions taken by a person to make whatever he [sic] is doing consistent with face" (p. 12). Facework encompasses numerous behaviors, including those that protect one's own face (what Goffman labels a "defensive" orientation) as well as those that affect the opponent's face (what he labels a "protective" orientation). Defensive facework includes attempts to *avoid* topics or activities that might reveal information inconsistent with a claimed identity and attempts to *correct* or repair threats to claimed identities. B. Brown (1977) and Pruitt and Smith (1981) list phrasing demands ambiguously, using disclaimers, hiding disagreement among constituents, and arguing that concessions do not set precedents as examples of avoidance behaviors in negotiation. They mention distributive bargaining tactics such as threats, warnings, refusals, and commitments as examples of corrective behaviors.

Negotiators have strong incentives to defend their face. Those who appear weak, for example, inadvertently encourage their opponent to make aggressive demands (Pruitt & Smith, 1981) and risk losing the trust of their own constituents, who in turn may constrain their latitude to search for integrative agreements (Roloff & Campion, 1987). B. Brown (1968) demonstrates that negotiators who appear weak subsequently will sacrifice tangible monetary gains to regain face. Negotiators also employ facework to influence their opponent's identities. Given the mixed-motive nature of negotiation, participants have incentives both to protect and attack their opponent's face (Wilson & Putnam, 1990). Bargainers may attack their opponent's face when they perceive that their opponent is attacking, is resisting a warranted persuasive appeal, is showing indifference toward their constituents' needs, or is failing to make reciprocal concessions or to bargain in good faith (B. Brown, 1977; Putnam & Jones, 1982). Bargainers may protect their opponent's face to defuse cycles of conflict escalation, to allow the opponent to concede without loss of reputation, or to help the opponent moderate his or her constituents' excessive demands (Fisher & Ury, 1981; Pruitt & Johnson, 1970). Examples of protective facework include qualifying criticism, complimenting positive qualities, and attributing joint concessions to external factors or to a common enemy.

Negotiation scholars working within both the social-psychological and the discourse-interactional perspective have elaborated Goffman's discussion of face and facework. These traditions make different conceptual assumptions about face and employ different research designs and message analysis systems to analyze facework.

THE SOCIAL-PSYCHOLOGICAL TRADITION

Social psychologists have emphasized the importance of face in negotiation for at least 30 years (Deutsch, 1961; Schelling, 1960). A number of studies directly investigate preconditions, forms, and effects of face saving. The authors share assumptions about how facework should be conceptualized and studied.[2] After describing these assumptions, illustrative research is reviewed.

SHARED ASSUMPTIONS

Scholars within the social-psychological tradition make conceptual assumptions about the nature of facework as well as about the relationship between communication, face, and context. To highlight these assumptions, Table 8.1 summarizes information about the measures of face and facework, the independent and outcome variables, and the bargaining tasks employed in these studies.

Social-psychological scholars usually focus only on what Goffman (1967) labels defensive facework. Studies examine avoidance and corrective practices such as: (a) making extreme initial offers; (b) using threats, commitments, and putdown statements; (c) blocking the opponent's goal attainment; and (d) refusing to make concessions (see Table 8.1). Only Tjosvold (1977a, 1978; Tjosvold & Huston, 1978) examines protective facework, and his research centers on the effects of only one protective tactic, compliments.

A second commonality is that social-psychological studies analyze defensive facework in terms of the distribution of gross categories of bargaining tactics, such as the proportion of demands or threats to total utterances (Carnevale et al., 1979, Pruitt, Carnevale, Forcey, & Van Slyck, 1986). These studies ignore more detailed linguistic features of tactics, such as whether demands are performed baldly, on-record, or with redress (P. Brown & Levinson, 1978). They also ignore the sequencing of facework tactics.

A third assumption of this tradition is that communication is a mediating process, or is part of a linear chain between inputs (threats to the bargainer's face) and outputs (negotiation outcomes). Carnevale et al. (1979) hypothesize a "four variable causal chain: Surveillance makes bargainers feel that they should look strong, which leads to distributive behavior, which interferes with the development of integrative agreements" (p. 121). Studies include numerous measures of negotiation outcomes, including the percentage of participants reaching agreement, time to reach agreement, deviation of final agreement from initial positions, quality of agreement, and individual and joint profits (see Table 8.1). Although they examine how concerns about face affect communication, social-psychological scholars pay less attention to how communication may reshape face-saving concerns. By taking an exogenous perspective, these scholars often treat context as an externally imposed shell, one that influences bargainers' perceptions and tactics but remains beyond their control.

Consistent with these assumptions, social-psychological scholars employ experimental research designs. Investigators typically manipulate features of negotiation situations and observe the effects of them on self-reported concern about face, bargaining tactics, and outcomes. Most researchers also employ simulated negotiations that involve a limited number of predefined issues and payoffs, college student participants, and short time periods (see Table 8.1). Although these methods maximize internal validity, they raise concerns about whether findings will converge or diverge with studies of face in naturalistic negotiations (Pruitt & Kimmel, 1977).

REPRESENTATIVE STUDIES

Social-psychological scholars explore tactics that threaten face, situational features that increase concern about face, and effects of facesaving concerns on negotiation outcomes.

Face-Threatening Behaviors. Tjosvold (1974, 1977b) and Tjosvold and Huston (1978) investigate several bargaining tactics that negotiators perceive as face threatening. Initially, Tjosvold (1974) examines personal criticism. Midway through a simulation, participants in two conditions are criticized by the opponent (in a note that describes them as "weak" and "incapable") while participants in the other two conditions are not. Not surprisingly, participants who receive personal criticism feel more affronted, more insulted, and less powerful than do those who are not criticized.

Perhaps more troubling is that negotiators also perceive positional criticism as face threatening (Tjosvold & Huston, 1978). Participants who receive critical feedback about their current bargaining positions midway through a simulation (in a note that describes their position as "rather weak and insubstantial") feel less effective and accepted than do participants whose position is affirmed. Apparently negotiators tend to take criticism of their substantive positions personally. These effects of positional criticism are reduced but not eliminated when confederates integrate such comments with protective facework that affirms participants' personal effectiveness (complimenting them as a "strong and capable person").

Finally, nonnegotiable demands can threaten face (Tjosvold, 1977b). In this study, experimental confederates initially disclose their resistance point and then refuse to make any concessions, while in the control condition, confederates start with a high opening demand and then make two concessions to the same resistance point. Participants feel more insulted by confederates who use nonnegotiable rather than

TABLE 8.1 Descriptive Information for Social-Psychological Studies of Face and Facework in Negotiation

Study	Bargaining Task	Independent Variables	Outcome Variables	Measures of Facework	Measures of Face
B. Brown (1968)	Modified trucking[a]	Feedback from constituents Opponent knowledge of payoffs	Total self-profit Mean self-profit	Number of trials and charge tolls costly to self Total self-cost from tolls	Importance of looking strong to opponent
Carnevale et al. (1979)	3-issue buyer-seller simulation[a]	Surveillance by constituents	Total joint profit Profits for each party	In-role patter Composite index of contentious behaviors	Importance of looking strong to opponent
Hiltrop & Rubin (1981)	1-issue buyer-seller simulation[b]	Size of concessions	None	None	Degree look strong
Johnson & Tullar (1972)	5-issue labor-management simulation[c]	Type of third party Level of face-saving concern	Difference between two sides' final offers	Concession size and rate over time	Importance of looking tough as a bargainer
Pruitt et al. (1986)	3-issue buyer-seller simulation[a]	Surveillance by constituents Gender of constituents Negotiator gender	Total joint profit Profit difference between two sides	Composite index of contentious behaviors	Importance of looking strong to opponent
Pruitt & Johnson (1979)	1-issue buyer-seller simulation[b]	Intervention by mediator Time pressure to settle Concession rate by opponent	None	Concession size after intervention	Perceived personal strength

Tjosvold (1974)	1-issue international simulation[b]	Personal criticism from opponent Orientation to tangible outcomes Use of threats by opponent	Percentage of participants reaching agreement Affective evaluation by opponent	None	Degree felt insulted by opponent Degree felt rejected by opponent
Tjosvold (1977a)	1-issue international simulation[b]	Nonnegotiable demand by opponent Constituent view of capable negotiator Race of opponent	Percentage of participants reaching agreement Affective evaluation of opponent	None	Degree felt insulted by opponent
Tjosvold (1977b)	1-issue labor-management simulation[b]	Affirmation of competence by constituents Self-presentation by opponent	Percentage of participants reaching agreement Evaluation of opponent	Affirmation of competence by constituents	Degree considered strong/capable by constituents
Tjosvold (1978)	1-issue international simulation[b]	Affirmation of strength by opponent Affirmation of position by opponent	Percentage of participants reaching agreement Affective evaluation of opponent	Affirmation by opponent	Importance of looking strong
Tjosvold & Huston (1978)	1-issue labor-management simulation[b]	Criticism of position by opponent Affirmation of competence by opponent	Percentage of participants reaching agreement Time to reach settlement	Affirmation of competence by opponent	Degree considered effective by opponent Degree position seen as strong by opponent

NOTES: a. This is a nonzero-sum task, for which integrative solutions are possible.
b. This is a zero-sum task, for which integrative solutions are not possible.
c. The author was unable to determine the nature of this bargaining task (zero- or nonzero-sum).

negotiable demands, even though the final demands in both conditions are identical.

In addition to the opponent's tactics, negotiators can threaten face via their own tactics. For example, negotiators often fear making concessions not only because of position loss (giving up ground without reason), but also because of image loss (appearing weak and foolish). Concession rate and image loss share a complex and reciprocal relationship. Both Pruitt and Johnson (1970) and Johnson and Tullar (1972) show that the size of concessions that participants make accounts for about 25% of the variance in degrees of self-perceived weakness. Hiltrop and Rubin (1981), however, report that the relationship between concession size and perceived strength is not totally linear. Their findings suggest the existence of a threshold level for making concessions, beyond which participants feel they have little face left to lose. Negotiators often refuse to make further concessions before reaching this threshold (see Tutzauer, Chapter 3, this volume). Indeed, negotiators with a high level of concern about maintaining face make fewer concessions during some phases than do those with less concern about face maintenance (Johnson & Tullar, 1972).

Intervention by third parties in some cases allows participants to make concessions without losing face. In two studies, Pruitt and Johnson (1970) report nonsignificant correlations between concession size and perceived strength when concessions are suggested by a mediator. Apparently intervention allows negotiators to shift responsibility for concessions from themselves to the mediator and to frame concessions as a fair rather than a weak move. In a follow-up study, Johnson and Tullar (1972) find that deadlocked participants who receive recommendations for concessions from mediators do not make larger subsequent concessions than participants in a "no intervention" condition. This finding, however, may be contaminated since the experimenters also gave the control group a recommendation to reexplore issues and generate additional alternatives.

Culture and Bargaining Tactics. An important limitation of the research just reviewed is the exclusive use of American participants. Cultural background undoubtedly influences how bargaining behaviors are perceived, since it shapes views of communication and negotiation. Individualist and low-context cultures, such as in the United States, prefer direct styles of communication in which intentions are displayed clearly in talk. Discrepancy between what is said and what is meant is minimized and disagreements are resolved through competition or collaboration. Collective and high-context cultures, such as in Japan, prefer indirect styles of communication in which intentions are conveyed implicitly via the socio-cultural context. Discrepancy between what is meant and what is said is common and dis- agreements are resolved through avoidance or accommodation (Graham & Sano, 1984; Ting-Toomey, 1988; M. Zimmerman, 1985). Japanese and Americans also hold differing views of the purposes, phases, roles, and decision-making processes of negotiation. Given these differences, bargaining behaviors that are acceptable between American negotiators (e.g., explicitly saying "no" to an opponent's proposal or discussing positions early in a negotiation) are extremely face threatening in Japan (Graham & Sano, 1984; M. Zimmerman, 1985).

Situational Features That Magnify Face Concerns. Negotiators claim desired images with their own constituents as well as their opponents (Wilson & Putnam, 1990). Several social-psychological studies investigate features of the representative-constituent relationship that influence the salience of face concerns, including surveillance and feedback (see Turner, Chapter 10, this volume).

Two studies directly investigate the effects of surveillance on desire to maintain face. Carnevale et al. (1979) find that male negotiators who believe that they are being observed by a constituent report a higher need to appear strong than do unobserved negotiators. Pruitt et al. (1986) replicate this finding for both male and female negotiators who are under surveillance by constituents of either gender.

In addition to surveillance, critical performance feedback from constituents influences concerns about face. In a well-known study (B. Brown, 1968), participants bargain with a more powerful confederate who uses an exploitive style and then they receive either negative feedback (they look "weak," "foolish," or "like a sucker"), positive feedback (they "played fair" or "looked good"), or no constituent feedback. Participants desire to "appear strong" significantly more often after they receive negative feedback rather than after they receive positive or no feedback.

Research by Tjosvold (1977a, 1978), however, indicates that positive as well as negative feedback can increase face concerns. In his first study, participants receive constituent feedback that is either highly positive or only moderately positive. Negotiators who receive extremely positive feedback are significantly *less* likely to reach agreement in subsequent bargaining than are those who receive moderate feedback. In a second study, in which feedback comes from an opponent rather than a constituent, participants who receive extremely positive feedback feel more concern about looking strong than do those who receive moderate feedback. These findings indicate that the relationship between feedback valence and concerns about face is not simple, and that the content and intensity of feedback also influence face concerns.

Effects of Face Concerns on Bargaining Outcomes. How do face-saving concerns affect negotiation outcomes? Many scholars assume that as face concerns become more salient, both defensive facework and destructive outcomes are more likely (B. Brown, 1968, 1977; Carnevale et al., 1979; Deutsch, 1961; Folger & Poole, 1984). According to B. Brown (1977): "In some instances, protecting against loss of face becomes so central an issue that it swamps the importance of the tangible issues at stake and generates intense conflicts that can impede progress toward agreement and increase substantially the costs of conflict resolution" (p. 275).

Several findings from social-psychological studies provide support for a linear, positive relationship between face concerns and destructive outcomes. Studies demonstrate that the same bargaining tactics or situational features that affect concern about face also are associated with: failure to reach agreement (Tjosvold, 1974, 1977a, 1977b, 1978), time to reach agreement (Tjosvold & Huston, 1978), lower joint or self-profit (B. Brown, 1968; Carnevale et al., 1979; Pruitt et al., 1986), poorer understanding of the opponent's priorities (Carnevale et al., 1979), and poorer interpersonal relationships (Tjosvold, 1974, 1977b). As direct evidence, Carnevale et al. (1979) report a moderate inverse association between concern about appearing strong and level of joint profit ($r = -.42$).

There are reasons to suspect, however, that the relationship between face-saving concerns and bargaining outcomes is more complex than these studies indicate. First, concerns about face do not always produce defensive facework. Pruitt et al. (1986) find that negotiators who are observed by constituents of either gender feel more concern about looking strong. This concern leads to more contentious behavior from representatives who report to male constituents but *less* contentious behavior from those who report to female constituents. Similarly, B. Brown

(1968) notes that participants who receive constituent feedback about looking weak tend to block their opponent's goal progress, *except* when the opponent knows that this retaliation is costly to the participants themselves.

Second, negotiators' responses to defensive facework may depend on their schemata (Bazerman & Carroll, 1987), frames (see Putnam & Holmer, Chapter 6, this volume; Neale & Bazerman, 1985b; Pinkley, 1990), and interaction goals (Wilson & Putnam, 1990). Tjosvold (1977b) reports that participants who believe that a strong negotiator "attempts to obtain tangible outcomes" are more willing to compromise than those who believe a strong negotiator always "resists intimidation." Similarly, Pruitt et al. (1986) argue that participants invoke gender schemata concerning what females (versus males) believe are appropriate responses to intimidation.

Third, increased defensive facework does not always lead to destructive outcomes. Putnam (1990) argues that contentious tactics such as threats simultaneously facilitate both integrative and distributive bargaining. The degree to which a threat facilitates each process depends on the wording, sequencing, and interpretation of the message. Consistent with this reasoning, Tjosvold (1974) observes that when opponents use threats, negotiators feel insulted, but they express better understanding of their opponents' priorities and may be more likely to reach agreement than no-threat negotiators.

Fourth, the effects of protective facework are not known. Research indicates that positive feedback mitigates the effects of positional criticism (Tjosvold & Huston, 1978) but also heightens concerns about appearing strong (Tjosvold, 1977a, 1978). Future social-psychological research needs to explore how negotiators integrate defensive and protective facework and how their uses of protective tactics, other than compliments, affect outcomes.

Over the past 30 years, scholars working in the social-psychological tradition have generated a sizable body of research that examines precursors, forms, and effects of face saving. Negotiators perceive personal and positional criticism, nonnegotiable demands, unqualified threats, and concessions as face-threatening tactics. Concern about face increases with constituent surveillance and feedback. Concern about face can foster distributive tactics and negative outcomes, although the nature of these effects needs clarification. A second tradition also has explored the role of face in negotiation.

THE DISCOURSE-INTERACTIONAL TRADITION

Scholars of conflict talk in the last 10 years offer specific insights about interaction patterns in negotiation, as well as general findings about the structures and functions of discourse (Brenneis, 1988; Donohue, Diez, & Stahle, 1983; Francis, 1986; Grimshaw, 1990; Maynard, 1985; Neu, 1988). Scholars in this tradition have conducted several exploratory studies of face and facework. These scholars hold assumptions that differ from the social-psychological tradition. Table 8.2 provides information about the type of bargaining discourse and contextual features that are analyzed, including the specific discourse forms and face concerns.

SHARED ASSUMPTIONS

Discourse theorists focus on both defensive and protective facework (Goffman, 1967). For example, research examines when negotiators hear directives as expressing disapproval toward their own and toward their opponent's face (Wilson et al., 1990) and how negotiators defend their own and protect their opponents' face during information exchange (Donohue & Diez, 1983).

A second common feature is that discourse studies focus on detailed linguistic features and sequences of facework. Some scholars center on the phrasing of particular speech acts, such as Weiss's (1988) analysis of 12 mitigators for requests. Others argue that negotiators communicate information about both parties' identities through any speech act; thus *all* negotiation talk can be analyzed as facework (Donohue, 1983; Kang, 1991). Discourse scholars view the "microscopic level of communication analysis" as "interesting and vital to our understanding of the process of negotiation" (Donohue et al., 1983, p. 250).

A third assumption of this tradition is that discourse and face are related reciprocally, rather than in a linear causal fashion. Participants can threaten face via their interaction, but through interaction they also can develop a new "working consensus" that redefines identities and hence reduces the need to save face (Wilson, Kim, & Meischke, in press; Wilson et al., 1990). Discourse scholars adopt an endogenous view in which context is created via interaction (Brenneis, 1988; Maynard, 1985). Given this assumption, Table 8.2 summarizes which discourse and contextual features are examined, but it does not assign the status of independent or dependent variables.

A final commonality is that discourse theorists treat "talk as primary," by viewing negotiation interaction as interesting in its own right rather than as an indicator of underlying face concerns or as a mediator between face concerns and bargaining outcomes (D. Zimmerman, 1988). Hence, discourse scholars produce detailed descriptions of how negotiators manage face in interaction. There are disadvantages, however, in rigidly adhering to this commitment. Discourse theorists offer few insights about relationships between facework and negotiation outcomes (see Table 8.2). In addition, no discourse study gathers perceptual data regarding participants' concerns about face. Perceptual data could offer insights about how each party contributes to interaction patterns.

Given these assumptions, discourse scholars employ quasi-experimental or case study research designs. Most researchers analyze naturalistic negotiations or lengthy simulations in which participants define issues and argue over utilities (see Table 8.2). Some scholars conduct quantitative analyses while others use examples to support claims. Unfortunately, some discourse scholars provide limited information about the nature of negotiations that they analyze (for an exception, see O'Donnell, 1990) and about the way they select examples and identify episodes. In general, the methods used by discourse scholars enhance external validity but limit the reader's ability to draw conclusions about complex causal forces.

REPRESENTATIVE STUDIES

Discourse studies of facework in negotiation typically elaborate or criticize issues raised by P. Brown and Levinson's (1978) theory of politeness. After summarizing their theory, this chapter reviews studies on openings, information exchange, autonomy management, and directive use.

Brown and Levinson's Politeness Theory. P. Brown and Levinson (1978) offer an account for numerous lexical, syntactic, and pragmatic similarities that occur across three disparate languages (English, Tamil, and Tzeltal). The authors attribute these similarities to people's universal desires to maintain face and to their abilities to generate defensive

TABLE 8.2 Descriptive Information for Discourse/Interactive Studies of Face and Facework in Negotiation

Study	Bargaining Task	Discourse Features Examined	Primary Face Want Examined	Contextual Features Examined	Measures of Outcome
Donohue (1983)	4 simulated teachers negotiations (professional reps.; 16 hours each)	All talk (every turn analyzed)	Both parties' negative face	Phase (opening moves of negotiations)	None
Donohue & Diez (1983)	4 simulated teachers negotiations (professional reps.; 16 hours each)	3-turn question-answer sequences	Both parties' negative face	None	None
Donohue & Diez (1985)	4 simulated teachers negotiations, 1 naturalistic teachers negotiation (100 hours), 1 naturalistic labor negotiation (phone company), 1 naturalistic divorce mediation (1-2 hours)	Choice of directive forms	Opponent's negative and positive face	Bargaining goals (discrepancy) Bargaining procedures (formality) Relational history (length)	None
Kang (1991)	1 naturalistic labor grievance (electricians), 1 simulated teachers negotiation	All talk (every thought unit): face strategies, task strategies, language intensity, lexical diversity	Both parties' negative face	None	None
O'Donnell (1990)	1 naturalistic labor/ management Quality of Work Life meeting (city gov't)	Use of politeness strategies (off-record, mitigators, etc.)	Opponent's negative and positive face	Bargaining role (labor vs. management) Bargaining side (same vs. opponent)	None

			Opponent's negative face	None	Proportion of total possible individual profit
Weiss (1988)	9 simulated international negotiations (6 issues; students)	Choice of directive forms (mitigators)			None
Wilson et al. (1990)	4 simulated labor grievance hearings (students; 2 hours each), naturalistic labor contract negotiations (published industrial cases)	Directives and subsequent arguments	Both parties' positive face	None	

NOTE: All discourse studies except Weiss (1988) employ tasks without predefined issues or utilities.

and protective facework. Building on Goffman (1967), they separate face into two concerns: the desire to have one's personality and possessions *approved of* by significant others (or "positive face") and the desire to maintain *autonomy* and be unimpeded by others (or "negative face"). According to P. Brown and Levinson (1978), certain behaviors are intrinsic "Face-Threatening Acts" (FTAs), that is, "by their very nature they run contrary to the face wants of the addressee and/or the speaker" (p. 70). The authors "make a distinction between acts that threaten negative face and those that threaten positive face" (P. Brown & Levinson, 1978, p. 72). Requests, orders, offers, and threats intrinsically threaten the hearer's autonomy; while criticisms, accusations, and blatant noncooperative activity are intrinsic FTAs for the hearer's approval. The degree of face threat from these acts depends on the power and distance between speaker and hearer, as well as on an act's relative offensiveness in a particular culture.

P. Brown and Levinson (1978) argue that a speaker defends his or her own face in part by protecting another's face. Yet, to accomplish instrumental goals, people perform FTAs. To manage the competing concerns of efficiency versus face, a speaker may use one of five "superstrategies": (1) perform the FTA baldly, on-record, without redress; (2) perform the FTA with positive politeness; (3) perform the FTA with negative politeness; (4) perform the FTA off-record (indirectly); or (5) do not perform the FTA. Each superstrategy is instantiated by linguistic "output strategies." Speakers use positive politeness, for instance, by intensifying interest in the hearer, by using in-group identity markers, or by making jokes. In sum, P. Brown and Levinson (1978) focus primarily upon protective facework.

Although several criticisms of politeness theory have emerged (Coupland, Grainger, & Coupland, 1987; Craig, Tracy, & Spisak, 1986; Kang, 1991; Lim, 1990; Lim & Bowers, 1991; Penman, 1990; Tracy, 1990; Wilson et al., 1990, in press), the theory has generated a large body of work in several disciplines and contexts (see P. Brown & Levinson, 1987). In negotiation, participants have concerns about both parties' autonomy and approval. Politeness theory does not predict that negotiators always will be polite, but rather that the degree to which they are polite versus impolite depends on the relative salience of multiple goals. Several discourse scholars apply the theory's insights to explore how negotiators manage their own and their opponents' desires for approval and autonomy (see Table 8.2).

Opening Moves. During the beginning of bargaining, "participants spend a great deal of time negotiating their conversational rights and obligations in addition to negotiating the issues of importance" (Donohue, 1983, p. 19). Opening moves include presentation of proposals plus initial questions concerning those proposals. Negotiators' desires to expand their own conversational rights (e.g., to control topics) while imposing obligations on opponents (e.g., to disclose information), but they must do this while maintaining a level of cooperativeness. Donohue (1983) lays out a six-step decision tree that maps one participant's initial request for information, the opponent's grant or refusal with or without redress, the participant's acceptance or counter request, and so forth. Using examples from naturalistic labor negotiations, he illustrates variations in how autonomy (negative face) gets managed in opening sequences.

Information Exchange. Participants attempt to control conversational rights and obligations beyond their opening moves. Donohue and Diez (1983) examine how autonomy is negotiated through three information-exchange sequences: unexpanded sequences (question-answer-acknowledgment), chaining sequences (question-answer-question), and arching sequences (question-question-question/answer). The researchers present examples of the latter two sequences that occur in simulated training negotiations between professional representative.

(1) Management: Do you have any proposals to offer?
       Labor: At this point I think we do have some proposals, and what we would like to propose to you is that you take back the consideration of reducing the force (pause) . . .
Management: Do you have any specific proposals in that area?
      Labor: At this point, no. (Chaining Sequence, p. 12)
(2) Labor: Well, there are some of our proposals that you didn't react to . . . Or did you wanna (pause)
Management: Which were you thinking of?
      Labor: In terms of salary, uh, (pause) cost of living increases (pause) you didn't respond to that. (Arching Sequence, p. 13)

By continuing to answer questions (i.e., by providing "preferred second pair parts"), labor in example (1) allows management to expand their conversational rights (Donohue & Diez, 1983). In contrast, arching sequences such as example (2) can signify struggle over who has the right to control topics and disclosures. Donohue and Diez (1983) observe that the likelihood that each sequence will occur depends on the form of the initial informational request. For example, interrogatives ("Will you tell us your proposal?") are more likely than imperatives ("Tell us your proposal") to initiate chaining sequences (see Gibbons, Bradac, & Busch, Chapter 7, this volume).

Autonomy Management. Aside from conversational topics, participants also negotiate control over proposals, arguments, and concessions. Although P. Brown and Levinson (1978) acknowledge that face needs are interdependent, their five superstrategies center primarily on the hearer's autonomy, and not on the speaker's own autonomy. In response, Kang (1991) develops a typology of strategies for coding how negotiators simultaneously expand, maintain, or constrain both parties' autonomy. He demonstrates that the self- and opponent dimensions of his coding system are relatively independent, since the degree to which a negotiator's message expands his or her own autonomy correlates only weakly with the degree to which it constrains the opponent's autonomy ($r = .12$). As expected, messages that constrain the opponent's negative face are likely to include competitive task strategies and intense language. Messages that constrain the negotiator's own autonomy are likely to include accommodating task strategies and less intense language.

Interpretation of Directives. Wilson and his colleagues (1990, in press) analyze how directives create multiple face threats. Directives are speech acts aimed at getting the hearer to perform a desired action (e.g., requests, commands, and questions; see Searle, 1976). According to politeness theory, directives are intrinsic FTAs primarily to an opponent's autonomy, since they elicit behaviors that the opponent would not have performed otherwise (P. Brown & Levinson, 1978, pp. 70-72).

Directives, however, also potentially threaten an opponent's desire for approval (positive face). Consider the following example from a naturalistic labor negotiation:

> *(3) Labor:* I suggest that you do a little more thinking about what the employee's fair share of this situation is.
>
> *Management:* Well, we've done plenty of thinking about it. (Wilson et al., 1990, pp. 8-9)

Here labor tries to constrain management's autonomy, while simultaneously expressing disapproval about the employee's share of the company's profits. Although some directives trigger multiple face threats, others constrain autonomy without expressing disapproval (see management's question in example 2). Politeness theory offers little insight about when directives will threaten positive as well as negative face. To address this issue, Wilson et al. (1990) analyze how negotiators project "definitions of the situation" via their directives (Goffman, 1959; Weinstein, 1969). They argue that directives threaten the opponent's positive face when the speaker implies that the preconditions for the opponent's compliance exist *before* the directive is uttered. That is, directives should be heard as criticizing the opponent when he or she already is expected and obligated to perform the requested action. For instance, the labor negotiator in example (3) implies that management *already should* have recognized that their salary proposal is unfair to the employees, as is evident in the way management's defensive response refers to the past. Wilson et al. (1990) also find that directives that imply that an opponent has failed to fulfill an obligation raise questions about his or her fairness, while those that imply that an opponent has failed to do something he or she has the *ability* to do raise questions about his or her task or communicative competence.

In addition, Wilson et al. (1990) show that negotiators can threaten their own positive face by using directives when the preconditions for the opponent's compliance do not yet exist. In example (4), management's positive face is threatened when labor asserts that management does not have the *right* to utter a directive.

(4) Management: I've tried to give you the reasons why I feel very strongly that the union should pass up this reopener.

Labor: And we feel just as strongly that you shouldn't in . . . under any consideration ask us to do that. You went into this contract with your eyes wide open, and that contract contains definite wage reopeners . . . (Wilson et al., 1990, p. 10).

Of course, participants may disagree about whether a negotiator's directive accurately portrays the current reality (see examples 3 and 4). Wilson and his colleagues are investigating how participants attempt to control definitions of the situation and negotiate a mutually agreeable "working consensus" (Goffman, 1967; Weinstein, 1969).

Use of Directives and Mitigators. Two studies investigate associations between directive form and negotiation contexts. Drawing on

Ervin-Tripp's (1976) work, Donohue and Diez (1985) analyze six forms of directives that vary in the degree to which they protect the hearer's autonomy. For example, direct imperatives ("Tell us what the cost factors are here") impose on the hearer more than do nonexplicit question directives ("Do you know the cost factors here?") which in turn impose more than do hints ("We can't figure this out").

Donohue and Diez (1985) predict that relationships exist between directive form and the contextual features of goals, bargaining procedures, and relational history. They conclude that highly face-threatening directives are likely to be used "when participants' goals are discrepant and a less cooperative context is apparent, when the procedures for conducting the negotiation are not as rigid, when participants have substantial relational history, and when the negotiation content is personally involving" (p. 315). They also argue that patterns of directive use can redefine contextual features, such as participants' role relationships, throughout a negotiation. Methods for teasing out the direction of such relationships would strengthen future research in this area (Poole & McPhee, 1985).

O'Donnell (1990) examines linguistic differences between an interpersonal and an organizational conflict episode, which occur during meetings between labor and management representatives in a "Quality of Working Life" program. The organizational conflict is an argument between a management and two labor representatives, while the interpersonal conflict occurs between two management representatives in front of the labor team. The managers perform most FTAs baldly, on-record in the interpersonal conflict, while labor uses off-record and negative politeness strategies in the organizational conflict. O'Donnell (1990) concludes, "In [the organizational] episode, there is less reciprocity with respect to . . . speech strategy than between interactants in [the interpersonal] episode; this difference reveals the greater power/status differentials that exist between the interactants in [the organizational] episode" (p. 227).

Although several studies support her claim that higher status is inversely associated with use of protective facework (see P. Brown & Levinson, 1987; Lim, 1990), O'Donnell's (1990) use of status to account for labor's politeness strategies contradicts several studies that show that labor tends to use attacking, offensive bargaining tactics while management uses defensive tactics (Donohue, Diez, & Hamilton, 1984; Fossum, 1979; Morley & Stephenson, 1977; Putnam & Jones, 1982; Putnam, Wilson, & Turner, 1990). O'Donnell's findings could indicate that the Quality of Working Life meetings analyzed in the study are more similar to small group than to negotiation interaction. However, her findings also may stem from drawing conclusions about status and facework based upon a sample of *n* = 2. Donohue and Diez (1985) also make their claims about relational history based upon only one naturalistic negotiation. Jacobs (1988) argues that the analysis of examples provides compelling support for some types of research claims, but not for ones about the distribution of conversational forms across contextual features like power. Given the pragmatic difficulties of obtaining large samples of naturalistic negotiations, discourse researchers may need to employ shorter simulations in future studies of context and directive use.

Aside from these studies, Weiss (1988) explores how the use of "mitigators," or syntactic devices that influence the offensiveness of a request, affects negotiation outcomes. Drawing on politeness theory, he develops a typology of 12 mitigators for requests. Arguing that mitigators can communicate politeness without reducing concern about substance, Weiss (1988) predicts a positive relationship between use of this protective facework and "negotiation effectiveness." To test this prediction, he analyzes mitigation use within simulated international negotiations.

Weiss (1988) reports that the most common mitigators are the use of indirect requests, inclusive pronouns, and simulation terminology or jargon ("give us *lv*"). His research hypothesis receives only mixed support. Of the 12 types of mitigators, 8 correlate positively with effectiveness, but 4 correlate negatively. Given these findings, the author may need to refine some of his mitigator categories.

Culture and Negotiation Discourse. P. Brown and Levinson (1978) argue that the desires for approval and autonomy are universal and that people in all cultures generate means for achieving them. However, they also posit culturally specific assumptions about face that raise questions about the generalizability of the findings just reviewed. Across different cultures, people: (1) perceive different speech acts as face threatening, (2) weigh power and distance differently when assigning magnitude of face threat, (3) desire approval from different types of "significant" others, and (4) view different types of people as having special rights to face protection (P. Brown & Levinson, 1978, pp. 247-258; 1987, pp. 13-15). Ting-Toomey (1988) elaborates on their list, arguing that conflict participants from different cultures vary in how they: orient to their own versus their opponents' face, value approval versus autonomy, see "substantive" and "relational" issues as separable, view face as an individualistic versus collective concept, and link face to the "here and now" versus the past and future.

Since discourse studies on negotiation are conducted primarily with "Western" participants, these differences across cultures raise serious concerns about external validity. For example, negotiations in Japan often open with an *aisatus*, an introductory meeting in which the highest status representatives control the interaction completely through a chaining sequence that avoids task-related topics (Graham & Sano, 1984, p. 2). This pattern suggests conversational rights and obligations are negotiated with dramatically different opening moves in the United States versus Japan.

In summary, discourse scholars have conducted detailed investigations of how negotiators define situations, negotiate rights and obligations, and manage desires for approval and autonomy through interaction. Most research draws on P. Brown and Levinson's (1978) politeness theory, although few studies succeed both at evaluating the theory and at offering unique insights about negotiation. Some studies focus on the form, sequencing, and interpretation of directives. Discourse studies are exploratory, charting out new areas that await systematic investigation.

CONCLUSION

Face and facework are prevalent concerns throughout negotiations. Participants attend to face concerns when they make opening moves, exchange information, use directives, respond to their opponents' tactics, adjust to constituent feedback, and offer concessions. Any comprehensive theory of negotiation processes and outcomes must incorporate the concept of face.

Scholars working within two different traditions, the social-psychological and the discourse-interactional, contribute to understanding the role of face in negotiation. Social-psychological scholars identify bargaining tactics that threaten face, situational conditions that magnify concerns about face, and ways in which face issues push negotiations toward destructive outcomes. Discourse scholars analyze how bargainers use lexical, syntactic, and pragmatic elements of facework to negotiate rights and obligations and to manage desires for autonomy and approval.

Unfortunately, scholars from each tradition rarely cite works from the other, even though both could benefit from cross-fertilization. In the future, social-psychological and discourse scholars should borrow analytic and methodological techniques from the other tradition, without compromising their own conceptual assumptions. For example, social-psychological scholars could gain new insights by analyzing protective as well as defensive facework tactics and by analyzing the linguistic details and sequencing of such tactics. Future research could examine the effects of "mixed" messages in which negotiators compensate for face-threatening tactics with compliments, mitigators, or accounts. Social-psychological scholars could attend to these issues without sacrificing assumptions of linear causation or preferences for experimental control. Similarly, discourse scholars could gain new insights from analyzing relationships between discourse patterns and negotiation outcomes. For instance, patterns of argument that follow face-threatening directives may signal which issues will get resolved integratively versus distributively (see Pruitt, 1981). Researchers could examine this issue without sacrificing assumptions about mutual influence or preferences for naturalistic negotiations (see Putnam & Wilson, 1989; Putnam, Wilson, Waltman, & Turner, 1986).

Both theorists and practitioners need additional insights about the role of face and facework in negotiations. Three questions seem important. First, how do negotiators coordinate face and substantive concerns? Participants enter into negotiations to resolve disagreements about substantive issues such as weapons systems (international), health insurance (organizational), or vacations (interpersonal contexts). Moreover, substantive and face concerns share several possible relations: Either may be most important, either may be an end in itself or a means to other ends, and either may set constraints on how the other is pursued. Wilson and Putnam (1990) present a framework for studying interaction goals that could be used to analyze how negotiators coordinate face concerns and substantive issues. They array interaction goals along two dimensions: content (instrumental, relational, and identity goals) and temporal abstraction (global, regional, and local goals). Global goals are relevant for the entire negotiation, regional goals pertain to a single bargaining session, and local goals drive small segments of interaction. Wilson and Putnam (1990) offer examples of conflicts between instrumental (substantive) and identity (face) goals at various levels of abstraction. They analyze how global goals set top-down constraints upon lower-level goals, such as when the global substantive goal of getting a raise leads a bargainer to form a regional goal of appearing tough during the first session. In contrast, they also illustrate how global goals may get redefined from the bottom up through shifts in lower-level goals, such as when a local goal of reciprocating an opponent's contentious tactics leads a bargainer to toughen his or her global resistance point on salary. Wilson and Putnam's (1990) framework could be used to examine questions such as whether expert versus novice negotiators differ in how they coordinate substantive and face goals. Both social-psychological (Neale & Bazerman, 1985a) and discourse (Craig, 1986) scholars analyze goals, and both traditions offer methodologies that could be used to evaluate Wilson and Putnam's (1990) framework.

A second question for future research is: How does culture influence the role of face and facework in negotiation? P. Brown and Levinson's (1978) politeness theory offers a framework for examining cultural differences in face and facework. Ting-Toomey (1988) presents several testable propositions that link cultures (individualism/collectivism; high-context/ low-context cultures) to the use of facework strategies in conflicts.

A final question for future research is: How are face concerns and facework related to negotiation outcomes? Most studies reviewed in this chapter examine the frequency of facework tactics (Carnevale et al., 1979; Pruitt et al., 1986; Weiss, 1988). Yet prior research on conflict escalation suggests that the sequencing of such tactics may be especially predictive of outcomes (Cronen, Pearce, & Snavely, 1979; Gottman, 1979; Putnam & Jones, 1982; Sillars, 1980). Putnam and Jones (1982), for example, discover that agreement dyads in a labor-management simulation follow a complimentary pattern, with labor specializing in offensive tactics and management in defensive tactics. Impasse dyads, in contrast, exhibit rigid symmetrical patterns of reciprocating both offensive and defensive tactics.

Both research traditions could explore the sequencing of facework tactics. Discourse scholars could undertake detailed analyses of how participants get into reciprocal cycles of face saving and attack, how linguistic resources such as topic shifts and semantic ambiguity can be used to get out of such cycles, and how cycles that lead to impasse differ from those that do not. Social-psychological scholars could examine situational features such as surveillance that may increase the likelihood of destructive cycles, as well as third-party interventions that can break such cycles. As anyone who has participated in an intense conflict knows, the payoffs from such work could be substantial.

NOTES

1. For a sampling of newspaper analyses that highlight concerns about face during the Persian Gulf Crisis, see: "U.N. Security Council Votes Embargo on Iraq; Saddam says seizure of Kuwait is permanent," *Washington Post,* August 7, 1990 (Newsbank, Persian Gulf Crisis, 1990, fiche 90, grid B2). "Iraq is seen set to level Kuwait: Saddam still defiant in New Year's visit to frontline troops," *Washington Post,* January 2, 1991 (Newsbank, Persian Gulf Crises, 1990, fiche 7, grid A10). "Could Bush afford to let Saddam stay?" *Washington Times,* February 19, 1991 (Newsbank, 1991, fiche 37, grid E10). "Hussein words on fine line between war and truce," *Miami Herald,* February 22, 1991 (Newsbank, 1991, fiche 37, grid D3). "Bush's dilemma close to 'nightmare scenario'," *Washington Times,* February 22, 1991 (Newsbank, 1991, fiche 37, grid E3). "Bush trying to 'defang' Iraqi leader," *Miami Herald,* February 23, 1991 (Newsbank, Persian Gulf Crisis, 1991, fiche 38, grid E3). "Bush gives Iraq until noon today to begin withdraw from Kuwait," *Washington Post,* February 23, 1991 (Newsbank, Persian Gulf Crisis, 1991, fiche 38, grid E7).

2. These assumptions are descriptive rather than prescriptive in nature. They describe common practices of the scholars who work within each tradition, rather than prescribe what is logically mandated by the tradition.

REFERENCES

Bach, G. R., & Wyden, P. (1968). *The intimate enemy: How to fight fair in love and marriage.* New York: Avon Books.

Bazerman, M. H., & Carroll, J. S. (1987). Negotiator cognition. *Research in Organizational Behavior, 9,* 247-288.

Brenneis, D. (1988). Language and disputing. *Annual Review of Anthropology, 17,* 221-237.

Brown, B. R. (1968). The effects of need to maintain face in interpersonal bargaining. *Journal of Experimental Social Psychology, 4,* 107-122.

Brown, B. R. (1977). Face-saving and face-restoration in negotiation. In D. Druckman (Ed.), *Negotiations: Social psychological perspectives* (pp. 275-299). Beverly Hills, CA: Sage.

Brown, P., & Levinson, S. C. (1978). Universals in language use: Politeness phenomena. In E. N. Goody (Ed.), *Questions and politeness* (pp. 56-289). Cambridge, UK: Cambridge University Press.

Brown, P., & Levinson, S. C. (1987). *Politeness: Some universals in language usage.* Cambridge, UK: Cambridge University Press.

Carnevale, P. J., Pruitt, D. G., & Britton, S. D. (1979). Looking tough: The negotiator under constituent surveillance. *Personality and Social Psychology Bulletin, 5,* 118-121.

Coupland, N., Grainger, K., & Coupland, J. (1988). Politeness in context: Intergenerational issues. *Language in Society, 17,* 253-262.

Craig, R. T. (1986). Goals in discourse. In D. G. Ellis & W. A. Donohue (Eds.), *Contemporary issues in language and discourse processes* (pp. 257-275). Hillsdale, NJ: Lawrence Erlbaum.

Craig, R. T., Tracy, K., & Spisak, F. (1986). The discourse of requests: Assessment of a politeness approach. *Human Communication Research, 12,* 437-468.

Cronen, V. E., Pearce, W. B., & Snavely, L. M. (1979). A theory of rule-structure and types of episodes and a study of perceived enmeshment in undesired repetitive patterns. In D. Nimmo (Ed.), *Communication yearbook 3* (pp. 225-240). New Brunswick, NJ: Transaction Press.

Deutsch, M. (1961). The face of bargaining. *Operations Research, 9,* 886-897.

Deutsch, M. (1990). Sixty years of conflict. *International Journal on Conflict Management, 1,* 237-263.

Donohue, W. A. (1983, May). *A conversation analysis of negotiation interaction: The structure of opening moves.* Paper presented to the annual meeting of the International Communication Association, Dallas.

Donohue, W. A., & Diez, M. E. (1983, May). *Information management in negotiation.* Paper presented to the annual meeting of the International Communication Association, Dallas.

Donohue, W. A., & Diez, M. E. (1985). Directive use in negotiation interaction. *Communication Monographs, 52,* 305-318.

Donohue, W. A., Diez, M. E., & Hamilton, M. (1984). Coding naturalistic negotiation interaction. *Human Communication Research, 10,* 403-426.

Donohue, W. A., Diez, M. E., & Stahle, R. B. (1983). New directions in negotiation research. In R. N. Bostrom (Ed.), *Communication yearbook 7* (pp. 249-279). Beverly Hills, CA: Sage.

Ervin-Tripp, S. (1976). Is Sybil there? The structure of some American English directives. *Language in Society, 5,* 25-66.

Fisher, R., & Ury, W. R. (1981). *Getting to yes: Negotiating agreement without giving in.* Boston: Houghton Mifflin.

Folger, J. P., & Poole, M. S. (1984). *Working through conflict: A communication perspective.* Glenview, IL: Scott, Foresman.

Fossum, J. A. (1979). *Labor relations: Development, structure, and process.* Dallas: Business Publications.

Francis, D. W. (1986). Some structures of negotiation talk. *Language in Society, 15,* 53-80.

Friedland, N. (1983). Weakness as strength: The use and misuse of a "My hands are tied" ploy in bargaining. *Journal of Applied Social Psychology, 13,* 422-426.

Goffman, E. (1959). *The presentation of self in everyday life.* Garden City, NY: Anchor.

Goffman, E. (1967). *Interaction ritual: Essays in face-to-face behavior.* Chicago: Aldine.

Gottman, J. M. (1979). *Marital interaction: Experimental investigations.* New York: Academic Press.

Graham, J. L., & Sano, Y. (1984). *Smart bargaining: Doing business with the Japanese.* Cambridge, MA: Ballinger.

Grimshaw, A. D. (Ed). (1990). *Conflict talk: Sociolinguistic investigations of arguments in conversations.* Cambridge, UK: Cambridge University Press.

Hiltrop, J. M., & Rubin, J. Z. (1981). Position loss and image loss in bargaining. *Journal of Conflict Resolution, 25,* 521-534.

Hu, H. C. (1944). The Chinese concept of face. *American Anthropologist, 46,* 45-64.

Jacobs, S. (1988). Evidence and inference in conversation analysis. In J. A. Anderson (Ed.), *Communication yearbook 11* (pp. 433-443). Newbury Park, CA: Sage.

Johnson, D. F., & Tullar, W. L. (1972). Style of third party intervention, face-saving, and bargaining behavior. *Journal of Experimental Social Psychology, 8,* 319-330.

Kang, K. H. (1991). *Face strategies in negotiation: Constructing and validating the coding scheme for the images of firmness and flexibility.* Unpublished doctoral dissertation, Department of Communication, Michigan State University, East Lansing.

Lim, T. S. (1990). Politeness behavior in social influence situations. In J. P. Dillard (Ed.), *Seeking compliance: The production of interpersonal influence messages* (pp. 75-86). Scottsdale, AZ: Gorsuch Scarisbrick.

Lim, T. S., & Bowers, J. W. (1991). Facework: Solidarity, approbation, and tact. *Human Communication Research, 17*, 415-450.

Maynard, D. W. (1985). The problem of justice in the courts approached by the analysis of plea bargaining discourse. In T. A. Van Dijk (Ed.), *Handbook of discourse analysis* (Vol. 4, pp. 153-179). London: Academic Press.

Morley, I., & Stephenson, G. (1977). *The social psychology of bargaining*. Cambridge, MA: Harvard University Press.

Neale, M. A., & Bazerman, M. H. (1985a). The effect of externally set goals on reaching integrative agreements in competitive markets. *Journal of Occupational Behavior, 6*, 12-32.

Neale, M. A., & Bazerman, M. H. (1985b). The effects of framing and negotiator overconfidence on bargaining behaviors and outcomes. *Academy of Management Journal, 28*, 34-49.

Neu, J. (1988). Conversation structure: An exploration of bargaining behaviors in negotiation. *Management Communication Quarterly, 2*, 23-45.

O'Donnell, K. (1990). Difference and dominance: How labor and management talk conflict. In A. D. Grimshaw (Ed.), *Conflict talk: Sociolinguistic investigations of arguments in conversations* (pp. 210-240). Cambridge, UK: Cambridge University Press.

Penman, R. (1990). Facework and politeness: Multiple goals in courtroom discourse. *Journal of Language and Social Psychology, 9*, 15-38.

Pinkley, R. L. (1990). Dimensions of conflict frame: Disputant interpretations of conflict. *Journal of Applied Psychology, 2*, 117-126.

Poole, M. S., & McPhee, R. D. (1985). Methodology in interpersonal communication research. In M. L. Knapp & G. R. Miller (Eds.), *Handbook of interpersonal communication* (pp. 100-170). Beverly Hills, CA: Sage.

Pruitt, D. G. (1981). *Negotiation behavior.* New York: Academic Press.

Pruitt, D. G., Carnevale, P. J., Forcey, B., & Van Slyck, M. (1986). Gender effects in negotiation: Constituent surveillance and contentious behavior. *Journal of Experimental Social Psychology, 22*, 264-275.

Pruitt, D. G., & Johnson, D. F. (1970). Mediation as an aid to face saving in negotiation. *Journal of Personality and Social Psychology, 14*, 239-246.

Pruitt, D. G., & Kimmel, M. J. (1977). Twenty years of experimental gaming: Critique, synthesis, and suggestions for future research. *Annual Review of Psychology, 28*, 363-392.

Pruitt, D. G., & Smith, D. L. (1981). Impression management in bargaining: Images of firmness and trustworthiness. In J. T. Tedeschi (Ed.), *Impression management theory and social psychological research* (pp. 247-267). New York: Academic Press.

Putnam, L. L. (1984). Bargaining as task and process: Multiple functions of interaction sequences. In R. L. Street & J. N. Cappella (Eds.), *Sequences and patterns in communicative behavior* (pp. 225-242). London: Edward Arnold.

Putnam, L. L. (1990). Reframing integrative and distributive bargaining: A process approach. In B. H. Sheppard, M. H. Bazerman, & R. J. Lewicki (Eds.), *Research on negotiation in organizations* (Vol. 2, pp. 3-30). Greenwich, CT: JAI Press.

Putnam, L. L., & Jones, T. S. (1982). Reciprocity in negotiations: An analysis of bargaining interaction. *Human Communication Research, 8*, 262-280.

Putnam, L. L., & Wilson, S. R. (1989). Argumentation and bargaining strategies as discriminators of integrative outcomes. In A. Rahim (Ed.), *Managing conflict: An interdisciplinary approach* (pp. 121-144). New York: Praeger.

Putnam, L. L., Wilson, S. R., & Turner, D. (1990). The evolution of policy arguments in teachers' bargaining. *Argumentation, 4,* 129-152.

Putnam, L. L., Wilson, S. R., Waltman, M. S., & Turner, D. (1986). The evolution of case arguments in teachers' bargaining. *Journal of the American Forensic Association, 23,* 63-82.

Roloff, M. E., & Campion, D. E. (1987). On alleviating the debilitating effects of accountability on bargaining: Authority and self-monitoring. *Communication Monographs, 54,* 145-164.

Schelling, T. C. (1960). *The strategy of conflict.* Cambridge, MA: Harvard University Press.

Searle, J. R. (1976). The classification of illocutionary acts. *Language in Society, 5,* 1-24.

Sillars, A. L. (1980). The sequential and distributive structure of conflict interactions as a function of attributions concerning locus of responsibility and stability of conflicts. In D. Nimmo (Ed.), *Communication yearbook 4* (pp. 217-235). New Brunswick, NJ: Transaction Books.

Ting-Toomey, S. (1988). Intercultural conflicts: A face-negotiation theory. In Y. Kim & W. Gudykunst (Eds.), *Theories of intercultural communication* (pp.213-235). Newbury Park, CA: Sage.

Tjosvold, D. (1974). Threat as a lower power person's strategy in bargaining: Social face and tangible outcomes. *International Journal of Group Tensions, 4,* 494-510.

Tjosvold, D. (1977a). The effects of the constituent's affirmation and the opposing negotiator's self-presentation on bargaining. *Organizational Behavior and Human Performance, 18,* 146-157.

Tjosvold, D. (1977b). Low-power person's strategies in bargaining: Negotiability of demand, maintaining face, and race. *International Journal of Group Tensions, 7,* 29-42.

Tjosvold, D. (1978). Affirmation of the high-power person and his position: Ingratiation in conflict. *Journal of Applied Social Psychology, 8,* 230-242.

Tjosvold, D. (1983). Social face in conflict: A critique. *International Journal of Group Tensions, 13,* 49-64.

Tjosvold, D., & Huston, T. L. (1978). Social face and resistance to compromise in bargaining. *Journal of Social Psychology, 104,* 57-68.

Tracy, K. (1990). The many faces of facework. In H. Giles & P. Robinson (Eds.), *The handbook of language and social psychology* (pp. 209-226). Chichester, UK: John Wiley.

Weinstein, E. A. (1969). The development of interpersonal competence. In D. A. Goslin (Ed.), *Handbook of interpersonal competence* (pp. 753-774). Chicago: Rand McNally.

Weiss, S. E. (1988, February). *Making negotiation demands: The concept and use of linguistic mediation.* Paper presented to the annual meeting of the Academy of Management, Anaheim, CA.

Wilson, S. R., Kim, M. S., & Meischke, H. (in press). Evaluating Brown and Levinson's politeness theory: A revised analysis of directives and face. *Research on Language and Social Interaction.*

Wilson, S. R., Meischke, H., & Kim, M. S. (1990, June). A revised analysis of directives and face: Implications for argument and negotiation. In F. van Eemeren, R.

Grootendorst, J. Blair, & C. Willard (Eds.), *Proceedings of the second International Conference on Argumenation* (pp. 470-480). Amsterdam, The Netherlands: SICSAT.

Wilson, S. R., & Putnam, L. L. (1990). Interaction goals in negotiation. In J. A. Anderson (Ed.), *Communication yearbook 13* (pp. 374-406). Newbury Park, CA: Sage.

Zimmerman, D. H. (1988). On conversation: The conversation analytic perspective. In J. A. Anderson (Ed.), *Communication yearbook 11* (pp. 406-432). Newbury Park, CA: Sage.

Zimmerman, M. (1985). *How to do business with the Japanese.* New York: Random House.

PART III

NEGOTIATION SITUATION AND CONTEXT

Chapter 9

NEGOTIATOR-OPPONENT RELATIONSHIPS

William A. Donohue and Closepet N. Ramesh

I can't even get to the table with these bozos. Hey, if they don't want to talk they can just suffer the consequences!

THIS QUOTE from an actual labor-management negotiation session characterizes a very important and often neglected area of negotiation research —relationship development. The problem is quite clear for most negotiators. Before they begin exchanging proposals, they must develop a working relationship that permits them to focus on the task. Greenhalgh (1987) articulates the problem clearly when he observes that relationship remains a crucial part of negotiation that researchers generally fail to explore. His description of the BATNA (Best Alternative to a Negotiated Agreement) concept is telling in this regard. Greenhalgh points out that inherent in the BATNA concept is the assumption that negotiators consider only the utility of their alternatives and not the parties' commitment to their relationships in deciding to abandon negotiations. He indicates that this assumption is practically absurd. Relationship generally has a higher value than zero in any negotiation.

This criticism suggests that the concept of relationship should occupy a more central role in negotiation research. To elevate the concept to its appropriate status, we must first determine what we know about relational development in negotiation and then offer some useful ways of conceptualizing this process. This chapter seeks to accomplish these goals by first defining our perspective on the construct of relationship and then reviewing research that informs this perspective.

HINDE'S APPROACH TO RELATIONSHIP

The task of defining the term *relationship* remains quite challenging because of the endless flood of books and papers that claim to expose the secrets of "close," "healthy," "happy," or "intimate" relationships. Even the National Council on Family Relations seems impressed by this largess as their family resources data bank on the topic of "relationship" contains nearly 35,000 citations (Kelley et al., 1983). For this review, we have chosen Hinde's (1979) conceptualization of *relationships* because of its clarity and breadth and its adaptability to the negotiation context. For Hinde, a relationship is a sequence of interchanges that is essentially dyadic, that occurs over an extended period of time, and that has specific cognitive and affective effects. The affective/cognitive states and the interchange sequences mutually inform one another about the status or condition of the relationship; hence they are relatively inseparable. Both must be examined to gain a conceptually defensible understanding of a relationship.

AFFECTIVE/COGNITIVE DIMENSIONS OF RELATIONSHIP

In the context of interacting, Hinde (1979) identifies five affective/cognitive issues that must be addressed when trying to study relationships. The first dimension is *expectation*. While interacting, communicators use knowledge about culture, the social context, and relational history to anticipate how the other party will react to given messages (G. Miller & Steinberg, 1975). Second, behavior is usually *goal-directed*. According to Hinde, interaction sequences are targeted toward specific ends with individuals continuously seeking feedback to assess success in achieving these goals (see S. Wilson & Putnam, 1990). Third, outcomes are influenced by individuals' *values*. Values are evaluative dimensions that negotiators employ to interpret outcomes. Fourth, Hinde indicates that *feelings*, or affective reactions including such "primary" emotions as happiness, surprise, fear, sadness, anger, disgust, and interest, warrant inquiry. Feelings of attachment and affective ties in relationships are also important to access. Finally, Hinde advocates tapping the extent to which participants *understand* or are familiar with one another. When individuals share a long history of interaction they use accumulated personal information to label their respondents' actions.

BEHAVIORAL DIMENSIONS OF RELATIONSHIPS

Hinde (1979) contends that these cognitive and affective understandings are intertwined with the behavioral sequences that carry relational information during interaction. Hinde advocates searching for both the content and quality of these behavioral sequences. The *content* of a relationship refers to categorizing of relational actions according to the global goal that behaviors seek to achieve (e.g., domination, affiliation). Relational *qualities* of interaction refer to the labeling of specific actions. What specific relational qualities or actions are aimed at achieving global goals? Is the negotiator interrupting and agreeing with the other party or person who offers a concession? For negotiators, Hinde's distinction appears to be the familiar strategy-tactic division with relational strategy acting as the content aspect and relational quality acting as the tactical aspect of relationships. This distinction is highlighted in examining negotiation behaviors that focus on relational development.

UNDERSTANDING RELATIONSHIPS IN NEGOTIATION

EXPECTATIONS

To review research on relationship development in negotiation, this chapter follows Hinde's (1979) framework. Expectations, the first area of research capturing the attention of scholars, centers on success and failure. Working from a game-theory format, McClintock and McNeel (1967) and Harrison and McClintock (1965) report that dyads achieving success in prior trials are significantly more cooperative in their behaviors than either those experiencing failure or those with no prior bargaining experience. In a game-theory type of negotiation, success is generally associated with some degree or kind of trust so that win-win proposals can be exchanged between negotiators. Apparently, trust carries over into future trials.

In a nongame-theory study in which participants could interact freely, Donohue (1978) confirms this finding by observing that individuals who expect to do well on subsequent negotiation trials are significantly more likely to be successful than those expecting failure, or than those with no clearly defined performance expectations (i.e., negotiators performing the task for the first time). This study concludes that expectations of success for bargainers are probably most powerful when they are based on past performance on the same kinds of tasks.

A second type of expectation deals with the extent to which negotiators anticipate future interactions with the same negotiators. In general, the research indicates that expectation for future interaction increases cooperation. For example, in the classical study in this area, Marlowe, Gergen, and Doob (1966) discover that a negotiator is less willing to exploit the other person when future interaction is anticipated. However, when the other person is perceived as egotistical and self-centered, the likelihood of exploitation increases, even when future interaction is anticipated.

Shapiro (1975) confirms this effect when he discovers that negotiators who anticipate future interaction are more likely to act equitably toward the other party in distributing resources. Slusher, Rose, and Roering (1978) refine this observation by examining the relative power of negotiators. They observe that as the relative power of the negotiator increases, cooperation increases, when the negotiator is committed to future interaction. The low-power negotiators become less cooperative with such commitments because they believe future interactions will be even more punishing than current interactions are. The authors suggest that these commitments may be most salient when power disparity is small.

In addition to power, two other variables mediate the cooperative effects of anticipated future interaction: resistance to yielding and capacity for self-monitoring. Regarding the former, Ben-Yoav and Pruitt (1984) note that when negotiators resist yielding to one anothers' demands, cooperative future interaction decreases contentious behavior because subjects believe they will have more opportunity to problem solve if they need it. With respect to self-monitoring, Danheiser and Graziano (1982) reveal that a negotiator's ability to monitor his or her own behavior to make it situationally appropriate influences anticipated future interactions. Such anticipations increase cooperation for high self-monitors and decrease it for low self-monitors. Apparently, the high self-monitor is more likely to be consistent across situations, so that anticipating cooperative future interaction increases cooperation during negotiation.

These studies indicate that the expectation of cooperative future interaction increases cooperation when: (1) individuals are not viewed as egotistical, (2) power is relatively balanced, (3) resistance to yielding is high, and (4) negotiators are relatively high self-monitors. Under these circumstances, negotiators enhance their joint benefits by increasing the likelihood of cooperative future interaction.

GOALS

Perhaps the most informative review of research dealing with goals in negotiation is offered by S. Wilson and Putnam (1990). They identify three primary negotiator goals: (1) instrumental goals that center on the distribution of resources, (2) relational goals that tap issues of power and trust, and (3) identity goals that address the problem of face or image. Relational goals are the most salient ones for this chapter. Many studies in negotiation seem fascinated with the construct *power.* Perhaps counterintuitively, most research indicates that balanced power generates the highest joint outcomes. Certainly, many trade books and popular training programs that advocate a high-power, "one-up" approach to bargaining would object to this finding, but it appears consistent across a variety of studies. For example, research shows fairly consistently that balanced power increases cooperative communication (Folger & Poole, 1984), improves outcomes in international negotiations (Strauss, 1979), increases agreement rates and creates better family outcomes in divorce negotiations (Kressel, 1985), and increases problem solving among interactants in community mediation sessions (McGillicuddy, Welton, & Pruitt, 1987).

The rationale for this observation is fairly clear. Balanced power decreases each side's ability to be contentious or unyielding because each side has the potential and resources to inflict penalties. This increased incentive to cooperate improves the climate for integrative problem solving. With both sides able to work together, they can help each other achieve their respective goals. Power imbalances facilitate oppression and ultimately the destruction of cooperative relations, which, in turn, discourages beneficial problem solving.

Research on trust has produced similar results. Millar and Rogers (1976) claim that trust is related to three variables: vulnerability (the potential of getting hurt by the other person), reward dependability (how much the parties rely on one another for resources), and confidence (consistency in behavior). Similarly, Greenhalgh (1987) defines *trust* in negotiation sessions as arising from a sense of commitment about the relationship, indebtedness, and perceived interdependence. He argues that assessing trustworthiness becomes critical to developing rapport at the beginning of negotiations. Negotiators want to know the limits of their states of interdependence and confidence as quickly as possible.

Most research reveals a positive relationship between the degree of negotiator trust and an increase in joint benefits. For example, Kimmel,

Pruitt, Magenau, Konar-Goldband, and Carnevale (1980) observe that bargainers with high aspirations and high trust produce more cooperative behavior and direct information exchange than do bargainers who do not trust one another. In a follow-up study, Pruitt and Smith (1981) confirm that trust is essential for integrative bargaining and for identifying high priority issues. In hostage negotiation, Cohen, Clairborn, and Specter's (1983), and Egan's (1975) studies reveal that increased trust removes emotional strain in hostage negotiation and thus permits increased cooperation.

However, too much trust, defined as either inappropriate self-disclosure (Rubin, 1983) or unreciprocated information about aspirations (Allen, Donohue, & Stewart, 1990), can hurt negotiators. In fact, Putnam and Jones's (1982b) review of bargaining research indicates that gradual disclosure of intentions stimulate cooperative outcomes. Telling it all at once before trust develops encourages exploitation. Thus, negotiators walk a fine line between trust and distrust. Building trust is a time-consuming and carefully orchestrated process.

VALUES

Not only do balanced power and appropriate levels of trust enhance negotiator relationships and outcomes, but also an understanding of each other's values enhances cooperative effects. For example, Druckman, Broome, and Korper (1988) manipulate the extent to which negotiators discuss their values prior to negotiation and then ascertain the effects of this discussion on outcomes. They find that when value discussions are open, participants report an improved negotiation climate and the negotiation produces more resolutions than when values are not discussed prior to negotiation.

What happens when parties discuss values during negotiation? In an interaction analysis of a simulated bargaining task, Zechmeister and Druckman (1973) find that subjects forced into a zero-sum, distributive payoff schedule focus on value statements to argue their positions. When subjects use integrative options to divide the payoff, they argue from positions based on fact and preference and avoid value-based arguments. In contrast to the findings from the Druckman et al. (1988) study, value discussions are associated with uncooperative interaction.

Research in cross-cultural communication provides an explanation as to why value clarification is difficult in a conflict context. Ting-Toomey's

(1985, 1988a, 1988b) research argues that cultures differ according to their individualistic or collectivist orientations. Collectivist cultures emphasize consensus decision making, use indirect face-negotiation strategies, and communicate in a context-dependent manner. That is, high context cultures rely on information preprogrammed in the receiver and in the setting, with only minimal information in the transmitted message. When people are collectivist oriented, they focus more attention on their own and less on other cultures. As a result, they develop a shorthand or telegraphed way of communicating. Messages are shorter because the context and background knowledge fills in the meaning that otherwise would be in the message.

Ting-Toomey (1985) points out that relationship information and message content are highly intertwined in collectivist cultures because of the stress toward homogeneity. As a result, attacking a person's position in the culture is the same as attacking the person. For example, in certain Asian cultures, disagreements constitute a challenge to the other person's face needs (see Wilson, Chapter 8, this volume). Hence, questioning another's position must be pursued indirectly. In individualistic, low-context cultures, relational and content messages are generally distinct. Thus attacking another's position is not an attack on the other person's face.

This research suggests that negotiating in collectivist cultures requires extensive relationship building prior to the bargaining. Indeed, Kume's (1985) review of differences between Japanese and American decision-making styles indicates that the Japanese demonstrate a greater need than do Americans to integrate relational issues into decision making. Since Japanese culture tends to be collectivist, and American culture is individualistic, this observation supports Ting-Toomey's claims.

More specifically, Cushman and King (1985) compare the negotiation practices of three cultures: Japanese, American, and Yugoslavian. They report that the Japanese are more concerned with relationship development prior to bargaining than are either the Americans or the Yugoslavians. Indeed, the failure of joint mergers between Americans and Asians can be traced to ignoring the need for relational development prior to negotiation (Black & Mendenhall, 1990; Lane & Beamish, 1990; Masse, 1981).

FEELINGS

Hinde's (1979) fourth dimension of relationship centers on affect or feelings. Although Hinde is ambiguous in his use of this concept, this chapter uses the term *affect* to encompass the entire range and intensity of human emotion and feeling. For our purposes, Mandler's (1975) approach to affect illustrates the role of emotion in developing negotiation relationships. Affect consists of both the activation of the Autonomic Nervous System (ANS) and the Cognitive-Interpretive System (CIS). Mandler believes that ANS arousal is a necessary condition for the CIS to occur. ANS arousal acts as a secondary signal system to initiate a meaning analysis of a stimulus situation. ANS arousal constricts focal attention to the stimulus situation to discover the source of the arousal, its nature, and its meaning.

The most basic issue relates to the fight-or-flight emotional reaction that individuals feel in response to such stressful situations as intense conflicts. Researchers have examined the fight-or-flight phenomenon (Brady, 1970; Roth, 1982; Salye, 1978) and its relation to negotiation performance. In general, these studies indicate that excessive stress, like that found during difficult conflict interaction, creates an intense physiological reaction that motivates the individual to either fight back or to withdraw from the situation. When that threshold level is reached, the ability to process proposals, requests, and other rational issues is often limited. As a result, trying to negotiate under these circumstances remains a futile activity.

Perceptions of emotions in the cognitive-interpretive system influence negotiation behavior in various ways. For example, a negative affective state leads to cognitive simplification processes (Janis & Mann, 1977; Staw, Sandelands, & Dutton, 1981). Simplification reduces the disputant's ability to think integratively since solutions like logrolling require complex thinking (Pruitt & Rubin, 1986). Negative affect may also lower the participants' incentives to make concessions on proposals (Gladwin & Kumar, 1986).

The interpretation of affect is also critical for negotiators. For example, Noller's (1988) review of marital communication research contends that marriages ultimately succeed or fail based on how couples handle negative affect. She finds compelling evidence that, in unhappy marriages, "demands for attention or communication by the wife are typically met with either physical or emotional withdrawal of the husband being met by increasing demands from the wife that are met by increased withdrawal" (Noller, 1988, p. 324). In happy marriages, negative affect is reciprocated. Couples confront it and ultimately discuss the issues associated with it.

In research on cross-cultural comparison, Matsumoto, Wallbott, and Scherer (1989) report significant differences in how cultures manage emotion. Specifically, Americans report feeling their emotions more intensely and for longer periods of time than do either the Europeans or the Japanese. However, these cultures do not differ in how they control or regulate emotion.

In summary, the expression or the interpretation of negative affect significantly influences relational development in negotiation by lowering trust between interactants (Higgins, 1987), influencing judgments of relational power and intimacy (Noller, 1988), and triggering attack-defend cycles of interaction (Donohue, 1981a, 1981b; Putnam & Jones, 1982b).

How do negotiators handle these emotions? For example, in a hostage taking situation, the hostage taker experiences heightened levels of emotional arousal. The police negotiator's primary task, therefore, is to reduce the hostage taker's level of excitement and to foster cognitive processing of alternative options (Lanceley, Ruple, & Moss, 1985; A. Miller, 1980). The negotiator must determine which messages will foster trust and rapport and which ones will reduce emotional arousal. Some techniques that police negotiators borrow from psychotherapy and counseling include active listening, paraphrasing, pauses, self-disclosure reciprocity, and open-ended questions (Fuselier, 1986; Lanceley, 1979; Strentz, 1983, 1986). These techniques enhance the negotiator's control over the interaction and reduce the hostage taker's level of emotional excitation (Fuselier, 1986; Fuselier & Van Zandt, 1987).

Rogan (1990), drawing upon communication-based conflict research, combines cooperative and integrative tactics, low levels of language intensity, and face concerns to reduce emotional arousal. Bowers, Metts, and Duncanson (1985) add to this list by controlling arousal through physiological leakage, paralanguage, kinesics, and lexical patterns.

UNDERSTANDING

In negotiation research, the concept of *understanding,* or having knowledge about the partner, is examined primarily from two perspectives: prior experience with an unfamiliar partner and bargaining with friends or intimates. In the first perspective, subjects that experience positive cooperative interaction prior to bargaining carry that cooperation with them into the negotiation (Oskamp & Perlman, 1965, 1966). Gruder

(1971) and Michelini (1971) also observe that positive prior interaction produces higher levels of cooperation.

However, other research reveals that any kind of prior experience enhances cooperation during bargaining. Harrison and McClintock (1965) report that dyads who experience task success immediately prior to negotiation are much more likely to cooperate than dyads who experience task failure prior to negotiation. But, after a one-week delay in performing the task, both the success and failure groups are more cooperative in negotiation tasks than are dyads with no prior experiences. In a follow-up study, McClintock and McNeel (1967) confirm this finding and discover that reward level significantly influences cooperation, with the high reward group more likely to exhibit cooperative interaction during negotiation than does the low reward group.

To explain the impact of prior contact on cooperation, Papa and Pood (1988) examine the effects of co-orientational accuracy on negotiation interaction. Co-orientational accuracy is the extent to which disputants know one another's positions on issues and each other's preferred conflict tactics. Using a simulated bargaining experiment, they observe that disputants who enter negotiation with high co-orientation accuracy spend significantly less time in competitively oriented conflict than bargainers with low co-orientation accuracy. Knowing another person's positions and tactic preferences suggests that the parties have developed a working relationship in the past. Hence, Papa and Pood contend that relational strength helps disputants move toward integrative communication in negotiation.

Intimacy, generally in the form of friendship, also emerges as a significant predictor of outcomes. In Swingle's (1966) research, bargainers are more likely to retaliate against good friends or complete strangers after experiencing harm in a negotiation than they are against disliked or neutral partners. However, Morgan and Sawyer (1967) note that negotiators who are friends cooperate more readily, are less likely to harm one another, and are more likely to be altruistic toward their partners than are negotiators who are strangers. More recently, Fry, Firestone, and Williams (1983) report that romantic involvement between negotiators decreases the likelihood of an integrative agreement, perhaps because the relationship makes it easy to demand or to resist.

Finally, individuals come to understand one another when the relationship is significant and satisfying for them. In studies on marital conflict (Burggraf & Sillars, 1987; Fitzpatrick, 1988; Sillars, Pike, Jones, & Murphy, 1984; Sillars, Weisberg, Burggraf, & Wilson, 1987; Witteman

& Fitzpatrick, 1986), couples who are satisfied with their marriages are likely to (1) be sensitive to one another's feelings, (2) confront one another and not avoid key issues that divide the couple, (3) avoid threatening and demanding comments, (4) listen to each other's comments, (5) stay with the fight and not run away, (6) spend time focused on individual needs, and (7) keep discussions centered on substantive issues and away from personality statements. Couples who demonstrate these characteristics move quickly to discuss proposals and to develop creative ways of resolving their differences.

BEHAVIORAL PATTERNS OF RELATIONSHIPS

To understand the behavioral patterns of relationships, researchers need to examine the strategies and tactics that negotiators use to reflect their relational intentions. Diez (1986) argues that bargainers communicate intentions through relational distance displays. She defines *relational distance* as the interactants' physical and psychological orientations toward one another with respect to power, solidarity, formality, and attraction. Thus understanding how negotiators manage these three parameters reveals how they negotiate their relationship. These parameters consist of role, social, and psychological distance.

ROLE DISTANCE

This relational parameter refers to the power and solidarity of the disputants as they seek to establish their roles in the negotiation. Considerable research in negotiation focuses on how negotiators use various strategies and tactics to manipulate power and solidarity. For example, establishing power and solidarity in negotiation surfaces in the classical distributive-integrative distinction. The distributive focus on individually oriented goals at the other's expense reflects a desire to establish dominance in the negotiation (Donohue, 1981a, 1981b; Putnam & Jones, 1982a; Putnam & Poole, 1987; Walton & McKersie, 1965). Tactics that are common in this orientation are threats that are used to punish and coerce opponents (Guyer & Rapoport, 1970; Leusch, 1976; Tedeschi, Schlenker, & Bonoma, 1973), or to induce compliance (Bonoma & Tedeschi, 1974; Brown, 1968; Tjosvold, 1973). Threats, of course, do not always work and can be characterized as "measures of last resort" (Tedeschi &

Bonoma, 1977; see also Gibbons, Bradac, & Busch, Chapter 7, this volume). In contrast, integrative strategies that emphasize joint gains send messages of solidarity. For example, Pruitt's (1981) list of integrative strategies stem from helping each other overcome the costs that might incur from a jointly selected outcome or from building a third alternative that bridges both individuals' goals. Messages of solidarity are also sent through demands and concessions. Research on opening bids reveals that even extreme opening bids given in a cooperative tone lead to more satisfactory joint settlements than opening bids that communicate mutual suspicion and defensive communication (Michelini, 1971; Sermat & Gregovich, 1966). Similarly, research that explores concessions reveals that positively delivered concessions elicit more cooperation from opponents and more reciprocal concessions than do negative or no concessions (Harford & Solomon, 1967; Oskamp, 1970; W. Wilson, 1971).

Promises also create a more cooperative context. Research indicates that they are used more frequently than threats (Cheney, Harford, & Solomon, 1972) and induce more compliance than threats do (Krauss & Deutsch, 1966), but only when source credibility is high or moderately high (Gahagan & Tedeschi, 1968). Cooperative opponents receive more promises than competitive bargainers do because the former are seen as more credible than the latter (Bonoma, Tedeschi, & Helm, 1974). Cooperative opponents become credible as each party invests more in the relationship and as solidarity improves.

Putnam and Poole (1987) emphasize that bargaining interaction is neither exclusively distributive nor integrative. Rather, this context exhibits both approaches depending on how the communication evolves over time. To understand how disputants interweave these two approaches to establish their relationship requires an analysis of the negotiators' interactions.

For example, Donohue's research (1981b) reveals that bargainers reciprocate attacking moves with more integrative moves to prevent the bargaining from reaching an impasse. In labor-management bargaining, Putnam and Jones (1982a) and Donohue, Diez, and Hamilton (1984) discover that participants reach agreements by using a complementary interaction system of labor-offensive, management-defensive strategies. Moreover, Putnam and Jones (1982a) claim that the symmetrical offensive exchange of attack-attack leads to an impasse. This research demonstrates that role relationship issues of solidarity and power are continuously negotiated during bargaining interaction.

SOCIAL DISTANCE

This relational parameter refers to the formality or informality of the relationship. In cooperative contexts, as individuals become warmer toward one another, their interactions also become informal with an increase in the use of humor, vulgarity, slang, personal reference, and chaotic turn taking. Greater use of complex vocabulary and sentence structure, less humor and vulgarity, and more rigid turn structures reflect a formal context (see Gibbons et al., Chapter 7, this volume; Diez, 1986; Gregory & Carroll, 1978). Understanding social distance is important for negotiators since building cooperative interaction typically involves moving toward informal decision contexts.

A number of studies examine the ways bargainers create formal and informal contexts. Diez's (1986) comparison of bargaining and caucusing interaction notes that negotiators use much more formal sentence structure and complex vocabulary choices during two-sided bargaining sessions than during their own caucusing sessions. The caucusing—as opposed to the bargaining—sessions exhibit more humor, less complex sentence structures, and shorter words. Turn taking is also chaotic during the caucusing sessions. Donohue and Diez (1983) observe this same formality when negotiators hold to rigid question-answer formats during proposal exchange. This formality is also communicated through a rigid turn-taking process in actual bargaining sessions (Donohue et al., 1984) and through formal argument sequences (Putnam, Wilson, & Turner, 1990).

However, when the interaction moves toward impasse, social distance becomes very informal. For example, in his study of couples in divorce mediation, Donohue (1991) reports that spouses who reach impasse turn to intense language use to communicate their thoughts. Intense language consists of repeated instances of profanity, sex, and death metaphors. Couples abandon any pretense to formality when they get mad, begin to attack one anothers' positions, or argue solely about relational issues.

Rogan and Donohue (1991) replicate this finding in their study of language intensity in hostage negotiations. In this context, negotiators increase language intensity as the situation becomes more confrontive. For example, during the initial moments of negotiation when the hostage takers spell out their demands, they use very intense language. In addition, they also interrupt frequently and use simple language and sentence structure. When the hostage taker starts to let the hostages go, the context returns to formality as signaled by increases in sentence length and decreases in language intensity.

These studies indicate that informal social distance is generally associated with confrontive, aggressive bargaining contexts. This finding makes sense given that informal contexts are, by definition, less rule-guided than formal ones. When issues become sensitive or individuals become aggressive, bargainers demonstrate less concern for structure and more concern for their own positions than they do in formal contexts.

PSYCHOLOGICAL DISTANCE

This dimension of relationship accesses the issue of affiliation. How much do individuals like each other, as reflected in their desires to become closer psychologically and physically? Researchers focus on several different behaviors to understand affiliation in conflict. For example, Gottman (1979, 1982) and his colleagues (Gottman, Markman, & Notarius, 1977; Mettetal & Gottman, 1980; Notarius & Johnson, 1982) analyze the verbal and nonverbal interaction of satisfied and dissatisfied marital couples. Their research indicates that the dissatisfied couples, as opposed to the satisfied ones, are: (1) much more likely to avoid confronting substantive issues, (2) less likely to negotiate differences (forward proposals and counterproposals), (3) more likely to reciprocate defensive verbal codes, (4) less likely to demonstrate reciprocal support for one another, and (5) less likely to listen attentively to one another. Noller's (1988) and Fitzpatrick's (1987, 1988) review of research in marital communication adds that these couples spin out of control by reciprocating negative affect without ever discussing the substantive issues associated with their feelings. Couples who are able to work through the conflict and get beyond the negative affect tend to have satisfying relationships.

Building on Gottman's (1979) research, Sillars and his colleagues (Sillars et al., 1984; Sillars et al., 1987) examine marital couples' interactions using Gottman's (1979) nonverbal affect scheme and Sillar's (1980) verbal conflict tactics. They discover that distressed couples distort the intent of one another's messages by focusing on nonverbal affect and ignoring substance. Couples in general, and dissatisfied couples in particular, focus on personality themes rather than on interaction themes, a pattern that leads to fault-finding and to focusing on problems over which people have little control. This attention to nonverbal affect and personalities promotes the use of distributive tactics, while a focus on substantive issues and interaction themes encourages integrative tactics.

A third research program that centers on psychological distance in negotiation examines verbal immediacy. Mehrabian and Wiener (Mehrabian, 1966a, 1966b, 1967, 1971; Mehrabian & Wiener, 1966; Wiener & Mehrabian, 1968) define *immediacy* as verbal and nonverbal choices that reflect an individual's desire to draw closer to persons and things liked, evaluated highly, and preferred, and move away from or avoid things disliked (see Gibbons et al., Chapter 7, this volume).

In negotiation studies on verbal immediacy, Donohue and his colleagues (Donohue, 1991: Donohue, Rogan, Ramesh, & Borchgrevink, 1990a, 1990b; Donohue, Weider-Hatfield, Hamilton, & Diez, 1985) reveal that: (1) structured negotiation interaction yields verbal immediacy and a desire to increase distance between parties, (2) relationally oriented bargaining produces language choices aimed at communicating directness and increasing the physical distance between parties, and (3) more substantive decision making yields the opposite pattern of indirectness and less physical distance than does nonsubstantive interaction. These results indicate that emotionally intense conflict discourages parties from editing their comments; they tell it like it is. However, they also show distaste for the process by wanting to escape from the situation. This push-pull process is the hallmark of distributive and difficult conflict episodes.

A CONTROL MODEL OF RELATIONAL MESSAGES

Perhaps the best way to integrate these results, and thus understand relationships in negotiation, is to place these dimensions in a systems framework (see Adams, 1990; Monge, 1977). The rationale for conceptualizing this research in a systems perspective lies in the role that relational messages play in negotiation. Based on studies of communication from a systems perspective (Watzlawick, Beavin, & Jackson, 1967), relational messages control the extent to which negotiators engage in substantive problem solving and ultimately reach satisfying agreements. Certain kinds of relational messages keep the negotiation focused on realistic issues, while other types move the focus to nonrealistic issues (Coser, 1956). In control systems terminology, relational messages can serve either a positive or negative feedback role. *Positive feedback* is information fed back into the system that moves it away from its desired outcome while *negative feedback* provides the system with information that corrects deviations from the desired goals. Certain relational messages function as positive feedback by distracting the negotiators from focusing on substantive problems. This chapter specifies the elements of a systems model and how these elements function.

A CONTROL MODEL OF
RELATIONAL MESSAGES IN NEGOTIATION

Three elements make up this system model: set point, system functions, and system environment. A *set point* is the global goal that interactants seek to achieve. The set point floats in relation to changing needs and conditions. In negotiation, the disputants typically establish the set point as reaching a mutually satisfying agreement. Failure to establish this set point indicates that one side or the other is unwilling to bargain in good faith.

The functions of the system are the sequencing or patterning of the elements that enable the set point to be achieved. Based on Hinde's (1979) model and our elaboration of it, the system elements consist of the three types of distancing messages that negotiators send to one another as they interact. The system functions include the sequencing of relational messages that keep the focus of the negotiation on realistic issues that move toward agreement, or keep the focus on unrealistic issues that move toward impasse.

Every system functions in some environment that places stress on it and either facilitates or hinders its functions. Too much stress compromises the regulatory functions of the system and pushes it to its limit. A reduction of stress facilitates movement toward its set point. For this research, Hinde's (1979) cognitive/affective relational dimensions function as system stressors or facilitators. Specifically, disputants' *cognitions* or their expectations, goals, and understandings of one another, and their *affective* orientations regarding values and feelings, either facilitate or hinder the communication system from doing its work.

INTEGRATIONS FROM THE SYSTEM MODEL

Distance. As previously indicated, every behavior in negotiation conveys information about the speaker's definition of role, social, and psychological distance. How do these elements function in negotiation to keep it moving toward mutually satisfying agreements? In examining role distance, research indicates that put-downs and negatively delivered concessions provide a positive feedback function (i.e., deviate the system from its set point), perhaps because they violate personal needs for a positive self-image (S. Wilson & Putnam, 1990). Yet, such integrative moves as opening bids given in cooperative tones or under system stress (high liking and understanding) provide negative feedback and keep the system within some cooperative limits. Promises and threats that function as compliance-gaining tactics perform similar negative feedback roles, particularly when the system has functioned for some time within cooperative limits. When the system moves toward impasse, however, threats and promises serve a positive feedback function and escalate the move toward impasse.

Perhaps the best example of how relational actions move the system either toward its set point or away from it appears in Putnam and Jones's (1982a) research. They discover that defensive moves by management serve as negative feedback functions in response to offensive moves by labor. Conversely, when management counters with offensive moves, the system shifts toward impasse.

The same kinds of system functioning emerge with social and psychological distance, as well as role distance. For social distance, establishing relatively formal distance and following specific discussion procedures function largely in a negative feedback capacity. However, more informal social distance and lack of structure lead the system to deviate from its set point. Similarly with respect to psychological distance, focusing on personalities and sustaining very direct levels of immediacy pushes the system toward impasse.

These results are consistent with the role distance literature because the tactics that escalate conflict are often delivered informally, violate structure, often accompany personality messages, and are direct. Hence, distancing messages have the capability to regulate the system in reaching its set point or to deregulate the system and escalate nonrealistic conflict.

Cognitive/Affective Orientations. Psychological orientations function as system stressors because the ones that bargainers bring into the setting greatly influence how they manage distance. The cognitive elements of expectations, goals, and understandings in Hinde's (1979) model serve as a useful illustration. The findings indicate that distance is decreased between parties, thereby regulating the system to reach its set point, when: (1) negotiators expect future interaction with an opponent they like but with whom they are not close friends; (2) they have had a chance to interact with the person and develop trust through gradual disclosure of personal information; (3) power is perceived as relatively equal; (4) the parties know one another's strategies and tactics; and (5) the relationship is judged as satisfying.

The affective elements of Hinde's (1979) model also influence relational systems in negotiation. That is, distance appears to decrease when disputants: (1) openly discuss values that underlie important positions, (2) use language choices that signal openness and directness, and (3) respond to emotional messages with reframing, questioning, and empathic strategies. These results are particularly critical in contexts (e.g., cross-cultural negotiation) that differ in values and language habits. Certainly, reacting emotionally to comments while using distancing language to hide values primes the negotiation system to fail. Signs of failure include fight-flight messages, cognitive simplification, and messages aimed at face concerns.

IMPLICATIONS AND CONCLUSIONS

This research overview underscores the importance of focusing on relational issues for negotiators as well as negotiation researchers. Certainly, ignoring distance patterns jeopardizes a negotiator's ability to reach an agreement and a researcher's ability to explain outcomes. Yet, inattention to the ways that the cognitive/ affective variables influence the sequencing of distancing messages also disadvantages both the negotiator and the researcher. The system framework may provide practitioners and researchers with a useful conceptual scheme for understanding how relational messages function in negotiation.

Another implication of this review is that focusing on the relational system may provide the best medium for understanding the forces of settlement and impasse in negotiation. Settlement seems likely when relational messages are either unnoticed (i.e., background features of the negotiation's substance) or are openly discussed in the interaction. Conversely, when relational messages become more important than substantive messages and disputants fail to discuss them, impasse is likely to occur.

For example, when negotiators: (1) exchange information, demands, and concessions under conditions of balanced power; (2) adhere to formal negotiation decorum; and (3) interact with openness and flexibility, relational messages become background features of the negotiation. Since disputants do not raise identity needs, relational messages fail to surface. However, when negotiations occur with power imbalances, minimal structure, and hostile interaction styles, face concerns become central in the dispute. Openly discussing relational issues regulates the system by clearing the air; ignoring them moves the system to impasse.

If relational messages become a unique medium for understanding outcomes, researchers and negotiators should make such analyses central to their work, as Greenhalgh (1987) argues. For example, researchers could conduct studies to examine if and when open discussions of relational problems facilitate system functioning. During periods of differentiation when relational issues are most likely to surface in negotiation, what strategies are useful for confronting such issues openly? Such discussions during periods of differentiation could conceivably reify the tension and further entrench the parties in a relational abyss. Hopefully, this chapter will be useful in generating questions about the role of relational development in negotiation.

REFERENCES

Adams, T. (1990). *Regulation and control in medicine: An introduction.* Unpublished manuscript, Department of Physiology, Michigan State University, East Lansing.

Allen, M., Donohue, W. A., & Stewart, B. (1990). Comparing hardline and softline bargaining strategies in zero-sum situations using meta-analysis. In M. A. Rahim (Ed.), *Theory and research in conflict management* (pp. 86-103). New York: Praeger.

Ben-Yoav, O., & Pruitt, D. G. (1984). Resistance to yielding and the expectation of cooperative future interaction in negotiation. *Journal of Experimental Social Psychology, 20,* 323-335.

Black, J. S., & Mendenhall, M. (1990). Cross-cultural training effectiveness: A review and a theoretical framework for future research. *Academy of Management Review, 15,* 113-136.

Bonoma, T. V., & Tedeschi, J. T. (1974). The relative efficacies of escalation and deescalation for compliance-gaining in two party conflicts. *Social Behavior and Personality, 2,* 212-218.

Bonoma, T. V., Tedeschi, J. T., & Helm, B. (1974). Some effects of target cooperation and reciprocated promises on conflict resolution. *Sociometry, 37,* 251-261.

Bowers, J. W., Metts, S. M., & Duncanson, W. T. (1985). Emotion and interpersonal communication. In M. L. Knapp & G. R. Miller (Eds.), *Handbook of interpersonal communication* (pp. 500-550). Beverly Hills, CA: Sage.

Brady, J. V. (1970). Endocrine and autonomic correlates of emotional behavior. In P. Black (Ed.), *Physiological correlates of emotion* (pp. 95-125). New York: Academic Press.

Brown, B. R. (1968). The effects of need to maintain face on interpersonal bargaining. *Journal of Experimental Social Psychology, 4,* 107-122.

Burggraf, C. S., & Sillars, A. L. (1987). A critical examination of sex differences in marital communication. *Communication Monographs, 54,* 276-294.

Cheney, J., Harford, T., & Solomon, L. (1972). The effects of communicating threats and promises upon the bargaining process. *Journal of Conflict Resolution, 16,* 99-107.

Cohen, L. H., Clairborn, W. L., & Specter, G. A. (1983). *Crisis intervention.* New York: Human Science Press.

Coser, L. S. (1956). *The functions of social conflict.* New York: Free Press.

Cushman, D., & King, S. (1985). National and organizational cultures in conflict resolution: Japan, the U.S., and Yugoslavia. In W. Gudykunst, L. Stewart, & S. Ting-Toomey (Eds.), *Communication, culture, and organizational processes* (pp. 115-133). Beverly Hills, CA: Sage.

Danheiser, P. R., & Graziano, W. G. (1982). Self-monitoring and cooperation as a self-presentational strategy. *Journal of Personality and Social Psychology, 42,* 497-505.

Diez, M. E. (1986). Negotiation competence: A conceptualization of the rules of negotiation interaction. In D. G. Ellis & W. A. Donohue (Eds.), *Contemporary issues in language and discourses processes* (pp. 223-238). Hillsdale, NJ: Lawrence Erlbaum.

Donohue, W. A. (1978). An empirical framework for examining negotiation processes and outcomes. *Communication Monographs, 45,* 247-257.

Donohue, W. A. (1981a). Analyzing negotiation tactics: Development of a negotiation interact system. *Human Communication Research, 7,* 273-287.

Donohue, W. A. (1981b). Development of a model of rule use in negotiation interaction. *Communication Monographs, 48,* 106-120.

Donohue, W. A. (1991). *Communication, marital dispute and divorce mediation.* Hillsdale, NJ: Lawrence Erlbaum.

Donohue, W. A., & Diez, M. E. (1983, May). *Information management in negotiation.* Paper presented at the annual meeting of the International Communication Association, Dallas.

Donohue, W. A., Diez, M. E., & Hamilton, M. (1984). Coding naturalistic negotiation interaction. *Human Communication Research, 10,* 403-425.

Donohue, W. A., Rogan, R., Ramesh, C. N., & Borchgrevink, C. (1990a, November). *Crisis bargaining: Tracking the double bind through verbal immediacy in hostage negotiations.* Paper presented at the annual conference of the Speech Communication Association, Chicago.

Donohue, W. A., Rogan, R., Ramesh, C. N., & Borchgrevink, C. (1990b, March). *The role of relational development in hostage negotiation.* Paper presented at the annual conference of the Central States Communication Association, Detroit.

Donohue, W. A., Weider-Hatfield, D., Hamilton, M., & Diez, M. E. (1985). Relational distance in managing conflict. *Human Communication Research, 11,* 387-406.

Druckman, D., Broome, B. J., & Korper, S. H. (1988). Value differences and conflict resolution: Facilitation or delinking? *Journal of Conflict Resolution, 32,* 489-510.

Egan, G. (1975). *The skilled helper.* Los Angeles: Brooks/Cole.

Fitzpatrick, M. A. (1987). Marriage and verbal intimacy. In V. Derlega & J. Berg (Eds.), *Self-disclosure: Theory, research and therapy* (pp. 131-154). New York: Plenum.

Fitzpatrick, M. A. (1988). *Between husbands and wives: Communication in marriage.* Newbury Park, CA: Sage.

Folger, J. P., & Poole, M. S. (1984). *Working through conflict: A communication perspective.* Glenview, Il: Scott, Foresman.

Fry, W. R., Firestone, I. J., & Williams, D. L. (1983). Negotiation process and outcome of stranger dyads and dating couples: Do lovers lose? *Basic and Applied Social Psychology, 4,* 1-16.

Fuselier, G. D. (1986). A practical overview of hostage negotiations. *FBI Law Enforcement Bulletin, 55,* 1-11.

Fuselier, G. D., & Van Zandt, C. R. (1987). *A practical overview of hostage negotiations.* Unpublished manuscript, SOARU, FBI Academy, Quantico, VA.

Gahagan, J. P., & Tedeschi, J. T. (1968). Strategy and the credibility of promises in the prisoner's dilemma game. *Journal of Conflict Resolution, 12,* 224-234.

Gladwin, T. N., & Kumar, R. (1986, September). *The social psychology of crisis bargaining: Toward a contingency model.* Paper presented at the International Conference on Industrial Crisis Management, New York.

Gottman, J. (1979). *Marital interaction.* New York: Academic Press.

Gottman, J. (1982). Emotional responsiveness in marital conversations. *Journal of Communication, 32,* 108-120.

Gottman, J., Markman, H., & Notarius, C. (1977). The topography of marital conflict: A study of verbal and nonverbal behavior. *Journal of Marriage and the Family, 39,* 461-477.

Greenhalgh, L. (1987). Relationships in negotiations. *Negotiation Journal, 3,* 235-243.

Gregory, M., & Carroll, S. (1978). *Language and situation.* London: Routledge & Kegan Paul.

Gruder, L. (1971). Relationships with opponent and partner in mixed-motive bargaining. *Journal of Conflict Resolution, 15,* 403-416.

Guyer, M., & Rapoport, A. (1970). Threat in a two-person game. *Journal of Experimental Social Psychology, 6,* 11-25.

Harford, T., & Solomon, L. (1967). "Reformed sinner" and "lapsed saint" strategies in the prisoner's dilemma game. *Journal of Conflict Resolution, 11,* 104-109.

Harrison, A. A., & McClintock, C. G. (1965). Previous experience within the dyad and cooperative game behavior. *Journal of Personality and Social Psychology, 1,* 671-675.

Higgins, E. T. (1987). Self discrepancy: A theory relating self and affect. *Psychological Review, 94,* 319-340.

Hinde, R. A. (1979). *Toward understanding relationships.* New York: Academic Press.

Janis, I., & Mann, L. (1977). *Decision making.* New York: Free Press.

Kelley, H. H., Berscheid, E., Christensen, A., Harvey, J. H., Huston, T. L., Levinger, G., McClintock, E., Peplau, L. A., & Peterson, D. R. (1983). *Close relationships.* New York: W. H. Freeman.

Kimmel, M. J., Pruitt, D. G., Magenau, J. M., Konar-Goldband, E., & Carnevale, P. J. D. (1980). Effects of trust, aspiration, and gender on negotiation tactics. *Journal of Personality and Social Psychology, 38,* 9-22.

Krauss, R. M., & Deutsch, M. (1966). Communication in interpersonal bargaining. *Journal of Personality and Social Psychology, 4,* 572-577.

Kressel, K. (1985). *The process of divorce: How professionals and couples negotiate settlements.* New York: Basic Books.

Kume, T. (1985). Managerial attitudes toward decision-making: North America and Japan. In W. Gudykunst, L. Stewart, & S. Ting-Toomey (Eds.), *Communication, culture, and organizational processes* (pp. 231-252). Beverly Hills, CA: Sage.

Lanceley, F. J. (1979). *The antisocial personality as a hostage taker.* Unpublished manuscript, SOARU, FBI Academy, Quantico, VA.

Lanceley, F. J., Ruple, S. W., & Moss, C. G. (1985). *Crisis and suicide intervention.* Unpublished manuscript, SOARU, FBI Academy, Quantico, VA.

Lane, H. W., & Beamish, P. W. (1990). Cross-cultural cooperative behavior in joint ventures in LDCs. *Management International Review, 30,* 87-102.

Leusch, R. F. (1976). Sources of power: Their impact on interchannel conflict. *Journal of Marketing Research, 4,* 382-390.

Mandler, G. (1975). *Mind and emotion.* New York: John Wiley.

Marlowe, D., Gergen, K. J., & Doob, A. N. (1966). Opponent's personality, expectation of social interaction, and interpersonal bargaining. *Journal of Personality and Social Psychology, 2,* 206-213.

Masse, M. (1981). The intercultural dialogue: Cornerstone development. *International Journal of Intercultural Relations, 5,* 203-214.

Matsumoto, D., Wallbott, H. G., & Scherer, K. R. (1989). Emotions in intercultural communication. In M. K. Asante & W. B. Gudykunst (Eds.), *Handbook of international and intercultural communication* (pp. 225-246). Newbury Park, CA: Sage.

McClintock, C. G., & McNeel, S. P. (1967). Prior dyadic experience and monetary reward as determinants of cooperative and competitive game behavior. *Journal of Personality and Social Psychology, 5,* 282-294.

McGillicuddy, N., Welton, G., & Pruitt, D. (1987). Third-party intervention: A field experiment comparing three different models. *Journal of Personality and Social Psychology, 53,* 104-112.

Mehrabian, A. (1966a). Immediacy: An indicator of attitudes in linguistic communication. *Journal of Personality, 34,* 26-34.

Mehrabian, A. (1966b). Attitudes in relation to the forms of communicator-object relationship in spoken communication. *Journal of Personality, 34,* 80-93.

Mehrabian, A. (1967). Attitudes inferred by non-immediacy of verbal communications. *Journal of Verbal Learning and Verbal Behavior, 6,* 294-305.

Mehrabian, A. (1971). *Silent messages.* Belmont, CA: Wadsworth.

Mehrabian, A., & Wiener, M. (1966). Non-immediacy between communicator and object of communication in a verbal message. *Journal of Consulting Psychology, 30,* 420-425.

Mettetal, G., & Gottman, J. M. (1980, November). *Affective responsiveness in spouses: Investigating the relationship between communication behavior and marital dissatisfaction.* Paper presented at the annual meeting of the Speech Communication Association, New York.

Michelini, R. L. (1971). Effects of prior interaction, contact, strategy, and expectation of meeting on game behavior and sentiment. *Journal of Conflict Resolution, 15,* 97-103.

Millar, F. E., & Rogers, E. L. (1976). A relational approach to interpersonal communication. In G. R. Miller (Ed.), *Explorations in interpersonal communication* (pp. 87-103). Beverly Hills, CA: Sage.

Miller, A. H. (1980). *Terrorism and hostage negotiation.* Boulder, CO: Westview.

Miller, G. R., & Steinberg, M. (1975). *Between people: A new analysis of interpersonal communication.* Chicago: Science Research Associates.

Monge, P. R. (1977). The systems perspective as a theoretical basis for the study of human communication. *Communication Quarterly, 25,* 19-29.

Morgan, W. R., & Sawyer, J. (1967). Bargaining, expectations, and the preference for equality over equity. *Journal of Personality and Social Psychology, 6,* 139-149.

Noller, P. (1988). Overview and implications. In P. Noller & M. A. Fitzpatrick (Eds.), *Perspectives on marital interaction* (pp. 323-344). Clevedon: Multilingual Matters.

Notarius, C. L., & Johnson, J. S. (1982). Emotional expression in husbands and wives. *Journal of Marriage and the Family, 44,* 483-489.

Oskamp, S. (1970). Effects of programmed initial strategies in a prisoner's dilemma game. *Psychonomic Science, 19,* 195-196.

Oskamp, S., & Perlman, D. (1965). Factors affecting cooperation in a prisoner's dilemma game. *Journal of Conflict Resolution, 9,* 359-374.

Oskamp, S., & Perlman, D. (1966). Effects of friendship and disliking on cooperation in a mixed-motive game. *Journal of Conflict Resolution, 10,* 221-226.

Papa, M. J., & Pood, E. A. (1988). Coorientational accuracy and differentiation in the management of conflict. *Communication Research, 15,* 400-425.

Pruitt, D. G. (1981). *Negotiation behavior.* New York: Academic Press.

Pruitt, D. G., & Rubin, J. Z. (1986). *Social conflict: Escalation, stalemate and settlement.* New York: Random House.

Pruitt, D. G., & Smith, D. L. (1981). Impression management in bargaining: Images of firmness and trustworthiness. In J. T. Tedeschi (Ed.), *Impression management in theory and social psychological research* (pp. 247-267). New York: Academic Press.

Putnam, L. L., & Jones, T. S. (1982a). Reciprocity in negotiations: An analysis of bargaining interaction. *Communication Monographs, 49,* 171-191.

Putnam, L. L., & Jones, T. S. (1982b). The role of communication in bargaining. *Human Communication Research, 8,* 262-280.

Putnam, L. L., & Poole, M. S. (1987). Conflict and negotiation. In K. H. Roberts & L. W. Porter (Eds.), *Handbook of organizational communication* (pp. 549-599). Newbury Park, CA: Sage.

Putnam, L. L., Wilson, S. R., & Turner, D. (1990). The evolution of police arguments in teachers' negotiation. *Argumentation, 3,* 129-152.

Rogan, R. G. (1990). *An interaction analysis of negotiator and hostage-taker identity-goal, relational-goal, and language intensity message behavior within hostage negotiations: A descriptive investigation of three negotiations.* Unpublished doctoral dissertation, Michigan State University, East Lansing.

Rogan, R. G., & Donohue, W. A. (1991, May). *Validation of a message content-based measure of language intensity in naturalistic conflict discourse.* Paper presented at the annual conference of the International Communication Association, Chicago.

Roth, W. T. (1982). The meaning of stress. In F. M. Ochberg & D. A. Soskis (Eds.), *Victims of terrorism* (pp. 37-57). Boulder, CO: Westview.

Rubin, J. Z. (1983). The use of third parties in organizations: A critical response. In M. Bazerman & R. J. Lewicki (Eds.), *Negotiating in organizations* (pp. 214-224). Beverly Hills, CA: Sage.

Salye, H. (1978). *The stress of life.* New York: McGraw-Hill.

Sermat, V., & Gregovich, R. P. (1966). The effect of experimental manipulation on cooperative behavior in a chicken game. *Psychonomic Science, 4,* 435-436.

Shapiro, E. G. (1975). Effect of expectations of future interaction on reward allocations in dyads: Equity or equality. *Journal of Personality and Social Psychology, 31,* 873-880.

Sillars, A. L. (1980). Attributions and communication in roommate conflicts. *Communication Monographs, 47,* 180-200.

Sillars, A. L., Pike, G. R., Jones, T. S., & Murphy, M. A. (1984). Communication and understanding in marriage. *Human Communication Research, 10,* 317-350.

Sillars, A. L., Weisberg, J., Burggraf, C. S., & Wilson, E. A. (1987). Content themes in marital conversations. *Human Communication Research, 13,* 495-528.

Slusher, E. A., Rose, G. L., & Roering, K. J. (1978). Commitment to future interaction and relative power under conditions of interdependence. *Journal of Conflict Resolution, 22,* 282-298.

Staw, B. M., Sandelands, L., & Dutton, J. (1981). Threat rigidity effects in organizational behavior: A multilevel analysis. *Administrative Science Quarterly, 26,* 501-524.

Strauss, M. A. (1979). Measuring inter-family conflict and violence: The conflict tactics (CT) scales. *Journal of Marriage and the Family, 41,* 75-88.

Strentz, T. (1983). *The inadequate personality as a hostage taker.* Unpublished manuscript, FBI Academy, Quantico, VA.

Strentz, T. (1986). Negotiating with the hostage taker exhibiting paranoid schizophrenic symptoms. *Journal of Police Science and Administration, 14,* 12-16.

Swingle, P. G. (1966). Effects of the emotional relationship between protagonists in a two-person game. *Journal of Personality and Social Psychology, 4,* 270-279.

Tedeschi, J. T., & Bonoma, T. V. (1977). Measures of last resort: Coercion and aggression in bargaining. In D. Druckman (Ed.), *Negotiations* (pp. 213-241). Beverly Hills, CA: Sage.

Tedeschi, J. T., Schlenker, B. R., & Bonoma, T. V. (1973). *Conflict, power, and games.* Chicago: Aldine.

Ting-Toomey, S. (1985). Toward a theory of conflict and culture. In W. B. Gudykunst, L. Stewart, & S. Ting-Toomey (Eds.), *Communication, culture, and organizational processes* (pp. 71-86). Beverly Hills, CA: Sage.

Ting-Toomey, S. (1988a). Culture and interpersonal relationship development: Some conceptual issues. In J. Andersen (Ed.), *Communication yearbook 12* (pp. 371-382). Newbury Park, CA: Sage.

Ting-Toomey, S. (1988b). Intercultural conflicts: A face-negotiation theory. In Y. Kim & W. Gudykunst (Eds.), *Theories in intercultural communication* (pp. 213-235). Newbury Park, CA: Sage.

Tjosvold, D. (1973). The use of threat by low power persons in bargaining. Doctoral dissertation, University of Minnesota, 1972. *Dissertation Abstracts International, 1,* 417-A (University Microfilms no. 73-18, 153).

Walton, R. E., & McKersie, R. B. (1965). *A behavioral theory of labor negotiations: An analysis of a social interaction system.* New York: McGraw-Hill.

Watzlawick, P., Beavin, J. B., & Jackson, D. D. (1967). *Pragmatics of human communication: A study of interactional patterns, pathologies, and paradoxes.* New York: W. W. Norton.

Wiener, M., & Mehrabian, A. (1968). *Language within language: Immediacy, a channel in verbal communication.* New York: Appleton-Century-Crofts.

Wilson, S. R., & Putnam, L. L. (1990). Interaction goals in negotiation. In J. Andersen (Ed.), *Communication yearbook 13* (pp. 374-406). Newbury Park, CA: Sage.

Wilson, W. (1971). Reciprocation and other techniques for inducing cooperation in the prisoner's dilemma game. *Journal of Conflict Resolution, 15,* 167-195.

Witteman, H., & Fitzpatrick, M.A. (1986). Compliance-gaining in marital interaction: Power bases, power processes, and outcomes. *Communication Monographs, 53,* 130-143.

Zechmeister, K., & Druckman, D. (1973). Determinants of resolving a conflict of interest: A simulation of political decision-making. *Journal of Conflict Resolution, 17,* 63-88.

Chapter 10

NEGOTIATOR-CONSTITUENT RELATIONSHIPS

Dudley B. Turner

Intra-organizational bargaining is a rich untapped domain for communication research.

—L. L. Putnam, 1985a, p. 236

THE VAST MAJORITY of research in bargaining and negotiation focuses on the two negotiators at the bargaining table, specifically, their actions and interactions and their outcomes. However, negotiators usually act as representatives who are influenced not only by the negotiating situation but also by their constituents (Druckman, 1977; Roloff & Campion, 1987). Viewing the negotiator as a representative adds complexity to the bargaining process. Rubin and Brown (1975) point out that simply having an audience physically or psychologically present affects the negotiator. Thus, concentrating primarily on the negotiator at the bargaining table limits an understanding of the overall negotiation process (Frey & Adams, 1972).

Druckman (1978a) claims that a negotiator's interaction with his or her constituents and with the opposing negotiator "are not regarded as being mutually exclusive during the course of a negotiation. They are complementary and intertwined, the one influencing the other in a reciprocal manner" (p. 108). Since negotiation at the table often hinges on communication activities in caucus sessions, research should focus on bargainer-constituent interactions (Putnam & Jones, 1982b). Putnam (1985a) proposes, "To understand the basis of interaction sequences at the table, researchers must extend their work beyond the bargaining dyad into the intergroup relations that constitute the negotiation event" (p. 236).

Much of what occurs in caucuses includes the process of reaching internal consensus between the negotiator and his or her constituents on what is an acceptable agreement with the other party. This process is often referred to as *intraorganizational bargaining* (Druckman, 1977; Walton & McKersie, 1965). No matter where the parties begin and no matter how diverse the ideas are within a party, negotiators and their constituents must come to an agreement before bargaining can be successfully completed. More than simply representing their constituents' desires, negotiators also mold and change their constituents' positions (Putnam, 1985b; Walton & McKersie, 1965).

Unfortunately, little research exists in this area. Communication studies of bargaining and negotiation often center on the strategies and tactics used at the table (Donohue, 1981a, 1981b; Pruitt & Lewis, 1975; Putnam & Jones, 1982a), but they rarely address the negotiator's interaction with his or her constituents nor the strategies and tactics used in caucus sessions.

This chapter examines the negotiator as a boundary role occupant who tries to balance the needs and desires of his or her constituents with the desires of the other party. After an overview of the boundary role literature, this essay reviews specific research concerning negotiator-constituent relations and message tactics.

A BOUNDARY ROLE PERSPECTIVE

A *role* consists of a set of activities or potential behaviors associated with a person's job or position in an organization (Kahn, Wolfe, Quinn, Snoek, & Rosenthal, 1964). Walton and McKersie (1965) describe a role as "a set of complementary expectations . . . prescribed by someone or some group" (pp. 283-284). Persons related to and affected by a particular role's activities are called the role set (Katz & Kahn, 1978; Kahn et al., 1964). A person's role set obviously includes other members of the same organization and may include persons outside of the organization. When role senders are located in a different social system or organization from the focal person, the focal person functions in a *boundary role* (Kahn et al., 1964).

Boundary role conflict occurs when one person, because of his or her position (job, function, role) and its duties, is subject to two (or more) sets of pressures from members of the role set such that compliance with one would make it difficult to comply with the other (Katz & Kahn, 1978; Kahn et al., 1964). Put more simply, it is when two role senders have mutually exclusive or incompatible goals (Putnam & Jones, 1982b). All boundary positions experience some conflict, but in roles such as a negotiator, the two sets of expectations are oppositional by definition. As Walton and McKersie (1965) explain:

> The boundary role occupied by the chief negotiator is the target of two sets of prescriptions about what the negotiator ought to do and how he should behave. That role expectations should originate from within his own organization should be obvious. In addition, a negotiator is often expected to behave with understanding and to act in a way that accommodates the needs of his opponent. (p. 284)

Negotiator roles involve three inherently communicative functions: representative, information processing, and agent of influence. Each function is bidirectional, outward and inward (Adams, 1976; Turner, 1990a). Directing functions outwardly occurs during bargaining with the other party, while directing them inwardly occurs during caucus interactions with constituents.

Since the negotiator's job entails inherent dilemmas of dealing simultaneously with individuals inside and outside of the organization (Druckman, 1973), the desired outcomes of one situation (e.g., between the negotiator and the union organization) often become sources of conflict for the other one (e.g., between the negotiator and management). In trying to balance these conflicting desires, the negotiator must deal with or work through such mediating factors as low trust or disagreement on bargaining goals with constituents, while simultaneously working with the other negotiator who has similar obstacles.

Although various aspects of this role relationship have been studied, this research has not centered on the communicative activities of the participants. In approaching the negotiator-constituent relationship from a boundary role perspective, communication becomes a pivotal factor in the negotiation process. Constituents must communicate their expectations to their negotiator before he or she can understand and perform this role. Often in research, communication has been ignored, assumed, or simply used as a tool to implement other experimental conditions.

Information that constituents communicate to their negotiator is rather obvious, such as their desired goals for each issue or how they want the negotiator to act while bargaining with the other party. However, information that does not deal directly with constituent expectations is not as obvious, even though it specifies certain restrictions on the negotiator, such as how much flexibility he or she has, or how much constituents trust him or her, or how closely constituents plan to monitor their negotiator.

The remainder of this chapter focuses on the research on negotiators and their constituents. The majority of this work uses the constituents' behavior as an independent or an antecedent variable and then measures its effect on the negotiator's behavior at the bargaining table. Less research is available on the communication between the negotiator and his or her constituents. However, relevant findings from both areas are summarized in this review.

CONSTITUENT EXPECTATIONS OF BARGAINERS

Constituent expectations can be grouped into three general areas: bargaining norms, goals on issues, and evaluations of the negotiator, often based on stated or implied expectations. Other research focuses on certain characteristics of the negotiator or on role restrictions that are communicated to the bargainer, namely, distance of the negotiator and constituent trust.

BARGAINING NORMS

In monitoring their representatives, constituents impose upon negotiators "certain expectations about how [they] will behave during the course of negotiations" (Walton & McKersie, 1965, p. 289). Past research has given bargainers directives but has not allowed them to discuss these guidelines with their constituents. Results show that when constituents tell their negotiators to cooperate or collaborate, it leads to more agreements in less time for a settlement than when they are told to compete or control (Benton & Druckman, 1974; Tjosvold, 1978). Benton and Druckman (1974) conclude that, "communications from constituents that moderate the competitive stance [of negotiators] . . . serve to reduce the boundary role conflict that interferes with obtaining agreements" (p. 149). However, negotiators who have a chance to discuss these directives might convince their constituents of a different strategy, depending on the situation, the parties involved, and the negotiators' experiences. Regardless of the unidirectional nature of these directives, constituents communicate how they want negotiators to behave and what they should strive to obtain.

PERCEIVED GOAL CONGRUENCE

A *goal* is the bargaining objective, or what is wanted from the bargaining or what a party is ultimately hoping to receive from the negotiation. Most research that uses laboratory simulations allows negotiators to determine their goals, or the researcher gives the goals to the negotiators. A few studies (Kogan, Lamm, & Trommsdorff, 1972; Tjosvold, 1978) allow joint decision making or discussion among negotiators and constituents prior to bargaining. Yet in almost all studies, there is no opportunity for the negotiator to revise those goals with his or her constituents once the bargaining begins. *Goal congruence* is "the extent to which the private goals of the negotiator and the goals of the constituents [match]" (Perry & Angle, 1979, p. 488). In most studies, goal congruence is assumed, or the negotiator revises goals unilaterally. In effect, the study fails to examine how the negotiator handles goal incongruence (see, for example, Breaugh, & Klimoski, 1977).

Prenegotiation contact and communication helps the negotiator clarify the constituents' desires and affects negotiator behavior (Klimoski, 1972; Klimoski & Breaugh, 1977). Cresswell, Murphy and Kerchner (1980) claim constituents influence bargaining outcomes if they communicate their expectations or desired outcomes for issues to their negotiator. More specifically, Neslin and Greenhalgh (1983) conclude that the preferences the bargainer takes into the negotiation strongly affect the outcomes of the process; therefore, the constituents should communicate their preferences accurately. A national survey supports this finding and links successful integrative bargaining to communicating constituent issues clearly and specifically (Peterson & Tracy, 1977).

When constituents convey goal congruence, the negotiator uses their ideas, desires, and proposals during bargaining. However, when constituents communicate disagreement with the negotiator's goals, the negotiator fails to convey their suggestions to the other party. Instead, he or she agrees with or builds upon ideas and proposals from the other party or from those generated during the bargaining itself (Turner, 1988, 1990a).

Turner's research differs from previous studies in that communication between constituents and their negotiators is sustained throughout the negotiation. In this situation, the constituents' desires may have less influence than in other studies since the negotiator has the opportunity to shape constituents' preferences during caucus sessions. Yet, negotiators must represent their constituents and are judged by them.

EVALUATIONS OF THE NEGOTIATOR

Simply knowing that constituents continually evaluate their negotiator affects his or her behavior. Klimoski (1972) reports that, "subjects who faced the possibility of an evaluation by their group took more time [to reach a negotiated agreement]" (p. 377). Often, however, constituents give feedback or evaluative information during the negotiation.

Specifically, the valence of constituents' evaluations influences the negotiator. Surveys of actual negotiators suggest that negative feedback from constituents lowers negotiator attitudes and leads to unsuccessful bargaining (Lambert, Dornoff, & Kernan, 1977; Peterson & Tracy, 1977). Communicating favorable feedback to the negotiator is linked to successful bargaining. In research reported by Rubin and Brown (1975), subjects who received favorable feedback from constituents engage in less retaliation during bargaining than those who receive derogatory remarks or no feedback at all. In like manner, Peterson and Tracy (1977) report that negotiators who receive praise or credit from their constituents engage in integrative bargaining.

NEGOTIATOR DISTANCE

Characteristics of the negotiator role also influence communication with constituents. Perry and Angle (1979) define *distance* as: a function of the negotiator's organizational centrality . . . the extent to which the constituents' goals are understood by the negotiator, and the extent to which the private goals of the negotiator and the goals of the constituents are congruent (p. 487-488). In more concise terms, "The distance of the negotiator from the constituency is a function of . . . organizational centrality, goal ambiguity, and goal congruence" (p. 490). Walton and McKersie (1965) explain the relationship between distance and goal congruence in a different manner saying, "differences in goal structure are more likely, the greater the organizational distance between groups" (p. 289). Hence, the negotiator may reduce his or her distance by communicating with the constituents about their desired goals.

In research on negotiator distance, distance is defined as (1) the status level or power of the negotiator in relation to the person(s) who he or she represents (see Carnevale, Pruitt, & Seilheimer, 1981; Organ, 1971) or (2) the negotiator's physical or psychological distance from constituents, whether or not the negotiator is a member of the group or organization (Breaugh & Klimoski, 1977).

Research that treats distance as status illustrates that superiors as negotiators experience greater shifts from their original positions, more satisfaction with decisions, and less time needed for agreement than subordinates as negotiators experience (Carnevale et al., 1981; Kogan et al., 1972; Organ, 1971). Research that examines the effects of group membership reports that negotiators who are group members are evaluated higher, stray from their positions to a lesser degree, feel they are more responsible for the solution, feel they have a better understanding of the team's viewpoint, try harder to uphold their positions, and are committed to their constituencies more than outsiders or nonmember bargainers are (Breaugh & Klimoski, 1977; Perry & Angle, 1979; Walton & McKersie, 1965). Yet, none of these studies examine the communication between the negotiator and the constituents. Interaction about desired goals or acceptable agreements is vital to the bargaining process, regardless of the negotiator's power or group member status.

CONSTITUENT TRUST IN THE NEGOTIATOR

Constituent trust in the negotiator is an important characteristic of the negotiator-constituent relationship. *Trust* is "the strength of belief of those represented that participants will behave so as to optimize the outcomes in terms of their constituents' objectives" (Cresswell et al., 1980, p. 274). It is central to negotiation and to the communicative activities involved. Why would constituents distrust their negotiator? Adams (1976) says, "To conclude a transaction, the negotiator may have to yield something or forego an outcome desired by his [or her] organization. Thus, there exists an apparent objective basis for distrusting the negotiator" (p. 1192). Trust is often gained through prenegotiation contact between the negotiator and constituents. Constituent trust affects the negotiator's behavior and interacts with other factors to influence bargaining outcomes (Frey & Adams, 1972; Klimoski & Breaugh, 1977; Lambert et al., 1977; Neslin & Greenhalgh, 1983; Wall & Adams, 1974). When negotiators perceive a low level of trust, they try to "establish that confidence or trust by conforming to the constituency behavioral norm" (Organ, 1971, p. 527). A negotiator's perception of constituent trust can be influenced by a single message. In the Frey and Adams (1972) study, the only difference between high- and low-trust groups is the initial message stating whether or not the negotiator is trusted; all other communications or actions from the constituents are identical. Yet the behaviors of negotiators in the two groups are significantly different. For example, negotiators in the low-trust condition employ fewer and more systematic concessions, experience more felt tension, and desire more flexibility than do bargainers in the high-trust condition. In low-trust situations, constituents may monitor the negotiator's actions, tell their negotiator what to do, and put him or her on the defensive. Negotiators in a low-trust situation not only follow their constituents' norms more closely, but also communicate their constituents' ideas, desires, and proposals more often than they do their own, and build less on the ideas generated during the bargaining itself (Turner, 1988, 1990a). Generally, when negotiators are not trusted, they are less flexible, show more distributive behavior, and communicate more competitively at the table than they do when trust is present (Organ, 1971).

High trust communicated to or perceived by negotiators leads to less felt tension and to more flexible behavior than does low trust. Trusted negotiators deviate from prescribed bargaining norms and communicate their own ideas rather than those given by their constituents (Brodie & Williams, 1983; Turner, 1988, 1990a, 1990b). As Organ (1971) explains, "To the extent that the negotiator feels he possesses the confidence of constituents, there would be less urgent grounds for conformity to behavioral norms in order to establish that confidence" (p. 527). In these studies, trust is communicated to the negotiators through an initial message. Constituents need to be aware of the impact a single message may have on the negotiator's behavior.

Low trust is often indirectly communicated to negotiators through constituent monitoring. When constituents indicate that they are monitoring a bargainer, this affects the negotiator's behaviors and attitudes. Compared to subjects who are not monitored, bargainers who think their constituents are observing them display stronger adherence to their constituents' norms and experience more tensions (Adams, 1976; Organ,

1971). Negotiators who are monitored also display less flexible bargaining (that is, slower, less systematic, and lower priority concessions) than do negotiators who are not monitored (Ben-Yoav & Pruitt, 1984; Carnevale, Pruitt, & Britton, 1979; Carnevale et al., 1981; Cresswell et al., 1980; Haccoun & Klimoski, 1975; Klimoski, 1972; Klimoski & Ash, 1974; Organ, 1971; Roloff & Campion, 1987).

Monitoring causes negotiators to be less influenced by and less responsive to information from the opponents than those who are not monitored (Clopton, 1984). This monitoring leads to lower rates of compromise, fewer deviations from initial positions, and more concern for satisfying constituents than does the absence of monitoring (Peterson & Tracy, 1977; Wall & Adams, 1974). Generally, negotiators behave rigidly and competitively when they are monitored by constituents; this rigidity, in turn, often leads to deadlocks or lower quality decisions.

Table 10.1 summarizes the findings reported in this section and indicates the messages that constituents convey to negotiators and the effects of these messages.

NEGOTIATOR-CONSTITUENT COMMUNICATION

Although the majority of negotiator-constituent studies focus on the negotiator's behavior, some research examines caucus activities and negotiator-constituent interaction. These findings are grouped into the categories of goal agreement and trust.

GOAL AGREEMENT AND COMMUNICATION

When constituents communicate disagreement with goals, negotiators perceive that conflict with constituents increases as the bargaining progresses, both in their own behaviors and in their constituents' behaviors (Turner, 1990b). These perceptions affect the negotiator's interactions with constituents.

Supporting team proposals and raising constituents' aspirations are strategies that negotiators use when goal congruence is high (Turner, 1988, 1990a). Bargainers not only indicate support for and agreement with team members' ideas but they also try to raise constituents' aspirations when goals are congruent. However, the opposite is not always true. Although some research suggests that negotiators may lower their

TABLE 10.1   Constituent Messages to Bargainers

Constituents ⟶ Negotiator₁ ⟶ Other Party	
(communicates to)	*(communicates to)*
Monitoring	competitive, distributive behaviors
	firmer positions (less flexibility)
	more low priority concessions
	slower concessions
Praise	less retaliation
	integrative bargaining
Criticism	more retaliation
	distributive bargaining
High Trust	less tension
	more use of negotiator's own ideas
	more deviations from prescribed bargaining norms
Low Trust	more tension
	use constituents' ideas and proposals
	competitive, distributive bargaining
	conform to constituents' bargaining norms
Cooperativeness	less competitive
	more agreements
Goal Congruence	use constituents' ideas and proposals
	integrative bargaining
Goal Incongruence	agree with and build on other party's ideas
	and proposals

constituents' aspirations or defend and clarify their own proposals in a low-goal congruence situation (Walton & McKersie, 1965), other studies do not support this finding (Turner, 1988, 1990a). For example in Turner's (1990a) research, negotiators argue for or against particular bargaining behaviors rather than for particular goals. Negotiators may use this approach to change aspirations indirectly, to pursue the goals that he or she feels are reasonable, or to disagree with constituents unobtrusively.

TRUST AND COMMUNICATION

The second category of research on negotiator-constituent communication involves trust. Negotiators who feel trusted perceive their constituents to be less demanding, less exploitive, and less hard on them than distrusted negotiators perceive (Frey & Adams, 1972; Organ, 1971).

TABLE 10.2   Negotiator-Constituent Communication

Constituents ⟶ *Negotiator* *(communicates to)*	*Negotiator* ⟶ *Constituents* *(communicates to)*
Goal Congruence	support constituent proposals and ideas raise constituent goal aspirations
Goal Incongruence	argue for more flexibility adjust personal goal aspirations increase conflict behavior try to change constituents' aspirations
High Trust	raise constituents' aspirations clarify and defend own proposals and ideas firmer messages to constituents
Low Trust	acquiescent statements to constituents

Distrust may lead to stifled, limited, or incomplete communication with constituents. Either type of interaction would affect bargaining outcomes.

The level of perceived trust significantly influences the way negotiators communicate with their constituents. Frey and Adams (1972) observe that negotiators send more acquiescent messages to their constituents in low- as opposed to high-trust situations. Although this study casts a computer as the simulated constituents, Turner (1988, 1990a) reports parallel results in face-to-face communication between negotiators and constituents. Negotiators defend their own proposals in caucuses when trust from team members is high. This openness or flexibility in high-trust conditions leads negotiators to try to raise their team members' aspirations. Earlier research indicates that distrusted negotiators feel inflexible and argue for their team's ideas and proposals (Walton & McKersie, 1965). These strategies, however, are not used frequently in caucus sessions (Turner, 1990b). Negotiator efforts to build constituent trust differ from directly confronting constituents in face-to-face interactions. Table 10.2 summarizes the research on negotiator-constituent communication during caucus sessions.

DIRECTIONS FOR FUTURE RESEARCH

There is a paucity of research on caucuses and intraorganizational bargaining and on the communicative strategies and tactics used in caucus sessions. As Roloff and Campion (1987) conclude, "Future research should study both communication between representatives *and* communication between representatives and their constituencies" (p. 162). Models of intraorganizational bargaining (Druckman, 1978a, 1978b; Walton & McKersie, 1965) are incomplete in understanding the impact of negotiator-constituent relations on intraorganizational bargaining. A basic model of intraorganizational bargaining, developed by Turner (1988, 1990a), draws on ideas from the literature on negotiation, role theory, and boundary role spanning. These studies also link caucus interaction with bargaining communication at the table.

Past studies treat the negotiator-constituent relationship as a medium for understanding negotiator attitudes, strategies, and outcomes. Few investigations center on how a negotiator handles his or her constituents. Several category systems exist for examining bargaining interaction at the table (Donohue, 1981a, 1981b). Researchers who use these systems (Pruitt & Lewis, 1975; Putnam & Geist, 1985; Putnam & Jones, 1982b; Putnam, Turner, Waltman, & Wilson, 1985; Putnam, Wilson, Waltman, & Turner, 1986; Turner, 1985) code bargaining interaction into such categories as threats, information giving, arguments, commitments, and promises. Yet they rarely take into account the negotiator-constituent relationship. If this relationship is included in a study, caucus interaction is coded with the same category scheme used for bargaining interaction. However, this research ignores the subtle subprocesses of intraorganizational bargaining.

Researchers must realize that caucuses are unique in their context and purpose. Applying bargaining strategies or group decision-making processes to caucus interaction is inappropriate. Development and fine tuning of coding strategies specifically for caucus sessions should continue. This development is necessary for investigating how caucuses influence bargaining and vice versa and for examining how communication facilitates both the inward and outward activities of a negotiator.

Figure 10.1 illustrates these complex inward and outward activities of negotiators. Central to these activities are the messages that constituents communicate to the negotiator. The positive and negative signs (+/−) beside each arrow indicate the relationships of the two variables. For example, more messages of high trust to the negotiator leads to more flexibility (+) and less competitiveness (−), with less acquiescent messages (−) to constituents in caucus sessions.

The effects of these bidirectional relationships are still unclear. As a representative, the negotiator must deal with constituent pressures, typi-

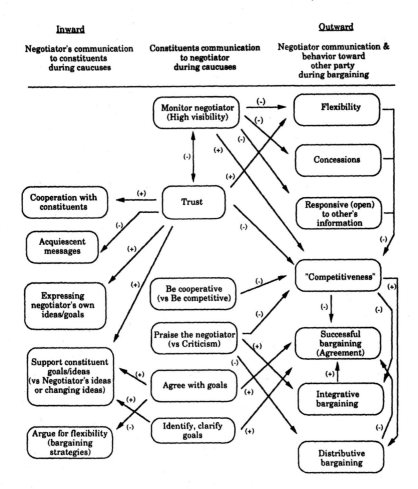

Figure 10.1. Inward and Outward Directed Communication

cally by demanding high outcomes or giving bargaining directives to "be tough." How do constituents influence their negotiator's bargaining? One model suggests that constituent pressure leads to tougher bargaining that often results in deadlocks (Ben-Yoav & Pruitt, 1984). A second model suggests that negotiators use constituent pressure to maintain or enhance a tough bargaining position and to induce concessions from the other party (e.g., "my people won't go for that," "my hands are tied," Friedland, 1983). This second approach implies that constituent pressure may not be a negative force and that negotiators can react to these pressures in different ways. The first two models posit linear cause-effect relationships.

A third model merges constituent pressure with other elements in the negotiation. Combining constituent pressure with concern for the other party results in negotiator flexibility, bargainer accountability to assure constituent satisfaction, and a creative solution that meets the goals of both parties (e.g., a "flexible-rigidity" approach, Pruitt & Lewis, 1975).

Measurement of the effects of constituent pressure on bargaining is rather limited. Variance from the constituents' original goals serves as an indirect measure (Roloff & Campion, 1987). Direct measures include reiterating constituents' arguments during bargaining (Turner, 1988, 1990a) or developing a creative agreement through problem solving (Carnevale et al., 1981). Yet even when such measures are directly linked to the bargaining, the caucus interaction is rarely studied.

Communication researchers must continue to deduce from the present negotiator-constituent research possible implications for caucus interaction and then test these implications. Turner's (1988, 1990a) model constitutes a starting point for testing links between negotiator-constituent relations in caucuses and ongoing bargaining at the table (see Figure 10.1). Ideally, researchers should use actual negotiations to validate laboratory experiments. However, many variables could still be studied in controlled settings.

Some links have been made between communication in the caucus and interaction at the bargaining table. More complete information is needed, however, to understand the interaction between the difficult, bidirectional boundary role of the negotiator. As Druckman (1978a) urges, "The interaction between the processes involved in this function [boundary spanning] remains a topic for investigation. Further elucidation awaits the results of [more] studies" (p. 109).

REFERENCES

Adams, J. S. (1976). The structure and dynamics of behavior in organizational boundary roles. In M. P. Dunnette (Ed.), *Handbook of industrial and organizational psychology* (pp. 1175-1199). Chicago: Rand McNally.

Ben-Yoav, O., & Pruitt, D. G. (1984). Accountability to constituents: A two-edged sword. *Organizational Behavior and Human Performance, 34*, 283-295.

Benton, A. A., & Druckman, D. (1974). Constituent's bargaining orientation and intergroup negotiations. *Journal of Applied Social Psychology, 4*, 141-150.

Breaugh, J. A., & Klimoski, R. S. (1977). The choice of a group spokesman in bargaining: Member or outsider? *Organizational Behavior and Human Performance, 19,* 325-336.

Brodie, D. W., & Williams, P. A. (1983). *School contract language.* Redmond, WA: Butterworth.

Carnevale, P., Pruitt, D. G., & Britton, S. D. (1979). Looking tough: The negotiation under constituent surveillance. *Personality and Social Psychology Bulletin, 5,* 118-121.

Carnevale, P., Pruitt, D. G., & Seilheimer, S. D. (1981). Looking and competing: Accountability and visual access in integrative bargaining. *Journal of Personality and Social Psychology, 40,* 111-120.

Clopton, S. (1984). Seller and buying firm factors affecting industrial buyers' negotiation behavior and outcomes. *Journal of Marketing Research, 21,* 39-53.

Cresswell, A. M., Murphy, M. J., & Kerchner, C. T. (1980). *Teachers unions and collective bargaining in public education.* Berkeley, CA: McCrutchen.

Donohue, W. A. (1981a). Analyzing negotiation tactics: Development of a negotiation interact system. *Human Communication Research, 7,* 273-287.

Donohue, W. A. (1981b). Development of a model of rule use in negotiation interaction. *Communication Monographs, 48,* 106-120.

Druckman, D. (1973). *Human factors in international negotiations: Social-psychological aspects of international conflict.* Beverly Hills, CA: Sage.

Druckman, D. (1977). Boundary role conflict: Negotiation as dual responsiveness. *Journal of Conflict Resolution, 21,* 639-662.

Druckman, D. (1978a). The monitoring function in negotiation: Two models of responsiveness. In H. Sauermann (Ed.), *Bargaining behavior* (pp. 344-374). Tubingen: Mohr.

Druckman, D. (1978b). Boundary role conflict: Negotiation as dual responsiveness. In I. W. Zartman (Ed.), *The negotiation process: Theories and applications* (pp. 87-110). Beverly Hills, CA: Sage.

Frey, R. L., Jr., & Adams, J. S. (1972). The negotiator's dilemma: Simultaneous in-group and out-group conflict. *Journal of Experimental Social Psychology, 8,* 331-346.

Friedland, N. (1983). Weakness as strength: The use and misuse of a "My hands are tied" ploy in bargaining. *Journal of Applied Social Psychology, 13,* 422-426.

Haccoun, R. R., & Klimoski, R. J. (1975). Negotiator status and accountability source: A study of negotiator behavior. *Organizational Behavior and Human Performance, 14,* 342-359.

Kahn, R. L., Wolfe, D. M., Quinn, R. P., Snoek, J. D., & Rosenthal, R. A. (1964). *Organizational stress: Studies in role conflict and ambiguity.* New York: John Wiley.

Katz, D., & Kahn, R. L. (1978). *The social psychology of organizations.* New York: John Wiley.

Klimoski, R. J. (1972). The effects of intragroup forces on intergroup conflict resolution. *Organizational Behavior and Human Performance, 8,* 363-383.

Klimoski, R. J., & Ash, R. (1974). Accountability and negotiator behavior. *Organizational Behavior and Human Performance, 11,* 409-425.

Klimoski, R. J., & Breaugh, J. A. (1977). When performance doesn't count: A constituency looks at its spokesman. *Organizational Behavior and Human Performance, 20,* 301-311.

Kogan, N., Lamm, H., & Trommsdorff, G. (1972). Negotiation constraints in the risk-taking domain: Effects of being observed by partners of higher or lower status. *Journal of Personality and Social Psychology, 23,* 143-156.

Lambert, D., Dornoff, R., & Kernan, J. (1977). The industrial buyer and the postchoice evaluation process. *Journal of Marketing Research, 14,* 246-251.

Neslin, S. A., & Greenhalgh, L. (1983). Nash's theory of cooperative games as a predictor of the outcomes of buyer-seller negotiations: An experiment in media purchasing. *Journal of Marketing Research, 20,* 368-379.

Organ, D. W. (1971). Some variables affecting boundary role behavior. *Sociometry, 34,* 524-537.

Perry, C. R., & Angle, H. L. (1979). The politics of organizational boundary roles in collective bargaining. *Academy of Management Review, 4,* 487-496.

Peterson, R. B., & Tracy, L. (1977). Testing a behavioral theory model of labor negotiations. *Industrial Relations, 16,* 35-50.

Pruitt, D. G., & Lewis, S. A. (1975). Development of integrative solutions in bilateral negotiation. *Journal of Personality and Social Psychology, 31,* 621-633.

Putnam, L. L. (1985a). Bargaining as task and process: Multiple functions of interaction sequences. In R. L. Street & J. N. Cappella (Eds.), *Sequence and pattern in communication behavior* (pp. 225-242). London: Edward Arnold.

Putnam, L. L. (1985b). Collective bargaining as organizational communication. In P. K. Tompkins & R. McPhee (Eds.), *Organizational communication: Traditional themes and new directions* (pp. 129-148). Beverly Hills, CA: Sage.

Putnam, L. L., & Geist, P. (1985). Argument in bargaining: An analysis of the reasoning process. *The Southern Speech Communication Journal, 50,* 225-245.

Putnam, L. L., & Jones, T. S. (1982a). Reciprocity in negotiations: An analysis of bargaining interaction. *Communication Monographs, 49,* 171-191.

Putnam, L. L., & Jones, T. S. (1982b). The role of communication in bargaining. *Human Communication Research, 8,* 262-280.

Putnam, L. L., Turner, D. B., Waltman, M. S., & Wilson, S. R. (1985, November). *Analyzing naturalistic bargaining from an argumentation perspective.* Paper presented at the annual convention of The Speech Communication Association, Denver.

Putnam, L. L., Wilson, S. R., & Turner, D. B. (1990). The evolution of policy arguments in teachers' negotiation. *Argumentation, 4,* 129-152.

Putnam, L. L., Wilson, S. R., Waltman, M. S., & Turner, D. B. (1986). The evolution of case arguments in teacher's bargaining. *Journal of the American Forensic Association, 23,* 63-81.

Roloff, M. E., & Campion, D. E. (1987). On alleviating the debilitating effects of accountability on bargaining: Authority and self-monitoring. *Communication Monographs, 54,* 145-164.

Rubin, J. Z., & Brown, B. R. (1975). *The social psychology of bargaining and negotiation.* New York: Academic Press.

Tjosvold, D. (1978). Control strategies and own group evaluation in intergroup conflict. *Journal of Psychology, 100,* 305-314.

Turner, D. B. (1985, April). *Labor negotiation: An argumentation analysis.* Paper presented at the annual convention of the Central States Speech Association, Indianapolis.

Turner, D. B. (1988). *Intraorganizational bargaining: The effect of goal congruence and trust on negotiator strategy use.* Unpublished doctoral dissertation, Purdue University, West Lafayette, IN.

Turner, D. B. (1990a). Intraorganizational bargaining: The effect of goal congruence and trust on negotiator strategy use. *Communication Studies, 41,* 54-75.

Turner, D. B. (1990b, November). *Intraorganizational bargaining and negotiator perceptions.* Paper presented at the annual convention of the Speech Communication Association, Chicago.

Wall, J. A., & Adams, J. S. (1974). Some variables affecting a constituent's evaluations of and behavior toward a boundary role occupant. *Organizational Behavior and Human Performance, 11,* 390-408.

Walton, R. E., & McKersie, R. B. (1965). *A behavioral theory of labor negotiations.* New York: McGraw-Hill.

Chapter 11

NEGOTIATION AUDIENCES:
THE ROLE OF THE MASS MEDIA

Sara U. Douglas

ALTHOUGH SOCIAL CONFLICT holds little interest to news producers, it is of vital importance to mass media news (Roloff, 1987). There is evidence, for example, that editors judge newsworthiness, in part, on the degree of conflict in the event (Atwood, 1970; Gans, 1979; Ward, 1967). Apparently, news consumers also are attracted to media accounts of conflict (Atwood, 1970). Some go as far as saying that without conflict there would be no news. The importance of negotiation to the media, however, is much less clear, and generally does not interest media producers. But, to the extent that negotiation is able to attract media attention and interest, conditions of the negotiations may change. This chapter examines the proposition that the media play a role in negotiation. That is, media are more than channels of communication; they are actively involved in the negotiation situation and perhaps in its outcomes. The proposition generates several questions. How and why is news of negotiations produced? What is the relationship between news production and negotiators? How might media affect the status and outcomes of negotiation? What is the role that media play in negotiations?

To address the first question, a framework suggested by sociologists Molotch and Lester (1974) is adopted. Although this framework does not discuss negotiation specifically, it is useful in examining the social construction of news and in reviewing related literature. This literature ranges from studies of labor-management negotiations to research on social conflict more generally. Studies of media access, media bias and power, and ongoing negotiator-media relations provide insights to examine the second question. The third question is addressed largely through reports of media effects research. Finally, the fourth question is considered from the perspective of the role of media as *tertius gaudens*. This idea, first suggested by Simmel (1950) and further elaborated by Arno (1984), is particularly pertinent to this chapter because of its applicability to negotiation. In this chapter the term refers to a situation in which interaction between negotiators and media suits media's own purposes. *Tertius gaudens* means "the third who rejoices."

MODELS OF NEWS PRODUCTION

Scholars typically use at least two relatively specific models to explain the way news is produced. These are the manipulative and the market models. The manipulative model proposes that news is selected to serve the interests of media owners, even though these interests may be opposed to those of the general public and may force departures from accuracy. The market model, in contrast, focuses on the interests of media audiences and the responsibility of news producers to provide them with what they want or need. What audiences want or need varies, but proponents of the model generally assume that news items are selected responsibly and portrayed objectively.

More recently, a number of media scholars have subsumed these and other simple models with the belief that both world events and news production of these events are complex social constructions (see Ettema, Whitney, & Wackman, 1987). Given this thinking, the challenge that scholars face is to examine these social constructions to understand the final product. News producers operate at three levels: news selection, news presentation, and assessment of the consequences of news for audiences as well as for future news production. The process is affected by a variety of factors, all of which are less contentious than the question of what happens to reality and objectivity in the process. The complexity of the debate is heightened by the recognition that news assemblers are not acting alone, but are part of a chain that typically includes news makers, news promoters, news assemblers, and news consumers. This series of intermediate social constructions suggests that the commodity ultimately produced by the news media is doubly manufactured. That is, the commodity "is a characterization of an event packaged so as to be 'sold' to the media and it is such characterization repackaged so as to be 'sold' to an audience" (Cohen & Young, 1981, p. 30).

Molotch and Lester (1974) suggest approaching the media not by looking for reality, but by looking for purposes underlying the strategies whereby one reality is created rather than another. In this conception of news, public events "exist because of the practical purposes they serve, rather than because of their inherent objective importance" (Molotch & Lester, 1974, p. 101). Moreover, media news content is viewed as the result of "practical, purposive, and creative activities" on the part of news promoters (those who identify an occurrence as having news value), news assemblers (newspersons, editors, and others who transform occurrences to public events by way of mass media), and news consumers. The social constructions employed by each link in the chain inhibits other interpretations that have not emerged as the construction of the event. Those groups at the end of the chain, typically the news consumers, are most disadvantaged by this process.

ASSEMBLING NEWS OF NEGOTIATIONS

Media power obviously is exercised through language (Carey, 1975; Gans, 1979; Gitlin, 1980; Morley, 1976; Tuchman, 1978). Carragee (1990) says, "Simply put, journalists and news organizations possess the important power of definition" (p. 4). Galtung and Ruge (1981) suggest that this power and the social construction of news are affected by two sets of factors: institutional settings that impose a range of bureaucratic and organizational constraints, and the frames of reference of the news assemblers. These factors contribute to what analysts call preestablished interpretive frameworks or "patterned stereotypes" that mediate the presentation of news as well as its selection. These factors may result in the systematic exclusion of alternative points of view and the simplification of complexities and problems (McColl, 1980).

BUREAUCRATIC AND ORGANIZATIONAL CONSTRAINTS

Carragee (1990), in explaining how media introduced Americans to the conflict between trade unions and the government in Poland, emphasized ways that news assemblers are influenced by the bureaucratic and organizational settings in which they work. Organizational and bureaucratic settings, in turn, undoubtedly are influenced by many things, including values and perhaps especially profits. Images of "shoestring budget newspapers," struggling community-run radio stations, and even the problematic exception of public radio and television provide substantial evidence that media industries generally are successful in their quests for profit. They have gained power and prestige along the way. Recognition of the changing structure of the media has contributed to the thesis of the manipulative model where owners dominate those who work for them. The web of media oligopoly power extends to a variety of political, legal, and social pressures that result in direct or indirect manipulation of journalists (Bagdikian 1983; Compaine, 1982; Murdock & Golding, 1977; Pertschuk, 1979).

Additional constraints arise from other structural properties of the media industry, especially the interconnectedness of the industries themselves, their ties to business, their dependence on advertising, and their relationships to government. Fishman (1980) argues that most bureaucracies reflect the establishment, namely government and private institutions. Research conducted by the Glasgow University Media Group (1976) concludes that broadcasting institutions are notably hierarchical with close links connecting them to a range of "official" and "acceptable" sources. They observe, "Given this emphasis it is difficult to structure news in a way that does not implicitly, at least, blame those groups or individuals who precipitate action that, in one way or another, is defined as 'disruptive' " (p. 204). This support for the system-as-it-exists explains why the media concentrate the bulk of their content on social conflict situations that present alternatives to the status quo.[1] Olien, Tichenor, and Donohue (1989) state, "Bureaucracies are designed not to resist change but to control the way change occurs and to mitigate consequences which are considered undesirable" (p. 142). Rada (1977) discusses media's stake in the status quo and claims that media personnel may be reluctant to be sympathetic to activities that might threaten their own position. Carragee (1990) notes that U.S. reports of the Solidarity movement in Poland avoid concerns inconsistent with traditional American politics. Herman (1985) observes that comparisons of paired news accounts of similar foreign events varied in interpretation along lines of U.S. foreign policy and political ideology. Olien et al. (1989) contend that mass media, given their deference to mainstream values, are visible agents of social control and conflict management. These authors note that in conflict situations, media accounts typically focus on the established rules that disputants are protesting and on whether the protesters are complying with socially accepted rules for expressing grievances.

It is this practice that earns media the frequently attributed role of legitimator, an entity that confers legitimacy on people, institutions, negotiators, and issues. However, although media has the *power* to confer legitimacy, research questions whether they actually use it this way. Frequently legitimacy already has been bestowed by higher sources of public authority and knowledge. The media's role, then, becomes that of *legitimist*, a supporter of legitimate authority, rather than the primary legitimator. Government regulatory agencies are prime examples of legitimate institutions because the public sees them as neutral, a perception that these agencies work hard to maintain. In labor-management negotiations, decisions by the National Labor Relations Board (NLRB), especially when supported in U.S. courts, are extremely helpful in convincing journalists of the legitimacy of labor's complaints (Douglas, 1986). In such cases, the media recognize these legitimated protests and spread the word to news consumers.

FRAMES OF REFERENCE OF NEWS ASSEMBLERS

Paletz and Entman (1981) argue that news is determined less by any external realities than by the internal logic of media organizations and personnel. According to these authors, bureaucracy in news organizations is characterized by hierarchy, division of labor, and standardized procedures, all seen as necessary to produce news efficiently. This strain toward efficiency has several important results. One is *pack journalism*, defined as "the frequent tendency of different reporters to write (and editors to assign) virtually identical political stories" (p. 19). While pack journalism fails to provide exciting accounts that differ from those of competitors, it is easy, speedy, and cheap. A second efficiency factor is the reliance on selected news sources. Paletz and Entman say that this reliance is both necessary and ingrained in journalists. The authors state, "Sources are crucial because most stories recount what someone says occurred, not what actually occurred" (p. 20). Sources, especially those that are well-known and powerful, can add legitimacy to news stories. However, even sources that are not totally trusted by the journalist are used, albeit with some type of warning that distances the journalist from possible source bias (Levy, 1981).

Although separating the individual journalist from institutional influences is not always easy, news assemblers clearly play active and creative parts in news selection and presentation. Journalists' basic knowledge of the subjects they cover varies a great deal, a factor that is reflected in the depth of their accounts. Only the largest media organizations can afford to have specialists on their staffs. Because of the national visibility of specialized correspondents (e.g., "our White House correspondent," "our economic analyst"), the expertise of journalists frequently is taken for granted, especially for national and international news. However, at the local and community level, usually the reporter who covers an impending crisis in teacher-school board negotiations is the same person who makes a routine check with the police desk and then rushes off to talk with demonstrators. Such people simply are unable to research the issues, backgrounds, and personalities involved in most of their assignments. Lack of depth in news stories frequently is attributed to media time or space constraints, but often it is due to the journalist's inability to learn as much as she or he could about a story.

Carragee's (1990) research demonstrates that this problem exists not only at the local level. Also specialized international correspondents who work for major networks operate within limited frames of reference. U.S. media coverage of the complex story of Polish Solidarity stressed the culturally familiar and neglected aspects that diverged from American political and cultural experience. True, some of this problem stems from the nature of television. Social and historical contexts that influence events and ideological orientations are not very amenable to television (Carragee, 1990). But journalists also possess the power of definition, and certainly they will be attuned to aspects of international stories that are culturally familiar, easier to understand, and easier to interpret.

Parallels between international and national stories abound. For example, a recent trend in labor-management negotiations is to focus less on salary and wages and more on complex issues such as job security, family leave, and employee rights. If journalists who are unfamiliar with the social and historical context of trade unions, as well as the processes of negotiation, mediation, and arbitration, are assigned to cover labor-management stories, they are likely to report only that which is understandable to them and to interpret it in a context of their own cultural familiarity.

In sum, negotiation issues as defined by the two parties can receive a number of different types of attention from the media, if they receive any attention at all. First, the views of both sides may be reported precisely as given to the media. This result could be justified on grounds of objective reporting and intrinsic interest to media consumers. Second, the issues as defined by the parties might be ignored in favor of another issue that is, in essence, created by the media. Perhaps the latter issue is better understood, makes more sense, or is seen as being in the media's best interests. Third, the negotiation issues as defined by only one of the parties might be reported. Fourth, the negotiators' issues might be taken apart and put back together again in ways that the media perceives they exist. Fifth, the gatekeeping and agenda-setting functions of the media might be activated, with the result that some issues are included, some are excluded, some emphasized, and some de-emphasized.

The second item noted above raises a related question. That is, do news assemblers *generate* problems? Do they have the power to heighten the intensity of the negotiations or to add new points that need to be considered by the negotiators? In their discussion of media and social conflict, Olien, Donohue, and Tichenor (1984) explicitly say no:

> [The media] may contribute to the process of public definition of a problem through dissemination of information, but they do not generate problem situations. To assume that the media create problems not only attributes awesome power to them, but it also places [them] in the ultimate role of controlling the type and direction of change in a system. (p. 14)

In contrast, Rakow (1989) argues that what gets published suits the purposes of the media industries. In her view, the media possess impressive power and use it not only to inform but to control. Her argument is persuasive; media indeed may have the ability to generate problem situations. However, the *consequences* of news assemblers' problem-generating actions may differ from what they intended. Media power to control also exists, but it is diffused by the complexity of the system. To believe that such power places media as the ultimate controllers of a system, as Olien et al. (1984) suggest, seems unreasonable. This position ignores the equally awesome power that other institutions possess.

NEGOTIATORS AS PROMOTERS OF NEWS

News promoters are individuals who have an interest in promoting certain occurrences for the public (Molotch & Lester, 1974, p. 104). Their purpose is to gain media access for the occurrences. Gaining media access is not particularly easy, but certain groups or individuals may be situated such that whenever they want an occurrence to be a public event, the media make it a public event. Such media status and favor, termed *habitual access* by Molotch and Lester, is bestowed upon only a limited few, such as high government officials, major corporate figures, and glamorous personalities. For example, if the negotiations involve the U.S. Secretary of State and the foreign minister of Israel, public event status is assured.

GAINING MEDIA ACCESS

Those who do not have such power and status must "make news" and this can be achieved by gaining "disruptive access," that is, by interrupting media's routine procedures and creating situations of interest to news people. Press conferences, demonstrations, and protests are examples. The key to the strategy of the news promoters is understanding what will interest the news assemblers. In social conflict situations, it is usually those trade unions, civil rights, and social action groups who have a grievance with the status quo that want to get media attention. They have a point to make and their issues vary in number and complexity. Researchers have studied labor-management negotiations to discern how one type of group—labor—gains disruptive access and to understand the strategies of groups that have relatively little power.

Conflict and negotiation revolve around power relationships. In a negotiation, labor is relatively powerless because trade unions may not possess sufficient resources with which to bargain. When media become involved, labor is at a second disadvantage because balanced accounts of labor-management stories are rare. Research in Australia, Great Britain, and the United States demonstrates that media coverage of labor-management negotiations frequently is biased in management's favor (Beharrell & Philo, 1977; Douglas, 1986; Douglas, Pecora, & Guback, 1985; Glasgow University Media Group, 1976, 1980, 1982; McColl, 1980; Mosco & Wasko, 1983; Rada, 1977). This bias, as McColl (1980) explains, "automatically militates against trade unions when they are involved in industrial action" (p. 426). A six-year study conducted by the Glasgow University Media Group (1976) provides evidence that television news in Great Britain not only tended to trivialize and sensationalize much labor news, but also tended to be "organized into highly selective patterns that implied a definite way of seeing and understanding industrial life" (p. 229). Young and Crutchley (1977) describe a demonstration in England against the Industrial Relations Act that the media portrayed as an irrelevant strike that no one wanted, an embarrassment, and an irrational nonevent. All these portrayals ignored the context of the event and the mounting industrial tension they represented. Workers typically are interviewed in rather chaotic situations (e.g., in groups, in noisy surroundings), while management representatives are interviewed in their offices and other settings that lend authority to their statements (Walton & Davis, 1977). McColl (1980) notes that news assemblers tend to see strikes as "labor news" rather than as "management news" or "business news," and to blame labor for disrupting the "normal" functioning of society (typified by the headline "Union threat on sheep exports").

Powerlessness encourages protest as a political activity (Lipsky, 1970). Organized protest may arise when negotiations break down or when negotiation, as an alternative, is not available. Lipsky's model of influence through protest shows the need for relatively powerless groups or institutions engaged in protest activity to activate other parties into the conflict in ways that will aid the protesters. The model is useful to communication scholars because Lipsky emphasizes that in the dynamics of protest politics, media provide the key to mobilizing additional support. There is, of course, always the risk that media may portray social advocacy groups negatively rather than positively. This portrayal could affect their perceived legitimacy and, depending on the degree to which they are seen as deviant, also could affect the level of negative coverage they receive (Shoemaker, 1982, 1984).

As the foregoing suggests, the ability to attract media's *attention* and the ability to attract media's *support* are quite different. Demonstrations, sit-ins, and strikes frequently are sufficient to attract media attention, but insufficient to attract media's support. Molotch and Lester (1974) contend that the reason media transform disruptive occurrences into disruptive public events is because these occurrences are problems for the relatively powerful. That is, news assemblers see such occurrences as events that "serious people" need to know about in order to plan a counterstrategy and "restore order" (p. 108). The media, therefore, focus not on the reasons for the protest, but on the need for the public to be aware of and informed about the activists' behaviors.

It is not enough then for negotiators to gain disruptive access to media. The case of the United Farm Workers in the 1960s illustrates this point. Cesar Chavez was a master at creating situations of interest to news people. Union picketing, leafleting, and demonstrations provided the media with visual interest, action, and color. But he found media support problematic even when he provided substantive evidence to prove his points. The visual qualities used to attract the media were insufficient to implement the consumer boycott of table grapes needed to achieve Chavez's objectives in this relatively powerless situation (Douglas, 1986; see also

Murdock's [1981] discussion of "event-oriented" press coverage that ignores causes and issues). A long-standing difficulty for unions is to fall back on strikes when negotiations fail. Unions "are caught in the contradiction of having to make demands against the very industry whose good fortunes they depend upon" (Parenti, 1980). Strikes may cause public inconvenience and, occasionally, real hardship; strikes may cause corporations to fail; and strikes can force workers out of jobs. From all points of view, the strike is a poor strategic choice—except as seen by the news assembler who may be attracted by the interest that strikes can provide.

MEDIA SOURCES AND MEDIA SUPPORT

In labor strikes and similar occurrences that have gained media attention, news assemblers frequently rely heavily, if not entirely, on sources from the protesting side. In a recent study of television coverage of automotive strikes, Pasedeos (1990) reports that more than two thirds of all automotive strike stories used a labor source while only one-third used a management source, and that a labor actor was present in almost all stories, while fewer than half had a management actor. Such attention to the protesting side might seem to give that side an edge. However, while Pasadeos does not address the direction (favorable/unfavorable) of the labor-management coverage, he considers the possibility that television journalists view a strike as a labor rather than a management event. Although the media may seek out sources and actors from only one of the negotiating sides, that side may not receive media support. Unless specific factors mediate against it, media's tendency is to to emphasize conflict and to defer to mainstream values. This tendency underscores the importance of the sophistication that negotiators bring to their role as news promoters (Lewicki & Litterer, 1985).

In the almost 30 years since Chavez learned the importance of media support, unions have become more sophisticated in improving their strategies to gain media and public support. The unprecedented media relationship that the Amalgamated Clothing and Textile Workers' Union developed in a multifaceted campaign against textile manufacturer J. P. Stevens in the 1980s is a clear case. First, the union gained legitimacy for its grievances through a legal component of the overall campaign that resulted in strong NLRB and court support. Additional legitimacy came through a corporate component whereby the union was able successfully to fight J. P. Steven's corporate power. What may have been most important, however, in gaining media's support, was the way the issues of the campaign were framed. They were strategically and successfully removed from a narrow labor interest framework and placed in a human rights context. This context broadened the story so that it interested a wider media audience than only textile workers and other union members. The negotiation issues, as they affected specific public groups, were explained to those groups—consumer groups, women's groups, both conservative and liberal politicians, student and religious leaders. Moreover, news assemblers in small- and medium-sized communities far from the Southern towns where the dispute actually was occurring watched as their students and city councils began to take stands, and began to understand the implications of the broad issues for their own communities. As one journalist wrote, "This issue affects people's lives. . . . Beyond that, the issue affects jobs—here and elsewhere—because if a large company like J. P. Stevens can thumb its nose at the law in the south, it may encourage other like-minded companies to move there" (Selkowe, cited in Douglas, 1986).

Fisher (1983) emphasizes that negotiating power, "the ability to affect favorably someone else's decision" (p. 150), must be enhanced before negotiations begin. He offers negotiators a list of helpful suggestions, one of which is the power of a good relationship. Although Fisher's interests lie with the two negotiating parties, a good ongoing relationship between a negotiator and the media, if it can be established, can help the two parties. Such a relationship encourages the negotiators to develop habitual as opposed to disruptive access. "Each side benefits from this ability to communicate. We may have interests that conflict, but our ability to deal with those conflicting interests at minimum risk and minimum cost is enhanced by a good working relationship" (Fisher, 1983, p. 155). Lewicki and Litterer (1985) observe that "media relations and 'image management' often become ends in themselves" (p. 232). Effler (1988) and Walsh (1988) specifically emphasize the need for effective, ongoing public relations programs to establish fair media attention during times of disputes and negotiations. Effler points to the National Football League's concern for its public image, its routinely good relationship with the media, and its adept public relations efforts during the players' strike in 1987. Walsh (1988), however, while in agreement with Effler, notes the following:

It would of course be naive to suggest that the trade unions should attempt, or could expect to succeed in the attempt, to reverse the media's traditional approach to covering their activities. . . . A pre-condition for success is an acceptance of the reality that the media have found a formula that is successful for their purposes. People in the media generally agree about the value and appropriateness of the techniques and methods used to gather and present the news. They have proved expedient and, for the commercial media, profitable. (p. 216)

NEWS CONSUMERS AND THE CONSEQUENCES OF NEWS

The manipulative model suggests that news consumers play a relatively passive role in the media effects process. However, scholars increasingly argue that news consumers assume an active part in the social construction of events, using procedures similar to those of news assemblers and news promoters (Molotch & Lester, 1974). News consumers interpret the news from the perspective of their individual values, beliefs, and knowledge. All of these are filtered through such factors as class, culture, demographics, experience, and history. Because part of this history and experience may be shaped by an individual's exposure to previous media messages, the potential constraints built into the interaction between consumers on the one hand and producers and assemblers on the other are formidible.

It is simplest for news promoters to think of news consumers as a mass public, to make appeals for favorable media attention, and to hope that those who respond sympathetically will help them achieve their negotiation goals. However, as marketers realized during the 1980s, the U.S. mass market has become fragmented. Because media cannot affect all consumers in the same way, news promoters may need to follow marketers' examples and learn how specific segments of the public might help them in their negotiations. Can the media provide a way to build alliances among news consumers? And, if favorable public attention is generated, can it affect the negotiations themselves?

The logical place for media to start building consumer alliances is with those consumers who are interested in and sympathetic to the message. Lewicki and Litterer (1985) note that two factors that affect audiences are the degree and the severity of potential outcomes of negotiations. The degree to which negotiations may affect news consumers ranges from strong direct effects through weak indirect effects to no effect whatsoever. A strike by the teachers in a local school district directly affects those parents with children in that school. If the strike is geographically distant, people may become involved indirectly if one side arouses their sympathies. Severity of the effects of a local school strike would be stronger for those with 10 children in school than for those with 2 children in school.

Media dependency theory suggests that the news interpretations of individuals emanate from their previous personal experiences as well as their previous media experiences with the subject. Smith (1987) contends that media dependency theory may explain differences in research results that indicate media effects are not one-way (from media to audience), but that mutual influences occur between media and audience. Adoni, Cohen and Mane (1984) observe that direct experience with issues helps account for the ways that news consumers interpret television news. This interpretation also includes biased perceptions of news reporting by consumers. Stevenson and Greene (1980) indicate that what consumers perceive as biased frequently is inconsistent with what is already in their heads. Similarly, Vallone, Ross, and Lepper (1985) demonstrate that partisans judge media coverage of controversial events as unfairly biased against the position they advocate.

Hartmann (1979), in exploring relationships between the presentation of industrial relations in the media and the way audiences perceive them, centers on differences between class subcultures rather than differences between individuals. In addition to providing evidence that media do not influence public conceptions directly, he argues that people in different class situations view industrial relations differently. He also observes that the "world of industrial relations as present in the media has more in common with a middle class view of the world than a working class view" and that "the media may help to sustain the prevalence of this particular framework as a way of making sense of industrial relations" (p. 476).

Although it is possible to segment and reach potentially interested and sympathetic audiences, such a process is not fast, simple, nor inexpensive. Moreover, it may be worth the effort only rarely. Olien et al. (1984), in a study of media coverage of a dispute about the proposed routing of a high voltage power line, claim that the distribution of public opinion on the issue was not a decisive factor in the outcome of the controversy. Arguments of the organized protesters proved futile. All major decisions in hearings and courts were in favor of the line and the state agency responsible for a final decision selected a corridor that deviated little from what the power associations preferred. The authors conclude that, "Such outcomes raise questions about media events as protest strategies" (p. 26). Several years later, the same authors added that, "Airing of the conflict gives the appearance of acknowledging, while not validating, the position of social protesters" (Olien et al., 1989, p. 155). This statement challenges news promoters with the need to gain media support as well as media attention. Still, news consumers are relatively weak as lobbyists, and there is widespread support for the conclusion of Olien et al. (1989) that consumers are relatively powerless in exerting authority and in influencing others.

In her analysis of the power of public opinion, Rakow (1989) asks the question, "What is 'information' without the ability to act?" (p. 178). Lewicki and Litterer (1985) agree and note that audiences to negotiations must be well-organized to exert leverage on one of the negotiators. Without organization, they have no means of presenting their group's interest.

> Even when a very large group of people may be negatively affected, they are *unlikely to have significant impact on the negotiations if the reaction cannot be brought to bear on the negotiators themselves. The reverse is also true: well-organized audiences can have significant effect on the outcome of negotiations even if their total numer is small.* (Lewicki & Litterer, 1985, p. 233; emphasis in original)

MEDIA EFFECTS ON THE NEGOTIATION PROCESS

Negotiations in their basic form involve two negotiators in private deliberations; each is responsible for his or her own interests and each possesses decision-making power. The preceding sections indicate the potential difficulties that occur when negotiations broaden and include others. Negotiators are aware that they represent constituencies and that other groups are observing their actions (see Turner, Chapter 10, this volume). As the social environment of negotiation becomes more complex, bargaining behavior changes significantly. Why then do negotiators want to become news promoters and make the negotiation situation even more complex?

Kochan and Katz (1988) offer a systems model that emphasizes how the process and outcomes of collective bargaining are influenced by the internal and the external contexts of the bargaining relationship. The external environment, which includes such factors as competition, technology, public policy, and social and economic change, offers opportunities to and imposes constraints on the negotiation process.

The challenge to the collective bargaining system comes not only from taking advantage of opportunities and minimizing constraints, but also from adapting to the dynamic nature of the environment. Kochan and Katz (1988) note that changes in the economy, public policy, and demographics, as well as social ideological shifts during the 1980s put organized labor at a distinct disadvantage.

The social environment plays a critical role in negotiations. One obvious concern of the media component of this environment is the aforementioned image of negotiators and the organizations they represent. These images include perceptions held by the public in general as well as those held privately, that is, by those involved directly in the negotiation. As the social context of negotiation becomes more complex, these images become increasingly public and vice versa. This public nature of negotiation entails more factors than the publicity that comes from media. As Lewicki and Litterer (1985) explain, audiences are individuals or groups "who are not directly involved in a negotiation, but to whom a negotiator will direct messages in an effort to influence the outcome of negotiations" (p. 214). They may be present or absent, dependent on or independent of negotiated outcomes, and eventually may become directly involved and play an active role in the negotiations. Audiences include team members, constituencies, and bystanders. Bystanders, including both media and news consumers, are not directly represented at the negotiation, but they may be directly or indirectly affected by negotiated outcomes (Lewicki & Litterer, 1985).

The existence of any audience influences negotiators because favorable audience opinion assumes increasing importance. However, negotiators find it hard to please both their constituencies, who want them to be firm, and their opposing negotiators, who want them to bargain (see Turner, Chapter 10, this volume, for a review of this work). Resulting pressures increase the possibility that negotiators will try to please their audiences rather than try to reach agreement (Lewicki & Litterer, 1985).

To widen the range of possible tactics, bargainers can control or manipulate the social environment of the negotiations. Through indirect communications negotiators can bring the opinions of others to bear on the opposing party (Lewicki & Litterer, 1985). Communicating through bystanders such as the media is one example:

Communication through the media is usually designed to reach *one's own constituency* or *interested audiences.* The quickest and most efficient way of letting one's own constituency know their negotiating posture is to represent that position in the media. . . . Communication may also be designed to *"activate" and win over interested audiences* who will communiate directly with the opponent. (Lewicki & Litterer, 1985, p. 232; emphasis in original)

Several media studies support Lewicki and Litterer's discussion of the social context of negotiations. One example is the research on state sunshine bargaining, a mandated process whereby certain sessions of negotiation are open both to the public and the media (Nigro & DeMarco, 1980; Pisapia, 1981; Sherman, 1980). Believing that participants will act more responsibly if they negotiate in public, the state legislatures of Florida and Kansas have mandated openness in public labor-management negotiations. In Florida the law includes all public employees and requires that all negotiations be open to the public. Opposition to the law has grown, however, generated by reports that the public presence increases negotiating time, restricts debate, makes compromise more difficult, and negatively affects outcomes. Feiock and West (1990) investigated these criticisms and conclude that while there are negative consequences associated with sunshine laws and the negotiation process (more time expended, inhibited dialogue, and difficult compromises), the "decisions and agreements resulting from open bargaining do not appear to be of substantially poorer quality than those resulting from closed bargaining" (p. 80). Citizens have no direct influence in such cases and structural access does not ensure public monitoring of labor negotiations. The little research done in this area suggests that closer examination of media selection, presentation, and long-term effects could be informative.

Attempts by negotiators to increase the visibility of negotiations entail a certain amount of risk. If the message is not realistic and superior to alternative sources of information, greater visibility works to a disadvantage (Roloff, 1987). In addition, negotiating parties must realize that the *opposing* side also can manipulate the social environment. Negotiators need to be sensitive to the ways media accounts affect them *during* the negotiation process. For example, do reports that favor the opposition make them more aware of and perhaps even sympathetic to certain aspects of the situation? Or do they become angry and less flexible? If the media complain about the fans' lack of consideration during baseball negotiations, do bargainers become aware of the ways in which the negotiation affects the public?

Finally, post hoc evaluations of media accounts of negotiations are valuable. Data from three studies support the hypothesis that groups and organizations in more established and dominant power positions apparently evalutate media coverage as being more favorable to their objectives than do groups and organizations in less established power positions (Donohue, Tichenor, & Olien, 1984). Members of less powerful organizations were more than three times as likely than those from more powerful organizations to judge media effects as harmful to their respective organizations.

Rada (1977) arrives at the same conclusion in a case study of strikers in Texas. In his words, "The media, in many cases, are reluctant to report or be viewed as sympathetic to community activities that might undermine their profit-making potential, threaten the community (business or otherwise) and their own position. For civil rights and other social action groups, the lesson has been bitter" (p. 113). Yet the opposite effect surfaces in some cases, namely, the Amalgamated Clothing and Textile Workers' Union- J.P. Stevens dispute. Post hoc opinions of both labor and management agreed that the media relationship developed by the union furthered union goals. Individuals from both sides believed that the union's corporate campaign strategy, with its vitally important media component was and would continue to be a necessary response by labor to the growth of multinational corporations. Undoubtedly both sides view media reporting negatively because most news promoters, if they could have done it themselves, would have presented it *differently*. But the more powerful organizations may be satisfied more frequently, and even the less powerful may be pleased with the outcome some of the time.

CONCLUSIONS: *TERTIUS GAUDENS*

The mass media in its coverage of strikes, labor-management disputes, and societal conflicts assume a variety of roles: party to the conflict, interested bystander, advocate, legitimator, mediator, arbitrator, agent in socially constructing the dispute, revolutionary, conduit of messages, truth-seeker, agenda-setter, watchdog, and guard dog. Undoubtedly other roles could be added. Much of the research focuses on one or several case studies that analyze and explain these particular roles. However, such a list raises troublesome questions. If more cases were studied, would more roles be identified? Do any patterns emerge among the various roles and the cases that they represent? Do the ascribed roles retain validity when detached from the case studies? And, finally, can one overarching role be identified? The answers to these questions are yes, apparently not yet, sometimes, and, arguably, yes. Time may provide answers to the first two questions; the second two are addressed below.

Some of the roles in the list indicate passivity (e.g., interested bystander, conduit), but they rarely are taken by media. A greater number indicate active states—specifically, party to the conflict, advocate, legitimator, mediator, arbitrator, agent, truth-seeker, agenda-setter, revolutionary, watchdog, and guard dog. Some imply bias or interests in a particular direction—namely, party to the conflict, advocate, legitimator, agent, agenda-setter, revolutionary, watchdog, guard dog. Others indicate some version of neutrality—for instance, interested bystander, mediator, arbitrator, truth-seeker. Most roles suggest that media are independent and not subject to control by others. However, "conduit" does not, and, more arguably, neither does "guard dog."[2] In spite of this suggested independence, a number of scholars argue against such a "fourth estate" view of media and find it difficult to consider them as necessary and independent channels for reporting social tensions (e.g., Beharrel & Philo, 1977; Compaine, 1982; Donohue et al., 1984).

Arno (1984), however, is one who supports press autonomy: "All this indicates that autonomy, as illusion if not fact, is important to the logic of the news reporting enterprise. And when structural conditions allow it, the forces, or the structural logic, that support press autonomy and opposition to control will assert themselves" (p. 233). He suggests that the way to investigate the news media as free agents is through their "third-party role."

When Arno uses *third party* to characterize media's role in conflicts, he refers to the "structural logic of third parties," or what Simmel (1950) calls "the sociology of three, when two are in conflict" (Arno, 1984, p. 231). The third party possesses autonomy, illusory or actual. Using Fisher's (1983) definition of negotiations, that is, two or more negotiators, the sociology would be four when three are in conflict, or six when five are in conflict. The difference is between a primary and a secondary party to the conflict, and the "number three is merely the minimum number of elements that are necessary for this formation" (Simmel, 1950, p. 162).

From this perspective, media's role as possible mediator is more easily understandable.[3] A position of mediation is a middle position, between two other parties, usually taken in an attempt to reconcile differences between the two. However, the typical middle position taken by the media is between media promoters and media consumers, not between the two negotiators. In such a role, media do not try to reconcile differences. In fact, their interest is likely to lie with continuation of the conflict.

Following Arno (1984) then, media fit the category of third parties that Simmel (1950) calls the *tertius gaudens,* "the third who rejoices." Media need societal conflict to function; they profit from the conflict of the other two (as do mediators and arbitrators). In addition, media's power derives from a *tertius gaudens* position; if one of the disputants gains control of the media, the third party position evaporates, as would its power. As Arno (1984) explains:

> Applying this kind of logic to the history of the news media in the United States, the emergence of objective, fair, informative newspapers and broadcast news from the beginnings of special interest propaganda sheets would seem to owe as much to the structural path toward self-aggrandizement offered by the role of the nonpartisan third party as to any free press ideology. Press freedom in the constitutional sense might well engender a plethora of competing, ideologically distinct media organizations, but it does not account for a growing centralization of print and broadcast news in the hands of profit-oriented corporations without any coherent political ideologies. As the news media become more expert in their jobs and less obviously partisan on issues, their prestige and authority increase, and correspondingly, their power as third parties grows. (p. 235)

Media are active in the pursuit of their own, usually narrow interests, both structurally and culturally defined. If a guard dog or other role is adopted, it is partly because that role serves media's interests. Media's tendency to act as free agents can be explained the same way. The *tertius gaudens* concept is more insightful and more useful than either the manipulative or market models; moreover, it casts media as active in the social construction of news. As an overarching media role, *tertius gaudens* makes sense. To the extent that media act in their own self-interests and increase their profits and power, certainly they rejoice.

Research in this area has grown and a number of directions might be followed. However, the various ideas in this research field need to be integrated. One step in that direction is to look for patterns that emerge across the various case studies. Scholars need to continue to study how and why news is selected and produced. We need to study the consequences of news at a macro level. For news of negotiation, little work exists in the latter area. We are increasingly challenged by international negotiations. Although this arena is routine in business and politics, international bargaining remains complex and problematic. The cultural and interpretive aspects of this process present some formidible obstacles but also may uncover some new insights into the more familiar, national media phenomena.

NOTES

1. Roloff (1987) reviews literature that focuses both on media as suppressors and instigators of cultural conflict. See also the "cultivation effect" literature (e.g., Gerbner & Gross, 1976; Gerbner, Gross, Jackson-Beeck, Jeffries-Fox, & Signorielli, 1978).

2. Olien et al. (1989) argue that media do not serve as watchdogs for a general public, but as guard dogs "for powerful interests and mainstream values" (p. 160).

3. This cannot be said of the role of *arbitrator,* a word that usually refers to one selected to settle differences between two negotiators by making final authoritative decisions.

REFERENCES

Adoni, H., Cohen, A. A., & Mane, S. (1984). Social reality and television news: Perceptual dimensions of social conflicts in selected life areas. *Journal of Broadcasting, 28,* 33-49.

Arno, A. (1984). The news media as third parties in national and international conflict: Duobus litigantibus tertius gaudet. In A. Arno & W. Dissanayake (Eds.), *The news media in national and international conflict* (pp. 229-238). Boulder, CO: Westview.

Atwood, L. E. (1970). How newsmen and readers perceive each others' story preferences. *Journalism Quarterly, 47,* 296-302.

Bagdikian, B. H. (1983). *The media monopoly.* Boston: Beacon.

Beharrell, P., & Philo, G. (Eds.). (1977). *Trade unions and the media.* London: Macmillan.

Carey, J. (1975). A cultural approach to communications. *Communication, 2,* 12.

Carragee, K. M. (1990). Defining solidarity: Themes and omissions in coverage of the solidarity trade union movement by ABC news. *Journalism Monographs.* Columbia, SC: Association for Education in Journalism and Mass Communication.

Cohen, S., & Young, J. (1981). The process of selection. In S. Cohen & J. Young (Eds.), *The manufacture of news: Social problems, deviance & the mass media* (pp. 17-33). Beverly Hills, CA: Sage.

Compaine, B. M. (Ed.). (1982). *Who owns the media? Concentration of ownership in the mass communications industry* (2nd ed.). White Plains, NY: Knowledge Industry Publications.

Donohue, G. A., Tichenor, P. J., & Olien, C. N. (1984). Media evaluations and group power. In A. Arno & W. Dissanayake (Eds.), *The news media in national and international conflict* (pp. 203-215). Boulder, CO: Westview.

Douglas, S. U. (1986). *Labor's new voice: Unions and the mass media.* Norwood, NJ: Ablex.

Douglas, S., Pecora, N., & Guback, T. (1985). Work, workers, and the workplace: Is local newspaper coverage adequate? *Journalism Quarterly, 62,* 855-860.

Effler, G. (1988). Off-the-field goals. *Public Relations Journal, 44,* 17-20ff.

Ettema, J. S., Whitney, D. C., & Wackman, D. B. (1987). Professional mass communicators. In C. R. Berger & S. H. Chaffee (Eds.), *Handbook of communication science* (pp. 747-780). Newbury Park, CA: Sage.

Feiock, R. C., & West, J. P. (1990). Public presence at collective bargaining: Effects on process and decisions in Florida. *Journal of Collective Negotiations in the Public Sector, 19,* 69-82.

Fisher, R. (1983). Negotiating power. *American Behavioral Scientist, 27,* 149-166.

Fishman, M. (1980). *Manufacturing the news.* Austin: University of Texas Press.

Galtung, J., & Ruge, M. (1981). Structuring and selecting news. In S. Cohen & J. Young (Eds.), *The manufacture of news: Social problems, deviance & the news media* (pp. 52-63). Beverly Hills, CA: Sage.

Gans, H. (1979). *Deciding what's news.* New York: Random House.

Gerbner, G., & Gross, L. (1976). Living with television: The violence profile. *Journal of Communication, 26,* 172-199.

Gerbner, G., Gross, L. P., Jackson-Beeck, M., Jeffries-Fox, S., & Signorielli, N. (1978). Cultural indicators: Violence profile no. 9. *Journal of Communication, 28,* 176-207.

Gitlin, T. (1980). *The whole world is watching: Mass media in the making and unmaking of the new left.* Berkeley: University of California Press.

Glasgow University Media Group. (1976). *Bad news* (Vol. 1). London: Routledge & Kegan Paul.

Glasgow University Media Group. (1980). *More bad news* (Vol. 2). London: Routledge & Kegan Paul.

Glasgow University Media Group. (1982). *Really bad news.* London: Writers & Readers.

Hartmann, P. (1979). News and public perceptions of industrial relations. *Media, Culture and Society, 1,* 255-270.

Herman, E. S. (1985). Diversity of news: "Marginalizing" the opposition. *Journal of Communication, 35,* 135-146.

Kochan, T. A., & Katz, H. C. (1988). *Collective bargaining and industrial relations: From theory to policy and practice* (2nd ed.). Homewood, IL: Irwin.

Levy, M. R. (1981, Summer). Disdaining the news. *Journal of Communication, 31,* 24-31.

Lewicki, R. J., & Litterer, J. A. (1985). *Negotiation.* Homewood, IL: Irwin.

Lipsky, M. (1970). *Protest in city politics: Rent strikes, housing and the power of the poor* (American Politics Research Series). Chicago: Rand McNally.

McColl, M. (1980). The mass media and industrial relations news: A case study. *Journal of Industrial Relations, 22,* 420-441.

Molotch, H., & Lester, M. (1974). News as purposive behavior: On the strategic use of routine events, accidents, and scandals. *American Sociological Review, 39,* 101-112.

Morley, D. (1976). Industrial conflict and the mass media. *Sociological Review, 24,* 245-268.

Mosco, V., & Wasko, J. (Eds.). (1983). *Labor, the working class, and the media.* Norwood, NJ: Ablex.

Murdock, G. (1981). Political deviance: The press presentation of a militant mass demonstration. In S. Cohen & J. Young (Eds.), *The manufacture of news: Social problems, deviance and the news media.* (pp. 206-225). Beverly Hills, CA: Sage.

Murdock, G., & Golding, P. (1977). Beyond monopoly: Mass communications in an age of conglomerates. In P. Beharrel and G. Philo (Eds.), *Trade unions and the media* (pp. 93-117). London: Macmillan.

Nigro, L. G., & DeMarco, J. J. (1980). Collective bargaining and the attitudes of local government personnel managers. *Public Personnel Management, 9*, 160-168.

Olien, C. N., Donohue, G. A., & Tichenor, P. J. (1984). Media and stages of social conflict. *Journalism Monographs.* Columbia, SC: Association for Education in Journalism and Mass Communication.

Olien, C. N., Tichenor, P. J., & Donohue, G. A. (1989). Media coverage and social movements. In C. T. Salmon (Ed.), *Information campaigns: Balancing social values and social change* (pp. 139-163). Newbury Park, CA: Sage.

Paletz, D. L., & Entman, R. M. (1981). *Media-power-politics.* New York: Free Press.

Parenti, M. (1980). *Democracy for the few* (3rd ed.). New York: St. Martin's.

Pasadeos, Y. (1990). Sources in television coverage of automotive strikes. *Journal of Broadcasting & Electronic Media, 34*, 77-84.

Pertschuk, M. (1979). Opening address. In Federal Trade Commission, *Proceedings of the Symposium on Media Concentration* (Vol. 1, pp. 1-5). Washington, DC: Government Printing Office.

Pisapia, J. R. (1981). Sunshine bargaining: A controversy examined. *Compact, 14*, 25-27.

Rada, S. E. (1977). Manipulating the media: A case study of a Chicano strike in Texas. *Journalism Quarterly, 54*, 109-113.

Rakow, L. F. (1989). Information and power: Toward a critical theory of information campaigns. In C. T. Salmon (Ed.), *Information campaigns: Balancing social values and social change* (pp. 164-184). Newbury Park, CA: Sage.

Roloff, M. E. (1987). Communication and conflict. In C.R. Berger & S. H. Chaffee (Eds.), *The handbook of communication science* (pp. 484-534). Newbury Park, CA: Sage.

Sherman, J. J. (1980). Government in the sunshine: How has it affected collective bargaining in Florida? In L. M. Miller (Ed.), *The impact of the media on collective bargaining* (pp. 27-36). New York: American Arbitration Association.

Shoemaker, P. J. (1982). The perceived legitimacy of deviant political groups: Two experiments on media effects. *Communication Research, 9*, 249-286.

Shoemaker, P. J. (1984). Media treatment of deviant political groups. *Journalism Quarterly, 57*, 115-121.

Simmel, G. (1950). *The sociology of Georg Simmel* (K. H. Wolff, Ed.). Glencoe, IL: Free Press.

Smith, K. A. (1987). Newspaper coverage and public concern about community issues: A time-series analysis. *Journalism Monographs.* Columbia, SC: Association for Education in Journalism and Mass Communication.

Stevenson, R. L., & Greene, M. T. (1980). A reconsideration of bias in the news. *Journalism Quarterly, 57*, 115-121.

Tuchman, G. (1978). *Making news: A study in the construction of reality.* New York: Free Press.

Vallone, R. P., Ross, L., & Lepper, M. R. (1985). The hostile media phenomenon: Biased perception and perceptions of media bias in coverage of the Beirut Massacre. *Journal of Personality and Social Psychology, 49*, 577-585.

Walsh, G. (1988). Trade unions and the media. *International Labour Review, 127*, 205-220.

Walton, P., & Davis, H. (1977). Bad news for trade unionists. In P. Beharrell & G. Philo (Eds.), *Trade unions and the media* (pp. 118-134). London: Macmillan.

272   *The Role of Mass Media*

Ward, W. (1967). *News values, news situations and news selections.* Unpublished doctoral dissertation, University of Iowa.

Young, J., & Crutchley, J. B. (1977). May the first, 1973—A day of predictable madness. In P. Beharrell & G. Philo (Eds.), *Trade unions and the media* (pp. 23-31). London: Macmillan.

AUTHOR INDEX

273

SUBJECT INDEX

ABOUT THE CONTRIBUTORS

JAMES J. BRADAC (Ph.D., Northwestern University, 1970) is Professor of Communication Studies at the University of California, Santa Barbara. His research focuses upon the role of language variables in person perception and social evaluation. He coauthored (with C. R. Berger) *Language and Social Knowledge*. He is currently completing a term as editor of *Human Communication Research* and is a Fellow of The International Communication Association.

JON D. BUSCH (M.A., University of California, Santa Barbara, 1991) is currently a doctoral student in Communication Studies at the University of California, Santa Barbara. His research interests include communication in relationships and language in social settings.

GERARDINE DeSANCTIS (Ph.D., Texas Tech University, 1982) is Associate Professor of Information Systems at the University of Minnesota. Her current research interests are computer-supported decision making and systems implementation in organizations. Her articles appear in journals such as *Management Science, Data Base, Academy of Management Journal, Information and Management,* and *Communications of the ACM*. She is currently an Associate Editor for *Information Systems Research, Management Science,* and *Organization Science.*

WILLIAM A. DONOHUE (Ph.D., Ohio State University, 1976) is Professor of Communication at Michigan State University. His conflict-related research interests include mediation and negotiation. He has published articles in *Communication Monographs, Communication Yearbook, Human Communication Research,* and *International Journal of Group Tensions*. His books include *Communication, Marital Dispute, and Divorce Mediation* and *Contemporary Issues in Language and Discourse Processes* (edited with D. Ellis).

SARA U. DOUGLAS (Ph.D., University of Illinois, Urbana-Champaign, 1983) is Associate Professor in the Division of Consumer Sciences, University of Illinois, Urbana-Champaign. In addition to her interests in mass media, her research focuses upon the textile industry and international textile trade and trade policy. She is author of *Labor's New Voice: Unions and the Mass Media* and has published articles in journals including *Media, Culture and Society, Journalism Quarterly,* and *Asian Survey.*

PAMELA GIBBONS (Doctoral Candidate, University of California, Santa Barbara) is Lecturer in Communication Studies at the University of California, Santa Barbara. Her research examines the role of language variation in memory and social perception processes. Her current work includes a coauthored paper (with J. Bradac and J. D. Busch) in *Language and Social Psychology* and a chapter in *Language and Social Cognition* (with D. Hamilton, S. M. Stroessner, and J. Sherman).

MAJIA HOLMER (M.A., San Diego State University, 1989) is currently working toward a Ph.D. in Organizational Communication and Philosophy of Communication at Purdue University. Her research focuses on the role of discourse in organizational domination, democratization, and bureaucratization.

MICHAEL E. HOLMES (Ph.D., University of Minnesota, 1991) is Assistant Professor at Purdue University. His research interests include hostage negotiation, computer-mediated communication, and group decision support systems. He has recently published articles in *The Police Chief* and *Journal of Organizational Computing.*

JERRY M. JORDAN (Doctoral Candidate, Northwestern University) is Assistant Professor of Communication at the University of Cincinnati. His research interests center on language behaviors and the cognitive processes underlying message production. He is currently researching the correspondence between social action plans and conversational discourse.

COLLEEN M. KEOUGH (Ph.D., University of Southern California, 1988) is Lecturer at the University of Southern California and consultant at Rockwell International Space Systems Division. Her study of argumentation in teacher-school board negotiations won the 1989 W. C. Redding Dissertation Award from the Organizational Communication

Division of the International Communication Association. Her other research interests include organizational culture and organizational development.

MARSHALL SCOTT POOLE (Ph.D., University of Wisconsin, Madison, 1980) is Professor of Speech Communication at the University of Minnesota. His current research interests are computer support for meetings, group decision making, conflict management, organizational communication, and interaction analysis methodology. Recent publications include an edited volume, *Communication and Group Decision-Making* (with R. Hirokawa) and the book *Working Through Conflict* (written with J. Folger). His article, "Group Decision-Making as a Structurational Process" (with R. D. McPhee and D. R. Seibold) won the Golden Anniversary Award for Outstanding Scholarship from the Speech Communication Association. He has served on the editorial boards of *Communication Research, Communication Monographs, Human Communication Research*, and *Academy of Management Review.*

LINDA L. PUTNAM (Ph.D., University of Minnesota, 1977) is Professor of Communication at Purdue University. Her current research interests include communication strategies in negotiation, organizational conflict, contradictory and paradoxical messages, and language analysis in conflict. She serves on the editorial boards of seven journals and has edited special issues on dispute resolution for *Communication Research* and *Management Communication Quarterly.* She is the coeditor of *Communication and Organization: An Interpretative Approach* (with M. Pacanowsky) and *Handbook of Organizational Communication* (with F. M. Jablin, K. H. Roberts, and L. W. Porter). Three of her articles and books have received best publication awards from the Organizational Communication Division of the Speech Communication Association.

CLOSEPET N. RAMESH (Ph.D., Michigan State University, 1991) is Assistant Professor at Northwest Missouri State University. His research interests include critical theory and hostage negotiations. Recent papers on hostage negotiations have been presented at the conventions of the International Communication Association and the Speech Communication Association.

MICHAEL E. ROLOFF (Ph.D., Michigan State University, 1975) is Professor of Communication Studies at Northwestern University. His research interests include bargaining and negotiation, social exchange within intimate relationships, persuasion, and interpersonal conflict resolution. He wrote *Interpersonal Communication: The Social Exchange Approach,* and coedited *Persuasion: New Directions in Theory and Research* (with G. R. Miller), *Interpersonal Processes: New Directions in Communication Research* (with G. R. Miller), and *Social Cognition and Communication* (with C. R. Berger).

DALE L. SHANNON (Doctoral Candidate, University of Minnesota) is a student in speech communication at the University of Minnesota. His current research interests include organizational communication with special emphasis on conflict and negotiation, negotiation support systems, group-decision support systems, and new technologies. He is also interested in quantitative research methods.

DUDLEY B. TURNER (Ph.D., Purdue University, 1988) is Assistant Professor in the School of Communication at The University of Akron. His research interests include negotiation, conflict management and pedagogical approaches in communication. His research has been presented at regional and national conferences and is published in *Communication Studies* and *Argumentation.*

FRANK TUTZAUER (Ph.D., Northwestern University, 1985) is Assistant Professor of Communication at the State University of New York at Buffalo. His research pertains to bargaining and negotiation, social networks, and the mathematical modeling of behavioral phenomena. Recent publications include articles in *Behavioral Science, Communication Research, Communication Yearbook, International Journal of Conflict Management, Progress in Communication Science,* and *Social Networks.*

STEVEN R. WILSON (Ph.D., Purdue University, 1989) is Assistant Professor of Communication at Michigan State University. He teaches classes in conflict and negotiation, interpersonal communication, persuasion, and social cognition. His research focuses on relationships between communication and cognitive processes during conflict and social influence episodes. He has written articles appearing in *Communication Monographs, Communication Yearbook, Human Communication Research, Central States Speech Journal, Management Communication Quarterly,* and *Research on Language and Social Interaction.*

Printed in the United States
1180000002B/163-180